THE CITY OF VINES

The original seal of Los Angeles, in use from 1854 to 1905, identifying it as the City of Vines. Courtesy of the Los Angeles Public Library.

THE CITY OF VINES

A HISTORY OF WINE IN LOS ANGELES

THOMAS PINNEY

Heyday, Berkeley, California
California Historical Society, San Francisco, California

The publisher is grateful to the Wine Librarians Association
for its generous support of this project.

Library of Congress Cataloging-in-Publication Data

Names: Pinney, Thomas, author.
Title: The city of vines : a history of wine in Los Angeles / Thomas Pinney.
Description: Berkeley, California : Heyday ; San Francisco, California :
   California Historical Society, [2017] | Includes bibliographical
   references and index.
Identifiers: LCCN 2016047274 | ISBN 9781597143981 (hardcover : alk. paper)
Subjects: LCSH: Wine industry--California--Los Angeles--History.
Classification: LCC HD9378.L67 P56 2017 | DDC 338.4/7663200979494--dc23
LC record available at https://lccn.loc.gov/2016047274

Cover Art: Workers in the vineyards of the Sierra Madre Vintage Company. Courtesy
of the California Historical Society at the University of Southern California.

Cover and Interior Design/Typesetting: Ashley Ingram
Printed in East Peoria, IL, by Versa Press, Inc.

Orders, inquiries, and correspondence should be addressed to:
   Heyday
   P.O. Box 9145, Berkeley, CA 94709
   (510) 549-3564, Fax (510) 549-1889
   www.heydaybooks.com

10 9 8 7 6 5 4 3 2 1

MIX
Paper from
responsible sources
FSC® C005010

To Catharine Alexander

CONTENTS

LIST OF ILLUSTRATIONS

PREFACE

The most striking fact about the history of winemaking in Los Angeles, city and county, is the completeness with which it has been forgotten. The trade has left hardly any material traces. If any buildings survive, they have been converted to other purposes so that their origins are unrecognizable, and the vineyards themselves have long since been swept away under the tide of housing. No one writes about the tradition of Los Angeles winemaking, few local histories make anything of the subject, and most people have no idea that the region was once the main source of California wine. When I tell people that I am writing about winemaking in Los Angeles, the invariable response is one of skeptical surprise: Whoever heard of that? And what can I find to write about?

Yet Los Angeles is where it all began, and where, for years, the main action was to be found. California wine meant Los Angeles wine. The whole California wine establishment descends directly from Los Angeles, and long after Los Angeles, city and county, had been outpaced as a player in California winemaking, it continued to be important.

My focus on the city and county of Los Angeles may seem an arbitrary limitation—why not write about all of Southern California? The fact is, nothing elsewhere compared in importance to Los Angeles. Until the turn of the twentieth century, the city and county of Los Angeles provided, overwhelmingly, the winemaking in Southern California. There were scattered growers and producers in Santa Barbara, Ventura, and San Diego Counties, but nothing to signify. San Bernardino

County, now imagined by most people to have been the major source of Southern California wine, did not in fact develop until the vineyards were beginning to be crowded out of L.A. County, and then it did so as a colonial development of the big Los Angeles wineries. The substantial vineyards in and around Rancho Cucamonga persisted into the 1960s, which is why people now think of the region as primary.

These two facts are why I have written this book: the fact that it was important, and the fact that it has been forgotten. I have enjoyed the work of putting together the case for giving Los Angeles its due. There is no doubt much more that might be known, but I have at least made a beginning.

That the missions made wine *is* generally known, but our information about how it was made, and how much of it was made, and what was done with it when it was made, is terribly thin. No one, so far as I know, has studied the question with any thoroughness. I have not been able to add anything to the subject; a patient study of the Spanish records would be required, and I am not competent to do that. There is a fair amount of information about the brief Mexican period, and after the American takeover in 1846–47 the record becomes reasonably full. I have, accordingly, given most of my attention to the hundred years following the American conquest down to the end of the story in the 1950s.

ACKNOWLEDGMENTS

My two major sources are, first, the Huntington Library and, next, the Shields Library of the University of California, Davis. The Huntington houses a rich collection of material from Southern California in the nineteenth century: the papers of Benjamin D. Wilson, of J. DeBarth Shorb, of L. J. Rose, and others provide a detailed view of the scene at the time. At Davis, the great library—developed to support the university's work in viticulture and enology, and now presided over by my former student Axel Borg—was an essential source of information, as were the records of the Bureau of Alcohol, Tobacco, and Firearms (BATF), the federal agency concerned with winemaking, now held in Special Collections at the Shields Library. The history of Los Angeles wine under Prohibition and in the years following Repeal would be impossible to write without the BATF papers.

Of the published work about Southern California winemaking, by far the most substantial and useful is Ernest Peninou's posthumously published *History of the Los Angeles Viticultural District* (2004). Charles Sullivan's series of articles about early California winemaking, published in the *Wayward Tendrils Quarterly* from April 2010 to October 2015, is another invaluable source of information, notable for its fullness and accuracy. Two exemplary works of reference were constantly useful: James D. Hart's *Companion to California* (1987) and Leonard Pitt and Dale Pitt's *Los Angeles A to Z: An Encyclopedia of the City and County* (1997); both volumes were published by the University of California Press.

A special word should be said about the collection devoted to the history of winegrowing in Southern California, held at California State Polytechnic University, Pomona, and developed under the direction of Danette Cook Adamson. It takes a broad view of history and is now a rich and growing collection not only of documents but of labels, posters, brochures, photographs, bottles, winemaking equipment, and other things associated with wines and vines as they flourished in Southern California.

Two friends, Gail Unzelman and Charles Sullivan, have, as always, provided indispensable help.

1

MISSION WINE

In May of 1769 the men and animals of the so-called Sacred Expedition were gathered near Loreto, on the Baja peninsula of Mexico, poised to begin their march into what is now California. Some four hundred cattle had already been driven northward by a group in advance of the main expedition, which was under the command of Captain Gaspar de Portolá. Another group had been sent around by sea and were to rendezvous with the overland marchers at San Diego Bay. The object of the expedition was to establish a Spanish presence in what, except for its coastline, was an almost wholly unexplored region stretching for hundreds of miles to the north along the Pacific. The expedition was called "Sacred" because the soldiers who provided the muscle were accompanied by Franciscan priests, whose charge was to set up missions, convert the Indians, and so prepare the land for productive settlement. The political meaning of the expedition was to forestall any occupation of the land by foreign powers—notably the Russians, who had made tentative moves in that direction, but also the English, who had a base in Canada from which they could move southward.[1] When the expedition began its march north, the modern history of California began, and with it the history of winemaking in California—although not all at once.

It was a precarious beginning. Only 126 of the original company of about 219, depleted by death or desertion, reached the expedition's first destination: the splendid bay where San Diego now stands. There,

Portolá, whose orders were to march to Monterey Bay to establish a colony there, dutifully collected half of the survivors, leaving a sickly remnant behind, and set out for his next destination, four hundred miles distant. There were further misadventures—Portolá marched right by Monterey Bay and instead discovered San Francisco Bay—and there were various hair-breadth escapes for both the marching group and the San Diego group. But the survivors hung on and managed to make a start on the three-pronged system of Spanish colonial enterprise: presidio, pueblo, and mission. This was a combination of army post (presidio), civilian settlement (pueblo), and church mission (the engine for converting or "civilizing"—the words were interchangeable—the Indians). The first presidios were at San Diego (1769) and Monterey (1770). To call them "forts" would be an overstatement; they were merely garrisons, without heavy fortification. The first pueblos were San José (1777) and Los Angeles (1781). The first missions were those at San Diego (1769) and Monterey (1770; relocated to Carmel in 1771).

The leader of the mission priests was, as every California schoolchild knows, Father Junípero Serra, a native of the island of Majorca, who had, among other things, been active in missionary work in Mexico for many years. He presided over the founding and the development of the California missions for fifteen years, and by the end of his tenure, which came only with his death in 1784, there were nine of these, scattered along the coast from the original foundation in San Diego in the south to San Francisco Bay in the north.

It is widely believed that vines were planted by Serra at San Diego in 1769, just as soon as the mission had been established.[2] There are some plausible reasons for the belief, the most important of which is, of course, the need for wine in the celebration of the mass. Besides, the Franciscans were Spaniards, accustomed to wine as an essential part of their diet, so what more natural than that they should at once have planted vines? There would have been no problem acquiring planting stock, since the missions of Baja California, where the Sacred Expedition had been assembled, already had productive vineyards.

But against the popular belief a number of stubborn facts must be set. As Roy Brady has shown in an important article closely reviewing the evidence, Serra did not set out from Baja until May 15.[3] If he had any cuttings with him, he would have needed to keep them dormant in cool and damp conditions, impossible to provide on the long, difficult march up the Baja peninsula. But suppose that Serra did have vine cuttings with him; in that unlikely case, and if he managed to keep them moist, they would have begun to leaf out almost at once in the warm climate of Baja, and that premature growth would have reduced the chances of a successful planting almost to zero. Serra's party did not reach the San Diego site until July 16, an impossibly late date for planting vines in any place, not to speak of such a dry place as San Diego. And no sooner were the sickly few soldiers and priests left alone at San Diego than the local Indians attacked, an attack that the enfeebled Spanish barely managed to repel. In these conditions, is it reasonable to expect that Serra planted vines—a crop, as Brady writes, "that would yield nothing for at least three years"?

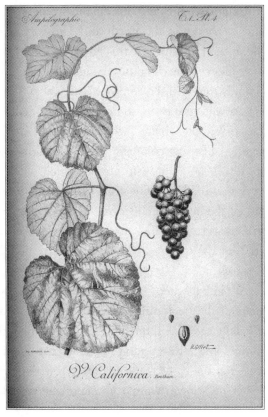

Vitis californica, the native California grape, but not a wine grape. From Pierre Viala and Victor Vermorel, *Ampelographie* (Paris: 1901–10). Courtesy of Special Collections, Shields Library, University of California, Davis.

Furthermore, there is evidence that the missionaries had no intention of supplying their own wants in this matter; instead, they brought wine with them, and had every expectation of receiving more by ship from Mexico, mostly from the old Jesuit missions in Baja. And so they did, for the next decade and more. It was expected that the first settlers would not achieve self-sufficiency for a long time, and so the port of San Blas, on the west coast of Mexico, had been set up specifically to supply the California venture. Mission records show that through much of the 1770s the harvests of such essentials as wheat, barley, and maize were small and uncertain, so that, in the words of one writer, "it is highly improbable that grapes would be planted before the cultivation of the necessary crops had been somewhat established."[4] Food came first; wine a distant second.

Finally, in making the case against a very early start to winegrowing in Spanish California, one may note that, although there are native grapes in California, they are unsuited for wine. The two native vine species—*Vitis californica* in the north and *Vitis girdiana* in the south—flourished along the banks of streams and rivers, and attracted attention at once as evidence that viticulture would succeed in the region. Serra himself, on only the second day after his arrival at San Diego, wrote that he had found wild grapes in abundance there.[5] Alexander von Humboldt, in his book about Mexico, which was based on his residence there in 1803, wrote, "The first colonists [in California] found, on their arrival there, in 1769, shoots of wild vines…which yielded very large grapes of a very sour quality."[6] The great botanist has it wrong—the native grape is sweet, the berries small—but he does testify to a general sense that the grapes were unfit for wine.[7] There were, no doubt, early winemaking trials of these grapes.[8] The results were such that the experiments were not continued.

All in all, then, it seems overwhelmingly improbable that 1769 marked the beginning of winegrowing in California. When the state officially celebrated the bicentennial of the industry in 1969, no one, so far as I know, rose up to protest against the historical error. Still, it was an error. But if the received notion is wrong, what is the correct version? When *did* winegrowing begin, and where, and with whom?

The missionaries were not indifferent to the prospect of growing their own wine. Strictly speaking, wine was a monopoly of the Spanish crown, as was the olive, and the planting of both vines and olive trees had been forbidden in Mexico, one reason among others why that country never developed a Mediterranean cuisine. But the rule was relaxed out of practical necessity in remote regions of the empire, such as Alta California and New Mexico. The Franciscans in California were free to plant grapes and make wine.[9] Serra repeatedly complained in his letters of the difficulties in getting a regular supply, and in 1777, in a letter to the viceroy in Mexico, he raised the idea of bringing in vines from Baja. Whether any were then imported, we don't know; but since Serra, eight years after the Sacred Expedition, writes about it as a thing to be done rather than a thing already done, it confirms the notion that the missions were slow to take up winemaking.

Two years after Serra's letter, however, the European vine had certainly arrived. Writing in March 1779, Father Pablo de Mugártegui of Mission San Juan Capistrano informed Serra that "snow is plentiful, wherefore, until the severe cold moderates and the floods subside, the vine cuttings which at your request were sent to us from the lower country have been buried."[10] Supposing that the cuttings in question were set out that spring, a small crop might be expected by the third leaf, in 1781, or a more substantial one by 1782.[11] Roy Brady, after considering all the possibilities, concludes that 1782 was the year of California's first vintage, that the place was the mission of San Juan Capistrano, and that the winemaker was Father Mugártegui. None of this is certain, but it is a good guess, much to be preferred to the received version of 1769, San Diego, and Serra.[12]

The vines that produced that first wine—and, in effect, all of California's wine for the next fifty years and more—were of what we call the Mission grape, a variety known through much of Spanish America under a number of synonyms, including Pais, Criolla, and Negra Peruana.[13] In California it was commonly called the Mission, since the missions were seen as its source. At other times it was called the Los Angeles grape after the most prominent region of California winemaking; or it

The Mission grape, the first variety—and for many years thereafter the dominant variety—in California vineyards. From a watercolor by Hannah Millard in *Grapes and Grape Vines of California* (1872). Courtesy of Special Collections, Charles E. Young Research Library, UCLA.

was called, quite wrongly, the "native" grape to distinguish it from grape varieties known to have been imported from Europe—these were called "foreign" or "European" grapes, although they were no more foreign or European than the Mission itself. Or it might simply be called the California grape.

Until quite recently the origin of the Mission variety was a mystery, at least to students of American viticulture. It is unquestionably a member of the species *Vitis vinifera*, the European grape, the source of most of the world's wine and all of the vine's noble varieties. But where did it come from? And was it known in the Old World? No one could say, although there were many unsupported guesses. Now, through sophisticated genetic analysis, researchers in Spain and Chile have determined that the California Mission grape is an old Spanish variety called Listán Prieto, no longer cultivated in Spain but still surviving on the Canary Islands.[14] The Baja vineyards would have been planted to this variety, and so the cuttings sent up to Capistrano were of Listán Prieto vines. They would have traveled by sea rather than over the arduous land route; only a very few ships visited California in those remote days, and among those very few the probable choice as the bringer of the vine is the *San Antonio*, in 1778, commanded by Don José Camacho. His name is unknown to the historians of wine, but he is, perhaps, the true Bacchus of California.[15]

The Franciscans could not know this, but when they planted those Mission cuttings at Capistrano they were about to succeed in doing what other settlers in North America, far on the other side of the mountains on the remote Atlantic coast, had been struggling vainly to achieve for almost two hundred years: that is, to grow wine. It is true that wine from vinifera grapes—the variety was the Mission—was already being produced on either side of the Rio Grande in the region of El Paso, on the Mexican border, now partly in Texas but then a part of Spanish New Mexico. Winegrowing there went back into the seventeenth century, and by the mid-eighteenth century El Paso had developed a substantial trade in wine and brandy south into the province of Chihuahua and north to Santa Fe.[16] El Paso winegrowing persisted into the nineteenth century but, after the American takeover, only in a much-diminished way; then it gradually faded out. A continuous supply of wine from vinifera in North America had a different source: California—specifically, Los Angeles.

Farther east, in the early coastal settlements of the country and in all of the interior regions that were settled behind the westward movement of the frontier, winegrowing of the traditional European kind had been tried everywhere, over and over again, and had always and everywhere failed. The vines of *Vitis vinifera*, planted at any point between the tip of Maine and the tail of Florida, and westward to the Mississippi, soon sickened and died. No one could understand why, and the question was all the more baffling because the would-be winegrowers saw abundant native vines flourishing all around them. The answer is a paradox: it is just because North America boasted so many varieties of native grapes—more than in any other part of the world—that the European grape would not grow. Native diseases had grown up with the native grapes, and the two had long since reached a sort of accommodation. But the innocent European grape—*Vitis vinifera*, the wine-bearer—knew nothing of the diseases that awaited it in the New World and was wholly unable to resist their onslaught. The list of pests and diseases native to North America is long, but leading the way are phylloxera (*Daktulosphaira vitifoliae*), a minute louse that feeds destructively on the roots of the vine; Pierce's disease (*Xylella fastidiosa*), a bacterial infection that shuts down the plant's water supply and so infallibly kills it; and three fungal diseases: black rot (*Guignardia bidwellii*); downy mildew (*Plasmopara viticola*), found in humid places; and powdery mildew (*Uncinula necator*), at home in dry climates. None of these things was then known in Europe, although phylloxera and powdery mildew have since been exported, with catastrophic results.[17]

What about the species of native grapes? They include *Vitis labrusca* (wild grape), *Vitis aestivalis* (summer grape), *Vitis riparia* (riverbank grape), and *Vitis rupestris* (sand grape), to name only a few of the more common species found throughout North America east of the Rockies. Practically speaking, none of them in an unsophisticated native state is fit for making wine. The berries are too small, the skin too thick, the seeds too large, the flesh too meager, the sugar too low, the acids too high, the flavors too wild, and so on through a long litany of defects. Wine can be made from such grapes if great quantities of sugar are added, but it is drunk only under duress.

The upshot of this situation was that the English colonies, and, later, the new republic of the United States, were wineless territories. The prosperous coast-dwellers could, and did, import European wines— Madeira was a special liking—but day in and day out Americans drank cider, or whiskey, or fruit brandies; the general taste for beer came later, with the heavy German immigration of the nineteenth century. South and west, Texas and California were Spanish territories, closed to foreign traffic, and even had they been open, they were too remote to affect the situation in the settled regions north and east. El Paso wine and brandy became briefly familiar to a small segment of the population in the days of the Santa Fe Trail after 1824. California wine would have to wait even longer to make it to the East Coast, but that tiny, obscure beginning made at Capistrano would, in time, grow into a revolution.

In the history of American wine, California offered a fresh start. Shielded behind the mountains and deserts that made traffic from the east almost impossible, it was free of phylloxera, of Pierce's disease, of black rot and downy mildew. And to these negative virtues one may add many of the positive sort. The climate of Southern California is Mediterranean—that is, one in which rain, in moderate measure, falls during the mild winters. Summers are hot and dry, essentially rainless. For general agriculture, although not always for the vine, irrigation is necessary. In compensation, the soil is fertile. The coast is often foggy, and that disturbs the ripening of such fruit as the grape, but only a few miles inland the effect of the fog is no longer felt. From that point on, grapes will grow anywhere in the valleys and on the hillsides of Southern California—not, of course, equally well in all places, but the vines will at least grow, as they could not be made to do in the distant East.

WINE AT THE MISSIONS

In order to understand the place of winegrowing at the missions, it is useful to know something of their purpose, practices, and economy.

The first thing to know is that the mission, in the Spanish system, was meant to be not a permanent but a temporary body. The idea was that once the natives had been baptized and set to work at peaceful pursuits, the purpose of the mission had been fulfilled and it would cease to exist.[18] For that reason, the missions owned no land but merely had the use of the huge unoccupied territory that lay all around them; when the Indians had absorbed their religious instruction and had learned the European arts, these lands would be divided among them and the Franciscans would move on. This scheme had in fact worked to some extent in Mexico, but in California the point at which the Indians would take over was never reached. And the missions, which were supposed to be temporary, grew more and more anomalous as they grew older. The Franciscans, it has been said, wanted it that way; they enjoyed the possession of undisturbed control over their California empire and had no wish to see it come to an end.[19] That is a hostile view. A more charitable view is that the Franciscans saw that their work was far from complete; they did not want to abandon an unfinished work.

There were never many Franciscans in early California—only two or three priests at each mission, and, at the system's greatest extent, only twenty-one missions. Thus, the Franciscans who carried out the work of the missions were a tiny handful scattered along the hundreds of miles of California's coastal valleys. As the missions developed, this handful succeeded in managing a large economic enterprise in which winemaking was a valued, although secondary, activity.

The Indians, once brought under mission control, were completely dependent upon the missions to which they belonged. They were called "neophytes," that is to say, novices, and novices they remained so long as the missions operated in California. The neophytes were gathered in villages—"rancherias" they were called—around the mission, where they could be instructed and disciplined (frequently by the lash) and where they were available to do all the work: tending the vast herds of cattle; digging the irrigation ditches; planting, cultivating, and harvesting the crops; and constructing and ornamenting the buildings, both sacred and secular. Work in the fields was carried out with primitive tools: digging sticks, machetes, hand rakes, and plows made of tree branches.[20] The work was mostly carried out under the supervision of mayordomos, who could either be Spaniards or mestizos. We regard the condition of the neophytes as slavery; to the Franciscans, it was a means of saving souls.[21] There is no reason to doubt the genuineness of that conviction, just as there is no reason to doubt that the neophytes bore a heavy burden. Several times the neophytes revolted, from as early as 1775 (San Diego) to as late as 1824 (Santa Barbara). As the French sea captain Auguste Duhaut-Cilly put it after his visit to California in 1827–28, nearly sixty years after the first mission had been founded, "If they [the neophytes] could all join together, they would certainly destroy the missions and take up again their former life."[22] But the system continued.

Those Indians who remained unconverted were called "gentiles." Although unbaptized, they might still work for the missions in one capacity or another, and as the settlement of Southern California developed, they might find work at one of the ranchos or in the pueblo of Los Angeles. In the census of Los Angeles for 1830, for example, gentiles outnumbered neophytes 127 to 71.[23]

The beginnings of the Spanish settlement of California were supported almost wholly by supplies from Mexico. Such support had to be continued for many years, but each mission and each pueblo aimed at self-sufficiency—food, drink, shelter, clothing, and all possible amenities would be provided by the labor of the people living in California. The pueblos, beginning with San José (1777) and Los Angeles (1781), were founded as agricultural communities so that they could help with the problem of supply, but the missions had to support the pueblos at the beginning, and the products of the missions continued to be the support of their Indian neophytes, gathered in rancherias around each mission. The Franciscans thus had to train their neophytes in worldly pursuits simply as a condition of survival. The methods of mission agriculture— the work that employed most of the neophytes—remained primitive. But even primitive agriculture was a big technological advance over the stone-age arts of the Indians, as were the many other sorts of work that were laid on them. At each mission, the church remained at the center, but it was surrounded by a whole range of secular activities, winemaking among them. Herbert Bolton listed the many tasks that the Indians performed:

> Each fully developed mission was a great industrial school, of which the largest, as in California, sometimes managed more than two thousand Indians. There were weaving rooms, blacksmith shop, tannery, wine-press, and warehouses; there were irrigating ditches, vegetable gardens, and grain fields; and on the ranges roamed thousands of horses, cattle, sheep, and goats....The women were taught to cook, sew, spin, and weave; the men to fell the forest, build, run the forge, tan leather, make ditches, tend cattle, and shear sheep.[24]

Most of the missions that were founded by Serra and his successor, Fermín Lasuén, were in what are now recognized as winegrowing regions in contemporary California, and most of them made wine back then.[25] Before his death in August of 1784 Serra was able to write that the missions were now "well looked after" with respect to wine.[26] An irregular spread of vineyards and of winemaking from mission to mission is recorded in the following years, so that, by the turn of the century, vines had been planted at all of the then-extant missions.[27]

Mission San Gabriel, the leading wine producer among the California missions. Painting by Ferdinand Deppe, 1832. Courtesy of the California Historical Society.

By 1810 wine was being made at fourteen of the missions; only those where the maritime climate discouraged grape growing (among them San Francisco, Santa Cruz, and Carmel) had to depend on their fellow missions for a supply of wine.[28] There are no statistics for mission wine, only incidental remarks and uninstructed guesses, so we don't know much about the scale of things. There is evidence, however, that many mission vineyards were small, only an acre or two, but even from so small a space the prolific Mission grape might yield enough to produce some hundreds of gallons of wine each season.[29]

Some idea about mission wines and winemaking can be gathered from the scattered information that survives. There is no point in reviewing the records of every mission, but a survey of winegrowing at the southern missions alone will make clear what tradition was inherited by those people who began making wine for themselves in and around Los Angeles toward the end of the eighteenth century.

To start with San Diego, the oldest and most southern of the missions, there are references to grapes at that place as early as 1781, and the Franciscans there were certainly making wine by 1784 and for the next five decades. When Richard Henry Dana called there in 1835, after the mission had been secularized, the meal he was given was accompanied by a decanter of wine—this, he said, was the "most sumptuous meal we had eaten since we left Boston."[30] At Mission San Luis Rey, next up the coast from San Diego, Duhaut-Cilly, who called there in 1828, found what he called "the best wine in all California," and since he had visited a number of the missions, from the northernmost at Sonoma to the southernmost at San Diego, his opinion carries some weight. He added, "I brought back some of this wine and still have a part of it. After seven years it has the taste of paxarete and color of white port."[31] This description—"paxarete" or "pajarete," a very sweet wine of Pedro Ximénez grapes made in the Spanish town of Paxarete—suggests that what Duhaut-Cilly brought back from California was the sweet white wine Angelica, which, with age, would tend to darken, and might, possibly, resemble an old and oxidized white Port.

San Juan Capistrano, next north, has, as we already know, the distinction of being the place where the first wine was made in California.

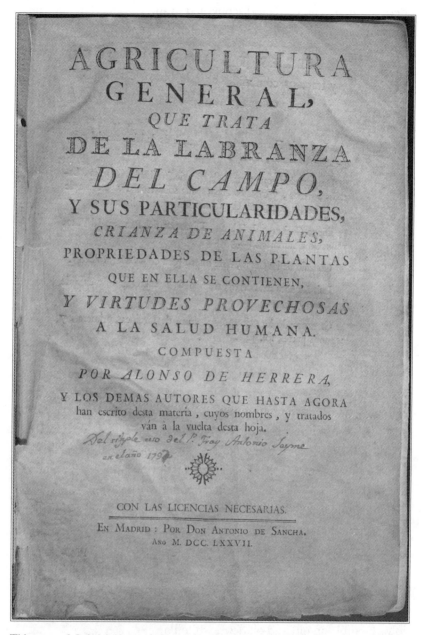

Title page of Gabriel Alonso de Herrera's *Agricultura general*, the 1777 edition of a work originally published in 1513, which helped guide winemaking at the California missions. Courtesy of the Santa Barbara Mission Library Archive.

It is not, however, distinguished beyond that in the story of California wine, although wine was steadily produced there. At Capistrano, Father Serra wrote, after what has been conjectured to be the first vintage in California, they had "already produced wine, not only for use at Mass but also for the table."[32]

The mission that seems to have succeeded best at winemaking—at least so far as volume is concerned—is San Gabriel, only about eight miles to the east of what was to be the site of Los Angeles, and thus the source of winemaking in the pueblo. Winegrowing at San Gabriel did not begin at a particularly early time in the history of the missions; the earliest extant reference to wine there is from 1796, but of course vines were planted before that date. Once begun, production never ceased to grow during the life of the mission.

The great flourishing of San Gabriel winemaking may be dated from 1806, when Father José María de Zalvidea arrived to take charge of the mission. He is remembered as a man of great energy and authority, who, in his twenty-one years of service there, made San Gabriel among the most prosperous of all the California missions. When he arrived he found already growing at San Gabriel a vineyard of some 3,000 vines from cuttings supplied from Baja California.[33] By 1818, when San Gabriel was reported to have 53,686 vines, the modest establishment that Zalvidea had found in 1806 was approaching a commercial scale of operation.[34] In 1834, the year in which Mission San Gabriel was secularized, the vineyard was reported to have then 163,579 vines, or approximately 160 acres, making it by far the largest producer among the California missions.[35]

One authority states that at meals at San Gabriel, wine was drunk "*ad libitum*," and Zalvidea is said to have kept a public table for visitors and travelers.[36] The hospitality of the mission is confirmed by one of the members of the first American party to enter California overland from the east: the group of trappers led by Jedediah Smith. The men arrived at the San Gabriel mission in December 1826, by which time Father Zalvidea had been sent in retirement to San Juan Capistrano. San Gabriel was now under the direction of Father José Bernardo Sánchez, who received Smith's party cordially and provided "plenty of good wine during supper," according to one of them.[37] Two years later Duhaut-Cilly, visiting the mission in hope of trade, was impressed by the "warm greeting of Padre Sánchez" as well as by the "splendid vines, which produce some very good wine. At that time they were loaded with ripe grapes, the purple and succulent clusters hanging down to the ground."[38]

The mission of San Fernando Rey de España, the other mission in today's Los Angeles County, was founded in 1797, sixteen years later than San Gabriel. Located about twenty miles north of the pueblo of Los Angeles, it, too, became one of the leading producers of wine in the mission era, as well as a source of food both for Los Angeles and for the presidio at Santa Barbara. The earliest report of winemaking there is from 1804, although one may suppose that it began a few years earlier. There are references to wine and brandy down to the secularization of the mission in 1835, and winemaking persisted there even after secularization. In that year, 1835, the two vineyards of the mission were reported to contain 32,000 vines, second in size only to San Gabriel among the California missions.

WINEMAKING AT THE MISSIONS

In remote and isolated early California the mission priests had to start from scratch with the process of winemaking. Practically all of them came originally from Spain, where some of them, at least, would have been familiar with the work of growing vines and making wine.[39] In addition to whatever practical knowledge they may have picked up, they also had some printed guidance. At the Santa Barbara mission there is a copy of a 1777 edition of a work originally published in 1513 called *Agricultura general* by Gabriel Alonso de Herrera; the volume is inscribed with the name of Father Antonio Jayme, who served for twenty-five years (1796–1821) at Mission Soledad, where he was the winemaker. The second part of this work is devoted to viticulture and winemaking and was, presumably, used as a guide to mission practice. The book shows the signs of regular use. It is also said that some missions used a work called *Libro de las secretos de agricultura, casa de campo y pastores* (Madrid, 1761).[40]

The cuttings of the Mission vine came originally, as we have seen, by ship from Mexico. Once a small vineyard had been established, there would be a growing supply of cuttings from that source to increase the vineyard size or to supply another vineyard at another mission, and so on. Vineyards would typically be small—a few acres usually—and several might be scattered in different locations. Some vineyards were enclosed by adobe walls, others bordered by hedges of cactus, and still others might have been protected by a common Southern California practice: close-set willow saplings that grew to form an animal-proof barrier.[41] The vineyard would be irrigated, perhaps twice in the growing season, and the vines trained after the Spanish fashion, that is, pruned to form a short, stout trunk so that each bushy, low-growing vine is self-supporting, the so-called head pruning method. This persisted as

A head-pruned vineyard in California, c. 1950s. This method of training went unchanged for more than 150 years. Courtesy of the Los Angeles Public Library.

the dominant form of training in California vineyards for most of the next two hundred years—one of the legacies of the missions, along with the Mission grape. The practice is well described in an account of the vineyards of Los Angeles in 1858:

> These vines are planted about five feet apart, and are not trained on supports or espaliers, but are kept closely trimmed, and are not allowed to spread or rise above about four feet from the ground. This produces a short, thick vine, which does not require support. Many of the vines were six to eight inches in diameter. These vines bear enormous bunches of fruit, weighing from one to three pounds and more.[42]

The need for irrigation would have encouraged planting the vines in straight, orderly lines, although there is some evidence that vineyards were also planted helter-skelter.[43] The vineyards at San Gabriel, according to Hugo Reid, were "intersected by fine walks," and perhaps they contained not only vines but a variety of fruit trees as well; there is evidence that mission vineyards were sometimes varied in this way.[44]

All of the work in the vineyard was done by Indians attached to the mission; for cultivating they used, it is said, "large ironclad hoes."[45] The workers were known as "vinaderos," and they, unlike the muzzled ox, were not denied any share in the produce of their labor. Reid, who knew the mission firsthand, wrote that the Indian men were given a weekly half-pint of brandy and the women a pint of wine.[46]

Since most of the mission vineyards were near the mission itself, transport of grapes was not a problem; there need be little interval between the time the grapes were picked and the time they were crushed.[47] The crushing itself, or, in this case, the treading, was notoriously done by the crudest of methods. One description says the treading was performed on a sloping ground covered with cowhides, hair side down. The grapes were piled on the hides, and then neophytes, clad only in breechclouts and with their hair tightly tied up, walked on to the grapes and trampled them. Each Indian had a pole to support himself in the slippery mass. The juice as it ran off the slope was caught in jars, and these were emptied into a large wooden cask to which the crushed grapes would be added and the whole fermented "for two or three months."

This description is from the 1830s and is somewhat suspect: Where did the large wooden cask come from? And how did a man support himself on such a surface with only a single pole? A later account, from the 1850s, describes the practice in the town of Los Angeles rather than at the missions, but it differs from the earlier account only in having the cowhide suspended to form a sort of pouch, its corners tied to four posts driven into the ground. H. H. Bancroft's description, from a period he refers to merely as California's "pastoral days," varies in some details. The treading is said to have been performed on a platform covered in clean hides, and the juice was caught in leathern bags before it was transferred to a "large wooden tub," where it fermented "for two or three months."[48]

Thus, or so it is said, was wine made in a country where timber was scarce and by a community largely without the usual tools and machines.

Brick *lagares* in which grapes were trodden, at the San Juan Capistrano mission. From Edith Buckland Webb, *Indian Life at the Old Missions*, 1952.

But there is a good deal of evidence to show that in general the methods used at the missions were by no means so primitive. However the earliest vintages may have been made, surviving evidence at several of the missions shows that crushing, by means of treading, was later done in low, brick-lined troughs or on floors made for the purpose; one such stone treading floor protected by a ramada survives today at Mission San Gabriel.[49] No doubt the Indians did the work, and no doubt they were dressed as described, but here they were working in a permanent structure rather than on an improvised cowhide setup. At Mission San José, under Father Narciso Durán, who was both winemaster and choirmaster there, the treading was accompanied by the singing of the choir, just as today in those Portuguese *quintas* where treading the grapes is still practiced.[50]

In addition to leathern bags and clay jars, barrels were also available as containers from an early period in California, since much of the provisions brought up from Mexico would have arrived in barrels.[51] Whether the Mission Indians ever managed to become coopers is not clear; a barrel was the one thing Robinson Crusoe never managed to make for himself on his desert island, and it may be that the missions met the same failure.[52] But they had barrels from one source or another; the crushed grapes and their juice would ferment very nicely in a sound and clean barrel. Other barrels would be used to store the wine after fermentation. It must be admitted that the information we have about containers at the missions—the tubs, casks, barrels, vats, and tanks so essential to winemaking—is scanty and unsatisfactory. When production was small the problem was perhaps not great, but when production grew, the need for large containers, especially for storage, would be acute. How the supply of such things was managed is a question to which I have no answer. Edith Webb, in her description of winemaking tools, refers only to "containers that were large."[53] Nothing of that sort has survived. Eugene W. Hilgard, writing in 1878, says of mission winemaking that "the entire caskage" consisted of "a few large, half-glazed earthenware jars (*tinajas*), from which the fermented wine was rarely racked off, being mostly consumed the same season."[54] Examples of large earthen jars survive at the Santa Barbara and San José missions, but I have seen no evidence that the mission workers were sufficiently skilled potters to have made such things.

How the pomace—the pulp, skins, seeds, and stems left after the fermented juice has been drawn off—was pressed in the early days is also not known. It is possible that at first there was no means for effective pressing; the pomace was simply discarded, and the so-called press wine that can be extracted from the pomace was lost. Charles Sullivan suggests that at first the pomace may have been squeezed between two long boards hinged at one end. Later, the ancient device of securing a tree trunk at one end and placing the free end over a container of pomace and bearing down on it may have been used. But by the turn of the century some form of screw press was in use.[55]

After fermentation, the wine requires cool and undisturbed storage, a fact that was understood by the Franciscan winemakers. At San Gabriel there still exists a small building used for the storage of finished wine. At San Fernando there is a cellar eighteen by forty-one feet, with an eight-foot ceiling, providing a storage space "cool, dry, and dark."[56] At San Juan Bautista a thick-walled adobe building served as a wine storehouse. Another such building is at the San Luis Obispo mission.

Winemaking under frontier conditions runs many risks, and the mission priests had little means for dealing with those risks. If the grapes come in overripe and loaded with sugar, the risk is that the fermentation will not run through to complete dryness but will "stick," leaving an unstable wine subject to diseases such as "tourne." If temperatures rise too high at the time of the vintage—as they more often than not do in California—the fermentation is adversely affected. Unwanted yeasts might cause unwanted flavors to develop in the new wine. And of course, left to itself and exposed to air, wine will turn to vinegar, a natural tendency that can be prevented only by artifice.

A winemaker today has such routine aids as cultured yeasts, sulfur dioxide as an antiseptic, refrigeration to manage fermentation, controlled cool temperatures for stored wine, and so on through a long list of tools and procedures, none of them available in eighteenth-century California. The wonder is that, in the early days when all was improvisation, the missions ever got anything worth drinking, and, having got it, were able to keep it in sound condition. Later, as methods and materials improved, they probably squeezed as much from the Mission grape as it was capable of giving.

The first priority for wine at the California missions was always quite clear: it was needed for the celebration of the mass. Wine for this purpose must be the pure juice of the grape, neither diluted nor turned to vinegar, although it may be fortified, since brandy is wholly derived from grape juice. No special aesthetic characteristics are required. Those qualities of body, aroma, and flavor such as are sought for not just by the connoisseur but by any wine drinker no matter how undemanding were not essential to mission wine. Given the simple requirements of the Franciscans, the Mission grape proved an excellent choice for their winemaking, although it had not been "chosen"; it was simply what they received from the vineyards of Baja. The Mission has all the qualities appropriate for a vine in a new and unfamiliar place, a frontier vine: it is undemanding about site and will grow anywhere, it withstands drought, and it bears abundant crops.[57]

Wine is required for the celebration of the mass—but not much wine. Only the priest at the daily mass drank the wine, and he needed only a sip. "A bottle might last a long time," I was told by a priest to whom I put the question. But could it be kept sound for a long time? Somehow it must have been. Wine for the mass had the clear priority, but practically speaking, once it was available in quantity, wine was for the table.

When considered as a source of palatable table wine, however, the Mission grape presents severe defects. Red wine from the Mission is poor stuff: the color is light and unstable, the flavor is dull, and the acid content is low, making the wine taste flat, a defect only intensified by the oxidization of the wine that was inevitable in the primitive conditions of mission winemaking. White wine from the Mission grape is no better, and the oxidizing effect quickly turns it brown. Fortified wines from the Mission are another story; they can be quite good, and such wines were soon produced at the missions, although just when it was that stills for distillation were introduced in order to produce the required brandy for making fortified wines (or for direct consumption), is not, so far as I know, on record.[58] The earliest reference to the production of brandy in California is from 1797, but without any particulars. The introduction of stills to transform the uninteresting wines of the Mission grape into brandy was, as Charles Sullivan has said, an event that changed the course of mission winemaking.[59]

One fortified specialty associated with the missions is the compound called Angelica (allegedly after the city of Los Angeles, although that origin is not clear of doubt). It is a white juice from the Mission grape to which brandy has been added. The brandy may be added either at the start to fresh juice or early in the process of fermentation, which is at once arrested by the high alcohol content of the brandy. But all of this was irrelevant to the main object of mission winegrowing, which was to supply the celebration of the mass. So long as that requirement was met, other considerations could be disregarded or postponed.

Probably most of the mission wine at the outset was red and unfortified, since that is the simplest wine to produce. But when the means of distilling brandy were obtained, then much of the wine was fortified. We have no information as to what proportion was so treated; as a mere guess one might say that at least half of the production was fortified. So long as the Mission grape dominated the wine production of California, sweet wines were preferred to dry. A large segment of the grape crop would thus have gone into brandy. Dry red and white table wines were probably in the minority.[60] One might also guess that brandy—*aguardiente*, as it was known in early California—was much more sought-after than any of the wines.

There is no evidence that wine from the missions was ever an item of any importance in the very limited foreign trade carried on by the missions. Under Spanish rule, which, in California, came to an end in 1822, all foreign trade was simply forbidden. Under Mexican rule, California was opened up to such trade, and foreigners—Yankees, Frenchmen, Englishmen—began to drift in to exploit the newly available opportunities. Hides and tallow from the immense herds that roamed the mission lands were the staple of trade; anything else was incidental.[61] However, mission wine *was* recognized as a possible item of trade, if not one that amounted to much.

There had always been traffic in wine and brandy among the missions themselves. The big producers, such as San Gabriel and San

Fernando, would send wine and brandy to those missions that could not provide their own, in return receiving credits from the recipients' earnings in the hide and tallow trades.[62] Once Mexican rule opened up the missions to foreign trade, wine was at least thought of as a possible item of trade. The trading firm of McCulloch, Hartnell and Co., operating out of Lima, Peru, signed a contract to deal in mission produce, including wine and brandy, in 1822. Whether any wine and brandy was actually shipped is not apparent. In 1823 Father Mariano Payeras, then president of the missions, signed a contract with the firm of Begg and Co. for trade; wine was named in the contract, but, again, there is no evidence of any shipments. In 1823 the government laid a tax of $8 on an exported barrel of brandy and $4 on a barrel of wine, but that may have been simply a prospective move rather than a genuine source of revenue.[63]

Duhaut-Cilly, in 1827, gives a full list of mission products without mentioning wine. He adds the observation, "The missionaries of Alta California sell only in order to maintain their establishments; few of them hoard riches."[64] In 1829 Alfred Robinson, in his enthusiastic account of San Gabriel, writes, "They make yearly from four to six hundred barrels of wine, and two hundred of brandy; the sale of which produces an income of more than twelve thousand dollars."[65] The quantity named seems exaggerated, although perhaps not by much.[66] But there probably were not $12,000 in all of California at the time, so that figure must surely be discounted. In any case, San Gabriel stood alone for the size of its winemaking; other missions could probably have contributed little or nothing to a regular trade, which would require a steady and dependable supply.

J. N. Bowman, at the end of his thorough survey of winegrowing in provincial California, states that mission wine was traded with Mexico, and with such ships and travelers as came to California, and with the Russians at Fort Ross.[67] That much seems safe to say, but there is no evidence to tell us what the scale of such irregular trade was. Brandy seems to have been the most saleable item; it would not spoil, as unfortified wine would, and of course it delivered a more powerful effect. In 1822, in order to help pay for the new church being built on the plaza at

Los Angeles, several missions, including San Gabriel and San Fernando, gave barrels of brandy rather than gifts of money.[68] For what it is worth, in the year before this, one of the soldiers in California is reported as having said of the brandy of San Fernando that it was "appreciated above any other."[69]

The era of the California missions came to an end following an act decreeing their secularization, passed by the Mexican legislature in 1833; such an end had long been in prospect—the missions, after all, were meant to be temporary—but that end had been evaded by one means or another on many occasions. Now it had come, although not at a single stroke.

The process began at San Diego and San Juan Capistrano in 1833, but proceeded irregularly: there was no plan or direction for carrying out the work of secularization, so the history is different at each mission. In general, the Franciscans were told that they no longer had any secular authority but were simply parish priests. The Indian neophytes were left to their own desperate devices. Some drifted off; some stayed at the mission but refused to work any longer. The priest in charge at San Juan Capistrano, having promised to pay off a debt with wine and brandy to be produced at the mission, suddenly had no workers and no way to meet his obligation.[70] The mission property was put under the control of an appointed administrator to await disposal by one means or another—ultimately, it all ended up in private hands that were not those of the Indians.[71] The Franciscans, deprived of their temporalities, allowed their buildings to decay and their cultivated fields to lie neglected. It was not that they allowed this but that they could do nothing about it. It is said that the vineyards at San Gabriel were ordered by Father Tomas Estenega, then the resident priest, to be uprooted, but that the Indians refused to do the work—whether from indifference or from unwillingness to see the source of their aguardiente disappear is not said.[72] For a time, in fact, the San Gabriel vineyards continued to be worked. The visiting inspector reported in 1839, five years after secularization, that "the vineyards...promise a much greater yield than last year. They have worked hard to enclose them with palisades; they are now all already so fenced except the large one which is being enclosed

Andrés Pico, great landholder, military commander, brother of Governor Pio Pico, and, for a time, guardian of the cellars of Mission San Fernando after its secularization. Courtesy of the Bancroft Library.

with ordinary sticks."[73] Evidently the property was worth keeping up, but this did not last; the visiting committee of the State Agricultural Society in 1858 found the vineyard, although containing "many thousand vines," to be "in a state of ruin." The fences had decayed, and the vines had long been exposed to the "ravages of stock."[74] In 1861 a visitor to San Gabriel reported that "nothing but the black stumps remain" of the vines.[75]

The San Fernando vineyards endured longer after secularization. The inventory made at the time of secularization reported 32,000 vines. In 1846 the vineyard (and all of the San Fernando Valley) was sold to the wealthy Spaniard Eulogio de Celis, then resident in Los Angeles, who, with a partner, Andrés Pico, made it "a successful enterprise." Pico, a bachelor, lived at the mission, where, according to historians Ruth Teiser and Catherine Harroun, he "entertained elaborately, singing Spanish songs for his guests, and staging bullfights in the plaza before the church." Wine from his vineyard and cellar he "bestowed lavishly upon his guests."[76] In 1847, Edwin Bryant, who was en route to Los Angeles with the California Battalion, recorded that at San Fernando he "drank, soon after [his] arrival, a glass of red wine manufactured here, of a good quality."[77] In 1854 the *Los Angeles Star* described the vineyards and olive groves of San Fernando as "superior to any in the state."[78] Whether they were or not, they must at least have been still in good condition. In the next year we learn that the San Fernando vineyards and gardens are tended by a Frenchman "who shares the profits of the sales of fruit, wine, and brandy with the proprietor"; perhaps the Frenchman did the work and Andrés Pico did the entertaining. When the visiting committee of the State Agricultural Society called on Don Andrés in July 1858, they found two vineyards each of 17,000 vines, and they were served both red and white wines from the mission's "cool, capacious, and well-stored" cellars.[79] But this story ended as it did with all the missions: there are references to the San Fernando vineyards as a productive source of wine and brandy through the '50s and '60s, but by 1880 only 1,700 "ancient" vines are said to have survived in the mission gardens.[80]

Long before this end, however, the mission vineyards had produced an uncounted number of private vineyards gathered in the pueblo of Los Angeles or scattered around what is now Los Angeles County. The vineyard at the San Gabriel mission was known familiarly as the *madre* vineyard, not because it was the earliest but because from it came that stream of vines which would make Los Angeles the fountainhead of California's wine industry.

2

SECULAR BEGINNINGS

EL PUEBLO DE LA REINA DE LOS ANGELES

The founding of the pueblo, now the city, of Los Angeles in 1781 was a very carefully prepared work.[1] The site, along the banks of the river then called Porciúncula,[2] was one that had been noted by the Sacred Expedition to California under Portolá. Father Juan Crespí, who kept a journal of the expedition, wrote on August 3, 1769:

> After crossing the [Los Angeles] river we entered a large vineyard of wild grapes and an infinity of rosebushes in full bloom. All the soil is black and loamy, and is capable of producing every kind of grain and fruit which may be planted.[3]

Twelve years later, Felipe de Neve, the governor of Alta California, whose idea it was to found pueblos in the province, came down from his capital at Monterey to Mission San Gabriel, where he could personally direct the founding of the new settlement. De Neve had chosen the site himself, a choice determined by the river.

The Los Angeles River, as it is now called, rises in the San Fernando Valley, over the hills to the north of the town, and at first flows to the east. It then turns south through a narrows, and from there, after a few miles and before 1825, it made a right turn to flow west into the Pacific near the present Marina del Rey. After a great flood in 1825 the river changed course and continued south, largely underground, to the ocean at San Pedro Bay.[4] The pueblo site is just below the river's passage through the narrows, a situation that allowed for the river to be dammed

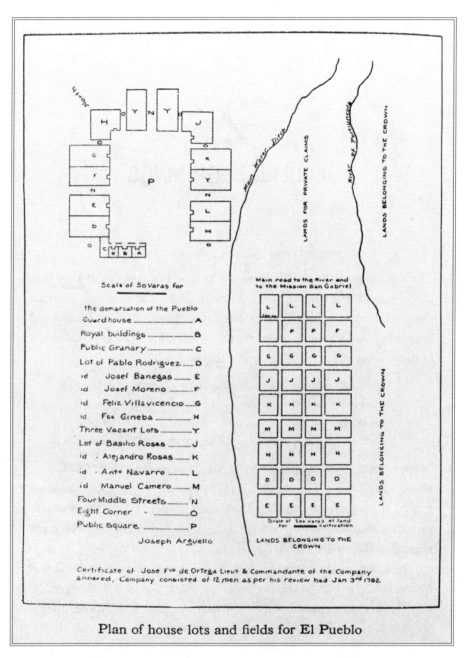

Plan of house lots and fields for El Pueblo

Diagram of the original plan of Los Angeles, with a key to the sites assigned to the settlers. Courtesy of the California Historical Society at the University of Southern California.

and for irrigation water to flow to the flatlands on the west bank of the river. The water was conveyed through ditches called *zanjas*, and these grew in time into a complex system, a circulatory system through which flowed the lifeblood of the community. A description of the system from 1858, when Los Angeles was still so small a town that the river could supply more water than was needed, is surprising to those who know the river in its present degraded state:

> The water [in the zanjas] is clear and sparkling as the bub-
> blings from a crystal fountain, presenting a striking contrast
> with the water in those portions of the State where mining
> muddies all the streams.
>
> The current is so great here, that, by a little attention, the
> most beautiful cascades and fountains may be constructed in
> almost any place where desired.
>
> After having passed through the Town, dispensing its
> blessings, this beautiful stream runs only about three miles,
> when it gradually sinks into the loose, sandy soil, and appears
> above ground no more.[5]

De Neve had drawn up elaborate directions for the design and regu-lation of the community that was to grow there. A pueblo—a civil set-tlement neither ecclesiastical nor military—was meant to provide, in the long term, a permanent basis for Spanish colonization and, in the short term, the food and other supplies that would make California self-sufficient. A civil community devoted to agriculture would be far better able to perform this necessary function than the priests at the missions or the soldiers at the presidios. Soldiers and priests had more than once been brought close to starvation when supplies from San Blas had failed to arrive. A stable community of farmers would put an end to that sort of anxious dependence.

From his base at Mission San Gabriel, de Neve supervised the rather slow, irregular process of assembling the settlers and assigning them their land. By Spanish law, a pueblo possessed 4 square leagues of land—roughly 28 square miles, or 17,713 acres—so there was a super-abundance of land available to the small band of *pobladores* in primitive

Los Angeles. Each family was given a house lot and four fields for the crops that they were to raise. To populate the new community, de Neve had managed to recruit only forty-four settlers, including fourteen families, from the provinces of Sonora and Sinaloa in Mexico. Their inducement was the promise of free land and supplies—"stock, tools, utensils, and a five-year moratorium on taxes in the new pueblo."[6] They were ordinary workers, including a mason, a blacksmith, and a carpenter; and they were a mixed lot: the adults counted "two Spaniards, one mestizo, two negroes, eight mulattoes and nine Indians."[7] Three of those recruited failed to make the trip; three others, with wives and children, were expelled a few months after the founding as "unfit." "Even those who remained were a motley bunch," as one writer has put it. "None of the men apparently could sign his name. None figured significantly in the development of Los Angeles. None had a great enough effect even to have a street or other public place named for him."[8] In short, "They left no impress on the city they founded."[9] Such judgments seem unfairly harsh. A small party, without education, without substantial external support, struggling for subsistence in a remote, alien spot—how could they be anything but obscure? Probably there was no leader among them, but then they had nowhere to lead apart from trying to grow things.[10] And it is also true that no one of any secure or prosperous standing could have been induced to join the original settlers of Los Angeles. Only people without prospects at home would be likely to venture.

The fact is that these nondescript and undistinguished settlers succeeded in doing the work that they were asked to do. The extant record of the early years is very bare, so we know little about the stages of their progress. What we do know is this: the mud-roofed shelters of willow and tule that had been the first dwellings became one-story adobe houses with roofs protected by tar, and the bottom lands along the river became fields of corn, wheat, beans, and, in time, vines. After five years, in 1786, the Spanish government no longer paid a subsidy to the settlers, but evidently they no longer required it. They were given title to their land and were left to provide for themselves. By 1790 they were producing 4,500 bushels of grain, and by the turn of the century "the pueblo was producing surpluses of wheat, corn, barley, and beans that it exported to the presidio at Santa Barbara."[11] That had been the plan, and it had worked.

The record of the early years in the pueblo of Los Angeles, as has been said, is largely blank; whereas the missions and presidios were required to make regular reports to the authorities in Mexico, the pueblos were not. But we can guess at the way things were going by the population figures that were added up from time to time. In 1791, for example, ten years after its founding, Los Angeles had grown to 139 inhabitants from the original 44. (There were no doubt some resident Indians, but typically they were not counted among the "gente de razón," as the Spaniards identified themselves.) The figure by 1800 is 315; in 1816, 560; in 1820, 650. In 1830, fifty years after its founding, the pueblo of Los Angeles counted 764 Spanish speakers and 200 Indians. The slow, almost glacial, process of growth was typical of all of provincial California, accounted for partly by the isolation of the country, partly by the jealous defensiveness exercised by the missions, and partly by Spain's prohibition of all foreign trade, a rule that operated until California became Mexican in 1822. The rule was broken by smuggling, but it certainly had an inhibiting effect on settlement.

When were grapes first planted in Los Angeles? To this question, the early settlers have left no answer.[12] It seems very unlikely that it could have been before grapes were established at Mission San Gabriel, and that may be dated before 1783, when vineyards are mentioned in the mission report for that year.[13] Once the mission vineyard had reached a productive age, say in four or five years, there would have been abundant cuttings available with every year's pruning. Were they all burned? Or did it occur to someone, either in the mission or the pueblo, that some of those cuttings might be planted elsewhere than at the mission? It is hard to believe that the idea never occurred to anyone.

What may have been the earliest secular vineyard—that is, one not belonging to a mission—in today's Los Angeles County was planted not in the pueblo but at one of the original land grants made in Spanish Alta California. This was Rancho San Rafael, of some 36,000 acres, granted to José María Verdugo in 1784, and now the site of, among other towns,

Map of the San Rafael grant of 1784, where, perhaps, the first non-mission vineyard in Southern California was planted, for José María Verdugo, the grantee. Courtesy of the Huntington Library.

Glendale, Flintridge, La Cañada, and Eagle Rock.[14] Verdugo, a soldier stationed at the San Gabriel mission, did not at first reside at his rancho; instead, he sent his brother there to build a house, plant a garden, and establish a vineyard.[15] Verdugo himself retired to his rancho in 1797, thirteen years after the grant of land had been made. It is reasonable to think that he found a vineyard already growing when he went to live at Rancho San Rafael. There are no particulars, so we don't know how large it may have been.

That a vineyard was in fact planted was confirmed in 1828, when Verdugo made out his will and gave the rancho vineyard to his daughter Catalina. To his son Julio, Verdugo willed a number of portable articles, including a barrel of aguardiente, and among the debts owed to Verdugo and listed as assets in the will is $170 owed by Teodocio José for aguardiente. Here, perhaps, is evidence that wine was made at Rancho San Rafael.[16]

THE FIRST LOS ANGELES WINE

The first reference to winemaking in Los Angeles itself that I know of is from the journal of a Yankee sea captain named William Shaler, who sailed up and down the California coast in 1805; he did not manage to visit Los Angeles, but he made notes. He reports that in Los Angeles "they are rapidly advancing in the culture of the vine and the wine produced here is of good quality."[17] Shaler's account of things in California, even though it comes at second hand, is generally reliable, and I see no reason to doubt his statement about "the culture of the vine." Growing grapes and making wine was apparently not something just begun in Los Angeles but a thing already established. We still do not know when the first vineyard was planted in the town, but it is easy to suppose that it happened almost as soon as the first planting at the San Gabriel mission. The two places were so closely associated that what the one was doing was certainly known by the other. There are many claims in later years about Los Angeles vineyards with vines sixty, eighty, or even one hundred years old, but most—probably all—such claims appear to be baseless. Jean Louis Vignes's old vineyard, for example, was said in 1853 to contain vines eighty years old, which would mean that they were planted in 1773, eight years before the founding of the pueblo. Such unconsidered claims are common.[18]

Let us be cautious and say only that, on Shaler's evidence, vineyards had been planted in Los Angeles by 1800 and that wine was available by 1805. From that point on it is possible, in an irregular way, to outline the development of what became the main business of the town. In 1809, Antonio Lugo, for many years thereafter a prominent name in Los Angeles, bought property in the town and soon after planted a vineyard of 8 acres. As Charles Sullivan has written, Lugo's is "the first name we can attach for sure to a Los Angeles vineyard."[19] He was a winemaker as well, for it is recorded that "old Don Lugo" made a sweet wine by the Spanish *arrope* method: "boiling grape juice to the consistency of syrup, then adding it to unfermented juice, thereby retarding fermentation."[20] Lugo's home and vineyard lay on the east side (that is, the river side) of San Pedro Street at Second Street (now in the Little Tokyo neighborhood), where he had a winery as well. This region, south of the plaza and open to the fields running down to the river on the east, was the main area for vineyards in Lugo's time and after, although

Antonio Lugo, "the first name we can attach for sure to a Los Angeles vineyard," according to Charles Sullivan ("Wine in California: The Early Years," *Wayward Tendrils Quarterly* 20 [October 2010]: 19). Lugo and his family were among the most prominent Californios in Southern California for many years. Courtesy of the California Historical Society at the University of Southern California.

vineyards also ran to the north along the river and irregularly to the west. Before it was San Pedro Street it was called Vineyard Street.[21] In time, nearly every home in Los Angeles had its patch of vines; grapes grew everywhere in the town and around it.

Lugo's vineyard, which was still producing in the 1860s, was among the larger ones in the town at the time that it was planted around 1809; by 1817 it had been joined by many more of the same or greater size. In that year, the governor, Pablo Vicente de Solá, reported to the viceroy that Los Angeles, with a population of 586, had 53,686 vines planted on 100 acres.[22] This figure has been doubted as too high, but I see no reason not to accept it. After seventeen or more years of active planting, that number of vines might easily have been set out. The real question is not the number of vines but the size of the market—that is, the number of people available to drink the wine. Supposing that the 100-acre figure is too high, we may use the 53,000-vine figure as equivalent to 53 acres. At a very modest estimate of 2 tons to the acre and 150 gallons of wine to the ton, the Los Angeles vineyards as they were described in 1817 would have produced about 16,000 gallons of wine for a population of 586 people, or about 27 gallons per capita, men, women, and children. This is a conservative figure.

Of course, not all of those grapes would have gone into wine: pests would account for some, others would be eaten fresh, and yet others would spoil or be left on the vine. Much of the wine was no doubt distilled into brandy, reducing the quantity of liquid but not its potency. And no doubt the "gentile" or "pagan" Indians—unbaptized Indians not connected with any mission—who did all of the work in vineyard and winery may have managed to drink up some of what they had made.

By what means the quantities of wine and brandy produced in Los Angeles in the first half of the nineteenth century were actually disposed of remains a puzzling question. Export is not the answer, and neither is trade among the California settlements, although there was some; we know little about local habits in this matter. And yet substantial quantities of wine and brandy were regularly made and somehow disposed of. John Albert Wilson, who had access to many ephemeral sources for his *History of Los Angeles County*, writes that around 1830 "the principal drink of the common people was aguardiente." Such a statement probably expresses only a vague notion that "they drank a lot" rather than a demonstrable fact, but the "common people" certainly had a generous local supply.

The list of Los Angeles vineyards in 1831 published in Wilson's *History of Los Angeles County* cannot be exhaustive, but it does suggest how widespread and how visible vinegrowing would have been in a town that still, in 1830, had only 764 inhabitants.[23] Wilson lists twenty-two vineyardists with Spanish names, from Alanis, Avila, Apablasa, Carillo, Lopez, and Moreno down to Valenzuela and Yorba. A few may be singled out. Máximo Alanis had been a soldier accompanying the band of original settlers in 1781; he now possessed Rancho San José de Buenos Ayres, the site of today's Westwood.

Manuel Requena, whose vineyard of some 8 acres extended along the east side of Los Angeles Street, a little south of Aliso, had a long and distinguished career of winemaking, since he was established before 1831. In his own time he was called, with more than a little exaggeration,

Manuel Requena, a "man of "a well-cultivated mind, and a high order of intelligence," who made prizewinning wines at his Los Angeles vineyard. Courtesy of the California Historical Society at the University of Southern California.

"the most successful producer of wines upon the Pacific coast."[24] In 1855, at the state fair, the wine he entered in the competitive judging baffled the committee, who could not classify it, but considered it "a wine of a fine quality and entitled to the first premium, $25."[25] When a visiting committee of the State Agricultural Society came to Los Angeles in 1858 they found his vineyard of 7,000 vines "all thoroughly cultivated and doing well," and the owner "a pure Castilian," a man of "a well-cultivated mind, and a high order of intelligence."[26] Requena was one of two Los Angeles winemakers whose wines were sent as a gift to President James Buchanan in 1857: Requena's contribution included white and red wines, brandy, and Angelica.[27]

Juan Ramirez, born in Santa Barbara in 1801, came to Los Angeles in 1828, built a house on Aliso Street, married into the prominent Avila family, and planted a 5-acre vineyard that was still producing an annual 20 tons in 1860.[28] At least four members of the great landholding Sepulveda family owned Los Angeles vineyards: Diego, Francisco, Henriques, and José. Francisco, a resident of Los Angeles since 1815 and alcalde of the town in 1825, appears to have been the first of the Sepulvedas to have a vineyard, if not in the town then at least close by it. His was planted around 1829, on a small part of the 30,000 acres of Rancho San Vicente y Santa Monica. José Sepulveda had a vineyard along Alameda Street in early Los Angeles, but I have no date for its beginning.[29]

The 1831 list is particularly interesting for its non-Spanish names. The revolution that brought an end to the Spanish empire in the new world reached California in 1822, when what had been Spanish became Mexican. Spain had forbidden all foreign trade; Mexico welcomed it, and from this time there begins a flow—or trickle—of "foreigners" into Southern California: mostly Frenchmen, Englishmen, and Americans, but with a sprinkling of others. More and more they took over, or began to develop, the businesses of the province, rather than joining the dominant pastoral life of the ranchos. Without ceasing to live by agriculture, Los Angeles became the market town for the surrounding countryside, the place where stores, tradesmen, and professional men could be found. Some of the foreigners became winegrowers, usually as only one of several roles they might play.

The best known of the pioneer American vineyardists is also the earliest, Joseph Chapman, who arrived in Los Angeles by a curious route. A native of New England, he had somehow become part of the privateering expedition led by Hippolyte Bouchard in 1818, an episode in the revolution against Spain. California was regarded by the revolutionaries as a loyalist territory, and so it was a proper object of attack. Bouchard and his men sacked and burned Monterey, destroyed Refugio Ranch west of Santa Barbara, and despoiled the mission of San Juan Capistrano, where it is said they "spilled the wine and spirits they could not drink."[30] Chapman did not participate in all of this destruction, since he had jumped ship at Refugio.[31]

The Californios were happy to take advantage of Chapman's gifts as a jack-of-all-trades. As W. W. Robinson has written, Chapman "knew how to build a grist mill, how to fell a tree, construct a schooner, splint broken bones, boss a gang of Indians, pull teeth, fashion farm implements, and make soap."[32] After several years in Los Angeles, Chapman was, in 1826, granted land along the Los Angeles River, where he set out a vineyard of 4,000 Mission vines and became a winemaker in addition to all his other trades. It is said that he learned winemaking while living at San Gabriel.[33] Alfred Robinson, who knew Chapman, said that he spoke "a mongrel language; English, Spanish, and Indian being so intermingled in his speech, that it was difficult to understand him." In addition, he was illiterate, and yet, as Robinson says, "his great ingenuity and honest deportment had acquired for him the esteem of the Californians."[34]

The fact that he ventured as a grape grower and winemaker in Los Angeles says a great deal about the prominence of that business in the town. Chapman already knew many trades when he arrived in Los Angeles, but winemaking was not among them. He took up that trade no doubt because wines and vines were what Los Angeles in the 1820s was all about. Chapman did not remain in Los Angeles. He died in 1849 in Santa Barbara. His son Charles inherited the vineyard, which was still productive in 1860.[35]

Richard Laughlin, a carpenter by trade, was one of the first Americans to reach Los Angeles by the overland route, with the party of James

Pattie in 1828. Laughlin remained in Los Angeles and planted a vineyard at his place on the east side of Alameda Street. Alameda Street, it may be noted, now running to the south through Chinatown, past Union Station and Little Tokyo more or less parallel to the river, was in the early days flanked by fields on both sides, many of them vineyards; it is the most common address for the pioneer vineyards. Laughlin's vineyard of 12 acres, in the care of his widow, was still producing in 1860.[36]

Matthew Pryor arrived in Los Angeles with Richard Laughlin in 1828 and, like Laughlin, planted a vineyard along Alameda Street.[37] George Rice and John Temple, who were in business together as storekeepers from 1827 to 1831, had a vineyard of 4 acres on the east side of San Pedro Street, the street leading south out of the pueblo to the landing place at San Pedro. There is no evidence that any of these four men made wine in addition to growing grapes, but it seems likely that Rice and Temple did, since wine was a part of their stock in trade;[38] there would have been no practical use for grapes from even a small vineyard except for making wine.

Louis Bauchet (or Bauchett, Bauchette, Bouchet, or Bouchette—the name appears to have given early writers unusual difficulty), a Frenchman and a cooper, arrived in Los Angeles in 1827 and did not plant but purchased an already established vineyard near what became Macy and Bauchet Streets—the latter being one of a number of streets in Los Angeles named for the vineyardists and winegrowers who once lived and worked there.[39] Bauchet died in 1847, but the vineyard, under his widow, Doña Basilia, was still producing in 1860.[40] Bauchet shares the honors with Chapman as the first of the "foreigners" from their nations to make wine in Los Angeles: Chapman was the first American; Bauchet the first Frenchman.

Yet another origin among the pioneers is provided by the man known as Juan Domingo. A Dutchman named Johann Gronigen came to Los Angeles by way of a shipwreck, that of the brig *Danube* in San Pedro Bay on Christmas of 1828. Gronigen, whose name gave trouble to the Angelinos, was called Juan Domingo because Christmas fell on a Sunday in 1828 (actually, it fell on a Thursday, but I repeat the received story). He elected to stay in Los Angeles, married a wife,

The winery of the Dutchman known as Juan Domingo, who was shipwrecked in San Pedro Bay in 1828 and remained in the city as a winemaker. From the lithograph of Los Angeles by Kuchel and Dresel, San Francisco, 1857. Courtesy of the Los Angeles Public Library.

planted a vineyard at Alameda and Aliso Streets, raised a family, and died there in 1858.

Ranches, as well as the pueblo of Los Angeles, might have had vineyards during this era, as has been noted of Verdugo's Rancho San Rafael. But there were not many ranches in Los Angeles County during the early years that are here in question—there were only about thirteen before 1830. It was not until after the secularization of the missions began in 1834, and the subsequent granting or sale of the vast mission lands, that the ranch life that has come to be synonymous with Mexican California came into full bloom. It is likely that most of the Los Angeles County ranches from the period of Spanish rule had vineyards, but so far as I can tell their produce was strictly for domestic consumption.

The labor in the vineyards of Los Angeles, city and county, was, for many years, mainly done by the local Indians, whether "gentile" or "mission." Mostly it was by the gentiles, for the mission policy was to keep Indian labor as its own. The Indians prepared the soil with their primitive plows—iron-tipped Y-shaped branches tied to the horns of the oxen that pulled them—and they planted the cuttings, cultivated the young plants, pruned and trained the vines, and picked the grapes and hauled them to the place of winemaking, where they did the treading and anything else that needed to be done. In Richard Steven Street's highly colored account of conditions in the vineyards of early California, where Indian labor was the main dependence for the first half of the nineteenth century, life was nasty, brutish, and short. The Indians fought murderously among themselves, and they were devastated by smallpox "regularly sweeping through the pueblo and killing as many as a dozen natives in a single day."[41] They were always in debt to their employers for little necessities—an indebtedness that kept them in peonage. Their pay went for brandy, or, as has been said, they were simply paid in brandy. Alcoholism finished off what the hard conditions of work had started, so that the Indian population sank dramatically. By Street's count, "only 219 natives remained in Los Angeles in 1860, compared with 2,014 a decade earlier."[42] This item from the *Los Angeles Star* for June 8, 1853, may stand as typical: "Found Dead—An Indian named Bacilio was found dead near the zanja at the upper end of town this morning. Justice Dryden and a jury sat on the body: verdict, 'death from intoxication, or the visitation of God.'—Bacilio was a Christian Indian, and was confessed by the reverend padre, yesterday afternoon."

Two descriptions of winegrowing in Los Angeles, one from 1828, the other from 1830, are, as is so often the case with early descriptions, quite contradictory. Captain Auguste Duhaut-Cilly, visiting Los Angeles in 1828, found, unlike most early visitors, that the town had an air of "liveliness, ease, and neatness." He observed that the two main crops were corn (that is, grain) and grapes: "The vines grow well here," he wrote, "but the wine and brandy that come from them are quite inferior in taste to the exquisite fruit from which they are made, and I believe that this inferiority must derive from the making rather than from the vintage." A few days later, when Duhaut-Cilly visited Mission San Gabriel, he noted its "splendid vines, which produce some very good wine."[43] The very good wine that he had at San Gabriel must have come from the same kind of grapes that had made the "inferior" wine in Los Angeles, so perhaps his idea is correct: the priests at San Gabriel had a better method than the citizens of Los Angeles when it came to winemaking. Yet there can have been no secrets about it: what the one place was doing must have been known to the other.

Alfred Robinson, who wrote in later years of the California he had known in 1830, in summarizing his account of the state's resources, wrote that "the vine is thrifty, and is cultivated every where; from which is made very excellent wine and brandy."[44] "Every where" is of course an exaggeration: at the time that Robinson speaks of, it meant that vineyards would be found at most of the missions and, especially, at Los Angeles, where Robinson was well acquainted, and whose wines and brandies he found "excellent" only a couple of years after Duhaut-Cilly had pronounced them "inferior."

There is no point in trying to reconcile such contradictions: any of a thousand reasons might account for them, and we have no way of knowing what the actual reasons were. But both men agree on the main fact: that wines and vines were an essential part of the life in the pueblo of Los Angeles. That fact is what made possible the next step in the story.

EXPANSION AND COMMERCIALIZATION

Jean Louis Vignes brought not only a highly appropriate name but a specialized knowledge to the Los Angeles of 1831. He came from the region of Bordeaux, a region synonymous with wine, and was by trade a cooper, a servant of the wine trade.[45] What lay behind his coming to California is not known. When he left the Bordeaux country in 1826 he was already forty-seven years old, and he left behind him a wife and four children. He traveled in the company of a Catholic priest, Alexis Bachelot, on a mission to Hawai'i, so Vignes was evidently not in bad odor with the church; Father Bachelot wrote gratefully of Vignes's assistance to the Catholic mission after their arrival in Hawai'i.[46]

Jean Louis Vignes, not the first by any means, but notably the most ambitious of the early winemakers in Los Angeles, where he settled in 1831. Courtesy of Special Collections, Charles E. Young Research Library, UCLA.

Vignes himself was part of a small group accompanying a young Frenchman who had a harebrained scheme to establish a plantation on land he expected to be granted. The expectation was groundless; no such grant was made, and Vignes was stranded in Hawai'i. For a time he lived hand to mouth. At another time he was in charge of a rum distillery, a useful experience for a man who would later make large quantities of California brandy.[47] After some five unrewarding years in Hawai'i he made his next move by sailing to California, landing at Monterey in May 1831 and then going south to Los Angeles, although just when is not known. He arrived, it is said, with a "stock of devotional ornaments and trinkets," which he sold in the town and at the mission with such success that he became "quite wealthy."[48] That would explain how he managed to acquire, in 1833, a substantial property in the heart of the vineyard region of the town—104 acres lying between Alameda Street on the west and the river on the east, from Aliso Street south to First Street.[49] The list of vineyard proprietors in Los Angeles in 1831 made by J. J. Warner assigns 5 acres to Vignes in that year.[50]

But the story is plainly incredible: How could the hamlet of Los Angeles, where barter was still a common practice, buy enough in the way of devotional trinkets to create a fortune? Besides, Vignes no doubt got his land as everyone did in the pueblo: by grant from the authorities.[51] As J. M. Guinn has written of Los Angeles in the 1830s, "There was not a land owner in it who had a written title to his lands."[52]

Aliso Street, where Vignes had his vineyard, was named for the landmark sycamore—El Aliso—that stood at the entrance to this property. It was sixty feet high and twenty feet in circumference, and when it died and was cut down in the 1890s it was estimated to be four hundred years old.[53]

When Vignes arrived in Los Angeles he would have found, as I have tried to make clear, a thriving scene of vine growing and winemaking going back over thirty years in the town and deriving from the winemaking at Mission San Gabriel before that. There would have been a ready supply of vines for planting; there would have been at least a working supply of essential winemaking equipment, some of it primitive, no doubt, but workable, and he would have found a pool of experienced Indian labor, ready to plant, cultivate, and harvest, including the crucial business of training and pruning the vines, and already experienced in the treading of grapes.[54] Everything necessary to develop a substantial vineyard and winery lay ready to his hand.[55] It is to his credit that he took the opportunity and made something more out of the situation than anyone had yet done, but one should not exaggerate the novelty of his work. Los Angeles was already known as "the city of vines," or, perhaps more accurately, as "a straggling village of adobe cabins, ox carts, grapevines and prickly pears."[56] The grape vines were the main thing.

The date of Vignes's first vintage is not known, but it is guessed to have been around 1837. By 1840 he is reported to have had 17,000 vines planted—roughly 17 acres by the usual Los Angeles measure.[57] By January 1843, he was enthusiastically described by William Heath Davis (who had known him since 1831) as having "the largest vineyard in California," from which came "California wines, of different vintages, some as much as eight or ten years old, of fine quality."[58] Vignes's El Aliso vineyard ultimately grew to contain 40 acres of vines, which were said to produce 1,000 barrels annually.[59] One can only guess at what the actual production was. Of the 40,000 vines growing in 1852, 32,000 were said to be of bearing age, from which one might, by a very conservative estimate, arrive at a figure of about 10,000 gallons, an unknown quantity of which would have been distilled into brandy. Vignes himself, when he advertised his place for sale in 1851, said that his 40,000 vines would "yield 1,000 barrels of wine per annum, the quality of which is well known to be superior."[60]

His was one of the substantial properties of the town. A lithograph of El Aliso from 1857—made after Vignes had sold the property, but presenting a scene probably not much different from what it had been in Vignes's day—shows a long, two-story adobe, the right-hand wing furnished with a gallery while the left-hand wing appears to have been the working winery. Barrels stand alone or are stacked outside the building, where a horse, hitched to a wagon loaded with barrels, awaits the driver. The sycamore for which the place was named stands at the left of the picture. Besides the great sycamore, another striking feature of El Aliso was an arbor covered in vines that ran a quarter of a mile down to the river through the vineyard.[61] This was one of the public attractions of the town where Vignes, a hospitable man, could entertain visitors or accommodate parties. It must have been a highly agreeable refuge from the treeless, dusty, unsanitary, undecorated Los Angeles of the Mexican years.

The El Aliso winery of Jean Louis Vignes, as shown in a Kuchel and Dresel lithograph of early Los Angeles (1857). The giant sycamore for which the property was named is at the left of the image. Courtesy of the Los Angeles Public Library.

It is often said of Vignes that he recognized the defects of the Mission grape at once and accordingly sent to France for superior varieties; these, according to William Heath Davis, "were put up with great care and sent from France to Boston; thence they came out in the vessels trading on this coast, to be experimented with in wine producing."[62] This is a quite assured statement, but so far no evidence has been found to confirm its truth. It should also be noted that the claim to be the first to bring new and better varieties of the vine to California has been made for several people. When Charles Kohler and John Fröhling set up a winery in Los Angeles in 1854, it is said that they immediately improved their vineyard with "cuttings imported directly from Europe."[63] Agoston Haraszthy, in Sonoma, has long been wrongly credited with introducing in the 1860s almost every variety known to California. There are many more claims and counterclaims for the honor of being "first."

There is no reason to doubt that Vignes did in fact send for varieties unknown to California "to be experimented with in wine producing." The idea would naturally occur to a Frenchman who knew better grapes, and there was nothing, except for the remoteness of California, to prevent his doing so. But if he did, no observable effect was produced. Los Angeles, and the rest of California, continued to make wine from the Mission grape, just as they always had, until as late as the 1880s. Fifty years after Vignes had arrived in town, the Mission was still the dominant grape in the Los Angeles vineyards.[64]

Charles Sullivan has closely examined the merits of the claim made for Vignes as the first importer of superior varieties to California. He finds it unpersuasive. Apart from Davis, no other observer of early California makes this claim for Vignes. Davis could not have gotten his information before his second visit to Vignes, in 1852, when, as Sullivan notes, "there was much talk in the California air about importing first class wine grapes from France to the Golden State." Yet there is no mention—newspaper or otherwise—of Vignes in this connection at the time. (The year 1852 was, incidentally, the year in which the first authenticated importation of such vines was in fact made.) There is simply no supporting contemporary evidence for the claim, just as there is no evidence that any difference was made to California winemaking at the time, or for a considerable time afterward.[65] The Mission grape dominated all the vineyards of California, north and south, for as long as Vignes lived and for many years after.

In 1838 Vignes was joined by his nephew, Pierre Sainsevain, who proved to be an asset not just to his uncle but to the trade at large during his long career in California winemaking.[66] It was perhaps on the young man's initiative that Vignes, in 1840, undertook to sell his wines up and down the state. California was then still quite thinly populated, but there were markets at San Diego, Santa Barbara, Monterey, and San Francisco (still called Yerba Buena at that date). If the people there wanted wine, Los Angeles was the place that it came from. Sainsevain loaded a schooner with white wine and brandy and called at these places to sell his uncle's wine, apparently with good success.

The venture seems not to have been repeated. There were, however, others besides Vignes who took part in the irregular trade in California wine. According to W. W. Robinson, Agustin Machado at the Rancho La Ballona, west of Los Angeles, was producing a white wine in the 1830s and after that "attained fame throughout California for its excellence." The wine sold for $10 per 18-gallon barrel at the ranch and for $25 up north, where Machado had agents.[67]

Some items from the papers of Thomas O. Larkin, a merchant resident in Monterey, where he also served as the American consul, give an idea of how the trade was carried on. Larkin seems to have had connections all over California, so that his place in Monterey served as a sort of distribution center. On May 5, 1839, John Temple, a merchant in Los Angeles since 1827 (Temple Street is named for him) wrote to Larkin to ask "what good San Gabriel wine will fetch and the probable quantity that can be sold." Larkin replied, "I think good wine will sell for fifteen hides per Bbbs," and he reported that "Sr. Celes sold his at 25$ cash, and offers his Brandy at 40$ cash." (Eulogio de Celis, a Spaniard resident in Los Angeles from 1836, had a vineyard at his place on Main Street south of the plaza.) Temple then wrote, "I shall send up some wine by Celis so if you wish to purchase you can do it of him."[68] Things could hardly be more casual than Temple's offer: the date of shipment, the quantity shipped, the kind of wine provided, and the price to be asked are all unspecified. Somehow it must have worked.

Left: Thomas Larkin, merchant and American consul at Monterey and active in the early and improvised California wine trade. Courtesy of the California Historical Society at the University of Southern California. Right: Don Juan Bandini and daughter Ysidora. Bandini figured prominently in the affairs of Mexican California. As administrator of the secularized San Gabriel mission, he supervised winemaking there. Courtesy of the California Historical Society at the University of Southern California.

"Good San Gabriel wine" was presumably wine from the still-intact vineyards of Mission San Gabriel, where Juan Bandini was the administrator and where, in 1840, he produced 400 barrels of wine and 135 of brandy.[69] Wine from Los Angeles was evidently a reliable source. To a ship's captain looking for supplies in 1841 Larkin wrote, "California wine I can obtain by sending to St Pedro," that is, to the port of Los Angeles.[70] William Wood, a surgeon with the Pacific Squadron of the U.S. Navy, in Monterey at the end of 1844, found that "two wines, red and white, products of the country, were also to be had in the shops."[71] These would certainly have been from Los Angeles.

Brandy was, at least in the Mexican era, more in demand than was wine. The reasons for this are obvious: brandy has much more potency; it was more economical to ship, since it is wine in concentrated form; the native wines were not particularly attractive; and brandy was much less liable to spoil during transit and after arrival. Brandy was, finally, macho. As Dr. Johnson once said, claret was for boys, port was for men, but brandy was for heroes. It was also for thugs, louts, and desperadoes.

When General Manuel Micheltorena, the newly appointed governor of Alta California, set out for Monterey in 1842, he was accompanied by several hundred soldiers, mostly recruited (or pressed) from Mexican jails, the word of whose reputation for unruly and destructive behavior preceded them. As this mob approached San Pedro, the merchant Henry Delano Fitch sent an inquiry to Larkin in June 1842: "Write me if you wish for any more Argte [aguardiente]. I expect there will be a good sale for it in Monterrey after the 500 men arrives." No doubt there was a great demand, but whether Micheltorena's men could pay for the brandy was another question. "At night, the gardens and vineyards were plundered, and the neighboring farms suffered greatly, from the frequency of the soldiers' visits."[72]

The improvised character of the wine trade appears in another item from the Larkin Papers. James McKinley, Larkin's agent in Los Angeles, writes to Larkin from Los Angeles on December 28, 1845, "I entend to leave this soon. I shall take to your pleace about two hundred barrels Aguardiente and some wine which I entend to sell at a cheap rate." A month later, on January 23, 1846, he writes again:

> Aguardiente will not be wourth above twenty dollar pr Bbls at Monterrey by the Mounth of April. There is a large quanty of it hear and there well be none shepped to Mazatlan this year so it well all have to be consumed in the Country. I have bought up considerable quanty of Wine and aguardiente but I am afraid I shall loss by wine. Agdte [aguardiente] however I was obliged to receive it or get nothing. I think it ought to bring twenty five dollars in cash.[73]

The scale of this transaction—200 barrels of brandy—and the evidence that there was a trade with Mexico (Mazatlán) are particularly interesting. It is reasonable to suppose that other merchants in California—Jacob Leese in Yerba Buena and Asa Fitch in San Diego, for example—also, like Larkin, had frequent dealings in native wine and brandy. At the producing rather than the selling end, there is record in 1843 of Hugo Reid trading in brandy with the ships that called at San Pedro and, on at least one occasion, making a trading trip with his wines to San Diego, Santa Barbara, and Monterey.[74] According to Larkin,

California exported 1,000 barrels of wine and brandy in 1846; presumably most of those barrels went to Mexico, and presumably more than one agent was involved in the trade.[75]

Vignes and his wines were prominent among the boasts of provincial Los Angeles. Early in 1843 Commodore Thomas ap Catesby Jones arrived in Los Angeles to apologize to Governor Micheltorena, temporarily resident in Los Angeles, for having captured Monterey, thinking that war had broken out between the United States and Mexico. When he learned his mistake, Jones took down the American flag, and, after lingering in the north, boarded his men and sailed to San Pedro. The apology was a festive affair. As soon as the navy men had rowed to the beach they were met by a cavalcade, including cooks who prepared a meal on the spot. Then there was a dashing coach ride to the pueblo (over a rough road seamed by gullies and ravines), for a dinner at the home of Don Abel Stearns attended by the governor and his retinue. The next day brought a banquet and a ball, followed by a supper and more dancing. Vignes then invited Jones and his officers to El Aliso and entertained them; if Abel Stearns had the finest house in the pueblo, Vignes at El Aliso had the most splendid show place. According to William Heath Davis (although he was not there) the Americans were "delighted" with the wines and were pleased to accept several barrels of "choice wine." Vignes expressed the hope that some of it might reach President John Tyler so that "he might know what excellent wine was produced in California."[76] Whether any of this wine actually reached the president I have been unable to learn.

Los Angeles might be ideally suited to the vine, as its many admirers never tired of saying, but no farmer can escape his enemies. In 1840, when Captain William Dane Phelps, master of the American bark *Moscow*, then anchored off San Pedro, called on Vignes, he was told that "were it not for the vermin this would be a first rate wine growing country, but they are so much troubled by the Wolves, Foxes, and a species of ground squirrel that destroys the Grape, that it is difficult to protect their vineyards from being stripped by them."[77] One wonders about the wolves: Were they coyotes? In any case, the four-footed pests were abundant. And there is more. In early Los Angeles one of the streets

at the western edge of the town was called Calle de Las Chapules—
Street of the Grasshoppers. In dry years, so the story goes, large hosts
of grasshoppers hatched to the west of the city; when they had eaten
everything there, "they took flight, and, flying with the wind, moved as
great clouds toward the east.... When the destroying hosts reached the
Calle de Las Chapules the vinatero knew his grape crop for that season
was doomed."[78] In 1859 we hear of a worm "somewhat resembling the
cutworm," and in that same year of a light harvest "a portion of the
crop was destroyed by mildew."[79] Jack rabbits chewed the young vines.
Bears and birds ate the ripe grapes.

Against birds the Angelinos had their own methods. Captain Phelps,
visiting Los Angeles again in September of 1842, as the grapes were
just getting ripe, set out to return to his ship by San Pedro Street at the
south of the town:

> As I passed by the vineyards, I observed that in the middle
> of each a scaffolding is erected on which an Indian boy is
> stationed in the morning and remains throughout the day
> with a hat full of stones and a sling, with which he keeps
> away the crows and blackbirds who otherwise would destroy
> half the crop.[80]

Besides the natural evils attendant on winegrowing, there was an
important social evil: the matter of drunkenness. The question of how
the large production of wine in provincial California was absorbed by a
small population has already been raised. A part of the answer, at least,
is that some people drank more than their share, especially of aguardiente. The problem had long been recognized in and around Los Angeles. An official report from San Gabriel in 1809 noted that drunkenness
there was "alarmingly on the increase."[81] In 1815 acting governor Luis
Antonio Argüello imposed severe restrictions on the sale of liquor, a sure
sign that it was being widely abused.[82] In 1827 Duhaut-Cilly, a friendly
observer, could not avoid remarking that although gambling was the
ruin of the Californios, "drinking degrades them even further."[83] Sir
George Simpson, an unfriendly observer, thought that the Los Angeles
he saw in 1842 was the "abode of the lowest drunkards and gamblers of
the country."[84] The abuse of liquor was general throughout California,

but Los Angeles—by far the biggest source of wine and brandy in the province—led all the rest in that matter.

After the end of the mission system in 1834, the mission Indians, who had been controlled by being kept at work for the missions, were turned loose to shift for themselves. Some rejoined the "gentile" Indians, some remained at the mission, some were put to work at the big ranches of the region, and some drifted to Los Angeles. There, together with a considerable number of gentile Indians, they were exploited as the cheapest possible labor, especially by the owners of vineyards and wine cellars, who were the chief employers of the place. The general practice, at least as it has been described by more than one observer, was to pay the Indian worker at the end of the week with a dollar or two with which he could buy aguardiente and stay drunk over the weekend. Or, to simplify the process, he was simply given his wage in the form of aguardiente. Either way, on Sunday, as he lay senseless in the street, he would be scooped up by the town marshal and his crew, dumped in a corral with the other drunks, and, on Monday, offered at auction to any bidder who could use his labor that week. The Indian was thus locked into a vicious circle from weekend drunk to weekend drunk, a circle that spiraled down to early death. And the city of Los Angeles had a modest source of revenue from the weekly auction.[85]

The problem of drunkenness, especially among the Indians, was not confined to Los Angeles. In September 1845, near the end of California's Mexican era, a late, desperate act was issued under Governor Pio Pico—a "Proclamation on Viticulture" that "prohibited people from buying grapes or wine from Indians who, besides drinking in excess, apparently had been stealing grapes and making wine on the sly, and thus undermining local winemakers and not paying the required taxes."[86]

Although native wines and brandy were in plentiful supply in Southern California, there is some evidence that the elite among the Californios preferred the imported stuff. A report on trade from Santa Barbara in 1827 argued that "the production of wine and brandy might be made profitable if foreign liquors could be excluded or heavily taxed."[87] Even more curious is Richard Henry Dana's disapproving observation made in 1835: "The Californians are an idle, thriftless people, and can make nothing for themselves. The country abounds in grapes, yet they buy bad wine made in Boston and brought round by us, at an immense price, and retail it among themselves at a *real* (12 ½ cents) by the small wine-glass."[88] This is curious on several grounds. Dana is wrong to say that the Californians could make nothing for themselves; as we know, they were making wine and brandy in abundance. But that makes it all the stranger that they should be willing to pay a great price for a wine imported not from France or Germany but from Boston!

There is record of wine being made at Boston in the nineteenth century. One company was reported in 1860 as having made 20,000 gallons annually from the wild grapes growing along the Charles River.[89] But, as any American dwelling on the East Coast knew—but as, evidently, the Californios did not—wine made from the unameliorated native grape is unfit to drink. It is hard to imagine what the Boston product tasted like: it would have needed a heaping amount of added sugar in order to reach an adequate level of alcohol, and if it were to survive shipment around the Horn to California, it must have been heavily fortified. It was doubtless badly oxidized as well. If the Californians bought this compound in preference to the native product, that must be attributed to the cachet clinging to anything "imported." They can't have drunk much of it. More sensibly, Spanish wines and Spanish brandy continued to be imported in the Mexican era of California.[90]

Jean Louis Vignes continued his business after the American conquest of California in 1846–47, but he was advertising his El Aliso for sale in 1851, evidently without success. Four years later he sold the place to his Sainsevain nephews, Pierre having been joined by his older brother, Jean-Louis, and together they took the vineyard into the American era.

For most of his active years Vignes had a neighbor and a friendly rival in Los Angeles. This was William Wolfskill, who had been a trapper and trader in New Mexico for some years before coming to California in 1831. Traveling over the Old Spanish Trail (neither old nor Spanish) he arrived in Los Angeles with a pack train freighted with New Mexico's sought-after blankets and other goods to trade for horses and mules. Instead of returning to New Mexico, he tried hunting for sea

William Wolfskill, who with Jean Louis Vignes was the pioneer of large-scale winemaking in Los Angeles. Courtesy of the California Historical Society at the University of Southern California.

otter, without much success, and then, in 1833, bought a small property in Los Angeles "containing some grape vines."[91]

By 1836 Wolfskill, who supported himself as a carpenter but grew more and more interested in the possibilities of his vines, secured a grant of land from the city and planted more vines. After two years he petitioned for and was granted 100 acres to the south of the pueblo, lying between present-day Alameda Street west to San Pedro Street and from Third Street south to Seventh Street. Here he began winegrowing on a substantial scale. There were already about 4,000 vines on the property; between 1838 and 1846 Wolfskill planted 32,000 more. The property was attractive enough that Wolfskill, soon after the American conquest, was offered $10,000 for his vineyard.[92] In 1856 and again in 1859 his vineyard was declared "Best in California" at the state fair. By 1858 Wolfskill had 60,000 bearing vines, and his winemaking establishment had four cellars with a total storage capacity of 100,000 gallons.[93]

Most of this expansion had been carried out even before the American conquest. Edwin Bryant, visiting Wolfskill's place in January 1847, described the vineyard as "young," although it already covered forty acres, from which were produced "180 casks of wine and the same quantity of aguardiente."[94] A cask, Bryant conveniently adds, "is sixteen gallons." Using the formula of 3 gallons of wine to make 1 gallon of brandy, it appears that Wolfskill made around 12,000 gallons of wine, a quantity that would just match what one would get from 40 acres producing 2 tons per acre yielding 150 gallons of wine per ton. Bryant reported approvingly of Wolfskill's wines: "He set out for our refreshment three or four specimens of his wines, some of which would compare favorably with the best French and Madeira wines."[95]

In the next year, another American observer inspected Wolfskill's place and reported on what he saw, in such a way as to make clear the very approximate and impressionistic character of early travelers' reports. This was Edward Buffum, a journalist who came out to California in 1847 with Stevenson's Regiment and visited Los Angeles in 1848. He wrote:

> An American, named Wolfskill, has here a vineyard containing thirty thousand bearing grape-vines, from which he makes annually a thousand barrels of wine, and two or three hundred of *aguardiente*, the brandy of the country. Some of this wine is a very superior article, resembling in its flavour the best Madeira, while another kind, the *vino tinto*, is execrable stuff. With proper care and apparatus, however, the grape of the *Pueblo* could be made to yield as good wine as any in the world; and the whole plain, twenty-five miles in extent, reaching to the beach at San Pedro, is susceptible of the cultivation of the vine.[96]

Bryant's 180 casks in 1847 have grown to Buffum's thousand barrels (capacity not stated) in the short space of a year. One despairs of such statistics, but practically they are the only kind available. Bryant's judgment on Wolfskill's red wine—"vino tinto"—as "execrable stuff" confirms the defects of the Mission grape. Both Bryant and Buffum say that Wolfskill's good wine resembles Madeira, by which they certainly mean a fortified wine, although whether red (port) or white (Angelica) is not said.

By 1849, according to John Albert Wilson's *History of Los Angeles County*, Wolfskill was sending wine north to San Francisco, now a flourishing market created by the gold rush. Wilson, unaware of early mission sales of wine, of Vignes's coastal venture back in 1840, of Hugo Reid, and of Larkin's traders, thought that Wolfskill was the "pioneer" in the export of Los Angeles wine. In an irregular way, as has already been shown, there was a more than negligible "export" before 1849. Wolfskill himself had at least thoughts of exporting his wine as early as 1842. He sent his brother John, then living at Sonoma, two barrels of aguardiente, among other items, and wrote that if he (John) wished to trade in wine and brandy with the ships visiting Northern California, he (William) "would deliver it as soon as it is made."[97]

Always curious and experimenting, William Wolfskill, at the same time that he was enlarging his vineyard, was planting every sort of fruit: pears, plums, quinces, apples, cherries, figs, lemons, and oranges—especially oranges. The Wolfskill grove had 2,200 trees by 1858. The committee of the State Agricultural Society, sent to inspect things in

Southern California that year, were almost overwhelmed by the splendor of Wolfskill's estate; it was, they thought, "quite superior to anything in the state."[98] Wolfskill now is better remembered for his pioneering work in establishing the citrus industry of Southern California than he is for his winemaking, but his winemaking was no mere sideline or afterthought. It was his first substantial business, carried on efficiently. By the late 1850s, however, he appears to have left the winemaking to others, selling his grapes and turning over to the buyer the use of his own winemaking establishment.[99] At his death in 1866, his will disposed of, among other properties, six named vineyards: Aguilar, Sotello, Brundige, Valenzuela, Scott, and Mulally, all in the pueblo of Los Angeles, as well as an unnamed one across the river to the east, the whole aggregating a good deal more than 200 acres.[100] His son Joseph carried on the business, which was still operating in 1888, although by that time winemaking was clearly subordinate to orange growing.

THE RISE OF THE RANCHOS

While Vignes and Wolfskill were building up their winemaking enterprises in the 1830s, the land grants on which the great Southern California ranches were founded began to proliferate. In what are now Los Angeles and Orange Counties only fourteen grants had been made under fifty-three years of Spanish rule; under Mexican rule, there were seventy-eight grants made in just fifteen years.[101] The grants were mostly made from the lands originally assigned to the missions, which had been shut down beginning in 1834. From that date there was a steady procession of new ranches, most of which had vineyards, at least some of which were quite extensive. At La Cañada de Santa Ana (1834), for example, Bernardo Yorba had, at his feudal estate, in addition to cooks, bakers, shoemakers, and so on, a "man to make the wine."[102] Rancho Paso de Bartolo Viejo (1835), near San Gabriel, had a vineyard; at Rancho Sausal Redondo (1837) there were 6,000 vines. Hugo Reid at Santa Anita (1839) cleared ground for 10,000 vines in 1840 and had 25,000 planted at the time he sold the place in 1847. Juan (or Giovanni)

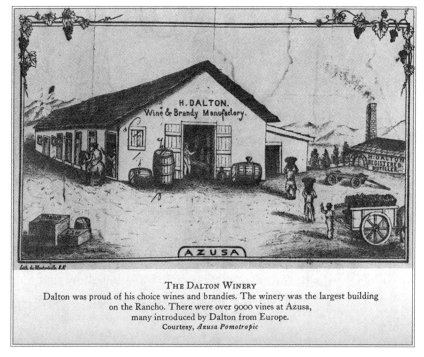

THE DALTON WINERY
Dalton was proud of his choice wines and brandies. The winery was the largest building
on the Rancho. There were over 9000 vines at Azusa,
many introduced by Dalton from Europe.
Courtesy, *Azusa Pomotropic*

The winery at Henry Dalton's Rancho Azusa, the biggest building on the property. Courtesy of the California Historical Society.

Batista Leandri, an Italian storekeeper in Los Angeles, bought Rancho Los Coyotes in 1841, where he had a vineyard from which, he told Alfred Robinson, he one day hoped to have the pleasure of "remitting a cargo of wines to the United States."[103] Leandri died in 1843, the hope unrealized, although the time was not very far off when the thing would be done. John Rowland and William Workman, who both came to Los Angeles in 1841, obtained the grant of the La Puente rancho in early 1842 and soon developed a substantial winemaking business there. So did Francis Temple, their neighbor and Workman's son-in-law, who planted 50,000 vines at La Merced Ranch (1845). Henry Dalton made wine from 50 or 60 acres of grapes at his Rancho Azusa (1845); when he acquired the ranch from Luis Arenas there were already 7,000 vines on the property, and one may suppose that Arenas had made wine from them. Dalton experimented with many different crops, but winemaking and brandy distilling were, according to Dalton's biographer, "the most important industry on the ranch."[104] All of this and more was done in the brief interval between the secularization of the missions in 1834 and the American occupation in 1847.

What the Americans found when they entered Los Angeles, then, was a town filled with vineyards surrounded by ranches with yet more vineyards.[105] No doubt the scattered signs of human settlement were dwarfed by the vast spaces of unoccupied Southern California, over which herds of horses and droves of cattle roamed at will. But so far as the human settlements were concerned, there could be no doubt about the primacy of the grape. The American soldiers, most of whom would never have seen a vineyard before and for whom wine was an exciting novelty, were quick to appreciate the Los Angeles product. Lieutenant William Emory, in January 1847, declared that the wine of Don Luis Vignes was "truly delicious, resembling more the best description of Hock than any other wine." Emory added that "many bottles were drunk leaving no headache or acidity on the stomach." At the same time, Dr. John Griffin, a surgeon with General Stephen Kearny's troops, discovered the wine of Los Angeles and found it "of fine flavour, as good I think as I ever tasted." Lieutenant Joseph Revere, of the navy, was especially smitten by the local speciality, Angelica, calling it "a delicious cordial." Doubtless the common soldiers were just as enthusiastic as their officers. Although it was reported that General Kearny had locked up a large store of wine and brandy so that Commodore Robert Stockton's sailors could not get at it, they can't have had any real difficulty in getting wine and aguardiente in Los Angeles, where both flowed in abundance.[106] Nor did they. A few days after entering the pueblo, one observer wrote, "one half of the army are drunk."[107]

Edwin Bryant's reflections upon the vineyards of Los Angeles as they appeared to American eyes in 1847 may stand for any number of similar responses. Bryant had come down from the north to Los Angeles at the end of 1846. There he boarded at a house where his eleven o'clock meal was accompanied by a bottle of native wine, and so too was his supper. After he had had a chance to look around, Bryant wrote:

The yield of the vineyards is very abundant; and a large quantity of wines of a good quality and flavor, and *aguardiente* are manufactured here. Some of the vineyards, I understand, contain as many as twenty thousand vines. The produce of the vine in California will, undoubtedly, in a short time form an important item in its exports and commerce. The soil and climate, especially of the southern portion of the country, appear to be peculiarly adapted to the culture of the grape.[108]

As a prophet, Bryant was right on target, although he could not have predicted what happened immediately next. Under the American military government, not much changed in any part of California during the first two years, but that period of quiet would soon be over. Before the occupation ended in December 1849, gold was discovered at Sutter's Mill (January 1848), and then, after official announcement of the discovery in December 1848, "the world rushed in."

3

AMERICAN LOS ANGELES

THE CITY OF VINEYARDS

One of the most striking illustrations of early Los Angeles was made in 1849 at the request of the city fathers, who, wanting to sell the lands belonging to the pueblo in order to raise some revenue, needed a map in order to manage the process. Only very primitive maps of the various land grants and properties in both the city and county had been made up to this point. Now, under the new regime, more formal procedures would be followed in order to make land titles secure. The American army of occupation had officers trained in engineering at West Point who could make a suitable map. As it happened, those officers had little to do, and the inflation of prices created by the California gold rush made it hard for them to live on their salaries, so they were not only allowed but encouraged to accept civil jobs.[1] One of these men, Lieutenant Edward O. C. Ord of the Third Artillery Regiment, was recommended to the Los Angeles people by his commanding general and, after due discussion, was hired to prepare the desired map for a fee of $3,000.[2] Ord and his assistant, William R. Hutton, surveyed the city, drew their map, delivered it in September, and collected their fee; the town officers, guided by the map, began to auction off the pueblo lands, and, one supposes, all parties were satisfied.[3] The hasty auction of the public lands of Los Angeles has since been condemned as a prodigal waste of a splendid patrimony. But we may at least be grateful to have the map, for it gives an idea of the economy of Los Angeles at the mid-nineteenth century more vivid than any other record.[4]

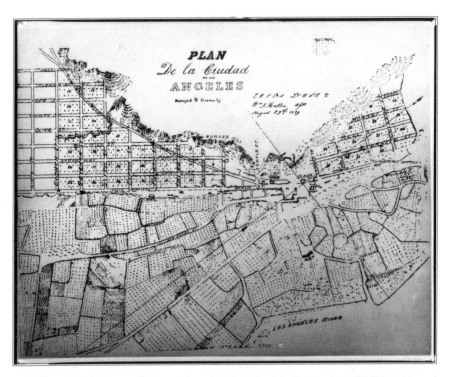

The 1849 Ord and Hutton map of Los Angeles, showing vineyards and other cultivated fields. Courtesy of the California Historical Society at the University of Southern California.

What the map makes graphically clear is the extent to which Los Angeles deserved its nickname as the city of vines. Left and right at the top of the map are imaginary blocks of neatly squared town lots, as they might be laid out after the city government had sold the land. Below these neat squares lies the actual town, straggling over a very small space at the center. The rest of the space, running down to the river and along it, is occupied by cultivated land on which vineyards dominate, not only in number but in the space occupied.[5] The pueblo appears as a minor appendage to a very large cultivated area, in which more than fifty vineyards have been counted.[6] The map shows only a part of the actual region devoted to agriculture at this point in Los Angeles's history; more vineyards lay south and north of the town, and were beginning to spread across the river to the east.

Vines were the first thing the traveler to Los Angeles saw: "The river," Edwin Bryant wrote in 1847, "is skirted with numerous vineyards and gardens, enclosed by willow hedges." Edward Buffum, in the same year, found that "the vineyards are lovely spots; acres upon acres of ground are covered with vines." Harris Newmark, coming up from San Pedro in one of Phineas Banning's coaches in 1853, entered Los Angeles for the first time by San Pedro Street, then known as Vineyard Street, "a narrow lane, possibly not more than ten feet wide, with growing vineyards bordered by willow trees on each side of the road." Vineyards stretched unbrokenly from the road to the river and south for a mile or more. Newmark adds the interesting note that in Los Angeles at that time wine was "a very cheap article, costing about fifteen cents a gallon," and was usually served free with meals.[7] Dr. Thomas J. White, newly arrived in Los Angeles in 1855, boasted, "There is no portion of the world, in all probability, that produces grapes in so great an abundance as Los Angeles." Captain (later General) E. D. Townsend, visiting California in 1855, declared Los

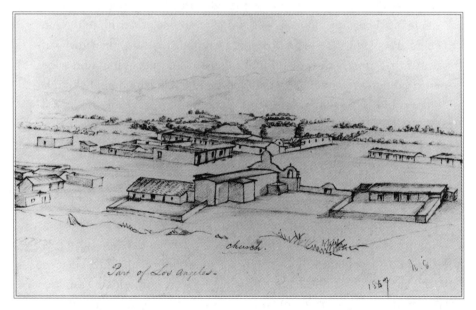

Los Angeles in 1847, showing the northern part of the plaza area and the church (in the center foreground). Detail of a sketch by William R. Hutton, who assisted Edward Ord in drafting the 1849 map of Los Angeles. Courtesy of the California Historical Society at the University of Southern California.

Angeles to be "the City of Vineyards."[8] Those vineyards were now on the verge of a new growth and prosperity.

The reason for that was the sudden creation of a new market by the gold rush to the northern foothill regions of California. The population of the entire state (although it was not yet a state) in 1848 is estimated at about 14,000 "gente de razón" and perhaps 100,000 Indians. Four years later, the state census put it at 260,000 white, while the Indian population was dwindling through poverty, disease, alcoholism, and other destructive forces.[9] Compared to the scale of things that had prevailed in California since its founding in 1769, this increase was immense, and its effects were powerfully felt in the south, especially in Los Angeles. Southern California remained an isolated backwater compared to the booming north: Los Angeles had only 1,610 people in 1850, an increase over the 1,250 of five years earlier, and nothing like the transformation that had overtaken San Francisco and Sacramento. But the farmers and vineyardists of Los Angeles now had a big and growing market for their wares, including fresh grapes as well as wine and aguardiente. There was a big demand for beef, too, so the cattle that had been the economic staple of Mexican California were briefly a source of wealth to the ranchero. People in the north, however, were quick to raise their own cattle, so that market dwindled for Southern California. Vines and wines were a different matter. They required some stable settlement before the vines could be grown and the wine made satisfactorily, and that condition had been obtained only in the south.

PERSISTENCE AND CHANGE

Many of the old Mexican names that figured in the early lists of Los Angeles grape growers and winemakers persisted under American rule: Alvarado, Capablanca, Ramirez, Requena, Rubio, et al. had all been at work before the conquest. Some new names were now added: Francisco Alvarado on the west side of town; Isidro Burruel, who produced wine from 100 acres of vines; Rafael Caravajal, a small producer; and, among the women, Maria Reyes were among those new to the list of growers and winemakers after 1847. The new Latino names were greatly out-numbered by those of the many foreigners who had been drawn to the business of winemaking in Los Angeles.[10] Among the Yankees, English, and Irish were Henry Barrows, a schoolteacher and the son-in-law of William Wolfskill; Ozro Childs, from Vermont, now a merchant in Los Angeles, who had a 12-acre vineyard south of town; and George Dalton, brother of Henry, of the Azusa Rancho, who set out a vineyard of 18,000 vines near Washington Street and Central Avenue in 1851 and was still cultivating them in 1880. Louis Wilhardt, whose 11-acre vineyard lay a mile north of the plaza, made a highly regarded white wine as early as 1849.[11]

Dr. Thomas Jefferson White, who came to Los Angeles from San Francisco in 1855, was distinguished as the first speaker of the California Assembly in 1849. In Los Angeles, he and his wife, according to Harris Newmark, made "quite an accession to our social ranks" and were much admired for their "frequent and lavish" parties.[12] White, besides practicing medicine, owned a drug store on Main Street, a vineyard next to Dr. Hoover's, and a winery in the basement of his house. That vineyard, as has been noted, was mistakenly thought to be the oldest in the town. When White bought it on arriving in Los Angeles it had 16,000 vines. White was evidently ambitious; Newmark says that he became "one of the leading winemakers," and by 1860 he had some 30,000 vines and was making from 12,000 to 14,000 gallons of wine annually. He had either an extraordinarily spacious basement or had found some other space as well. "He has adopted the only and true policy for enhancing the value of his wines," an account from 1860 declared, "viz. by keeping over each vintage from three to five years, thus giving sufficient age, which gives character to the wine. The great secret which has produced so much discredit to the California wines, has been in thrusting them into the market the first year."[13]

Talk about the need to age wine before putting it on the market was familiar at this time and for a long time afterward. J. DeBarth Shorb, when he was planning the big San Gabriel winery at the end of the 1870s, announced that he would hold his wines for three years before releasing them; this was a main theme in promoting the business.

Andrew Boyle, an Irishman who had been associated with Matthew Keller in Mexico, took this line in announcing the wine from his vineyard on Boyle Heights in 1863:

New Brand of California Wine!!

Paredon Blanco

Mr. Boyle, for the first time, offers his Wine for Sale, having preferred to wait until it had attained a mature age. He now offers the vintage of **1860**, which will commend itself to all connoisseurs.

To be sold in lots to suit purchasers. All orders left at BOYLE'S SHOE STORE, *Main street, near Commercial,* will meet prompt attention.[14]

"To be sold in lots to suit purchasers" reminds us that, outside of San Francisco, wine at this time would rarely have been sold in bottles. Customers would bring whatever container they might have, and that would be filled directly from the barrel. Five years after Boyle's notice, another ad in the *Los Angeles Star*, this one for the "PURE NATIVE BRANDY AND WINES" of P. Downey & Co., makes the same offer: "put up in packages to suit purchasers, at the shortest notice."[15]

The French speakers were well represented in Los Angeles. Michael Clement had a house and vineyard near the Los Angeles River in 1852, and Prudent Beaudry, a prosperous real estate developer originally from Quebec, had a vineyard on the heights across the river.[16] Major Ben C. Truman, writing in the *New York Times* in 1887, called the Beaudry vineyard one of the city's "oldest and best known" and added that Beaudry had "an immense winery."[17] Leonce Hoover (originally Huber), a Swiss who had served as a doctor in Napoleon's army, came to Los Angeles in 1849 and bought a vineyard, from José Serrano, with vines, so it was popularly said, a hundred years old.[18] The same sort of exaggeration seems to have affected Hoover himself. When a committee of the State Agricultural Society called on him in 1858, they were astounded to find that Hoover, so he assured them, drank nothing but his own wine all day long, except for a morning cup of coffee: "At his meals, when at work, around the social board, on retiring at night—at any and all times, he drinks his pure juice of the grape with perfect freedom, and, as he assures us, without the least intoxicating effect."[19]

Most of the names above, and many others that might be added, were those of people for whom winemaking was a sideline or a part-time occupation. Abel Stearns, for example, the biggest landowner and one of the wealthiest men in Los Angeles County, had a vineyard and winery that could not have occupied much of his time or interest. But the major players in Los Angeles wine were fully committed. In the 1850s, the first decade of American possession of California, they constituted a Big Three: the Sainsevain brothers, Matthew Keller, and the firm of Kohler and Frohling. The Sainsevain brothers, Pierre and Jean-Louis, had bought their Uncle Jean Louis Vignes's El Aliso winery in 1855 and at once set about enlarging it. In 1856 Don Pedro, as Pierre was known in Los Angeles, was planning an agency in San Francisco

Jean-Louis Sainsevain, who, with his brother Pierre, continued the Los Angeles winery founded by their uncle Jean Louis Vignes. Courtesy of the Huntington Library.

in order to establish the reputation of Sainsevain wines; he opened it in 1857 and earned a good name there for Los Angeles wine. By 1858, when they made 115,000 gallons of wine, the Sainsevains were the biggest producers in the state. In that year they had five cellars at their Los Angeles property, each 135 feet long by 15 feet wide.[20] About half of their annual production was from grapes from their own 40-acre vineyard; the other half came from purchased grapes. In 1858 they are reported as buying the crop and making wine at B. D. Wilson's Lake Vineyard, at Andrés Pico's San Fernando mission winery, and at John Rowland's La Puente ranch. When the vintage was completed the Sainsevains celebrated with a banquet for their workers.[21]

They invested heavily in an effort to make a sparkling California wine, importing an expert from France for the purpose. They had an apparent success: a Sainsevain "Sparkling California" was put on the market in 1858 and attracted attention as far away as New York, to which "three hundred dozen" of this wine at $12 a dozen was shipped each month.[22] But the low-acid Mission grape would never yield a decent base wine. Their expert had trouble controlling the "atmospheres"—the internal pressure created by the wine fermenting in bottle—and they accordingly suffered large losses from exploding bottles. Despite that, Sainsevain Sparkling California was produced in considerable quantity, more of it, in fact, than the Sainsevains could sell. It was soon recognized that the wine was poor stuff; by 1861 there were 165,000 bottles of unsold Sparkling California in the Sainsevains' cellars. In 1862 the venture into sparkling wine was shut down, although a writer for the *Atlantic Monthly* in 1864 said the Sainsevains were "still experimenting" to improve their sparkling wine.[23] In 1867 the El Aliso property was sold.[24]

Both Sainsevains continued successfully in the wine business, but no longer in Los Angeles. It was a disappointing ending to a once-prosperous business; visitors as recently as 1858 had said of the Sainsevain winery that "everything in and about this establishment indicates enterprise, science, and skill, enriched by large experience and noble philanthropy."[25] The philanthropy is unexplained.[26]

Ad for the ill-fated sparkling wine produced by the Sainsevain brothers. It is called "Sparkling California" in the main design but "Sparkling California Champagne" in the text below. From *Alta California*, December 12, 1857. Courtesy of the California State Library.

MATTHEW KELLER AND THE LOS ANGELES VINEYARD

A second major player in post-conquest Los Angeles was Matthew Keller, of the Los Angeles Vineyard. Keller was described by Harris Newmark, who came to town only a couple of years after Keller, as a "quaint personality," but of "real ability."[27] Another contemporary said Keller was a man of "intelligence, energy, and resolution," and added that he was a spiritualist as well.[28] A family member, after Keller's death, claimed that Keller spoke English, Spanish, French, German, and Gaelic.[29] Perhaps he did: there is good evidence for the English, Spanish, and French at any rate. He was certainly Francophile, as most good Irishmen were. He sent his son Henry to be educated in France when the boy was only eight years old; Henry never saw his parents again, both of them dying before he was summoned home. Keller put his French to professional use as well; he read the French literature about winemaking, and he corresponded with the great Louis Pasteur, who sent him a copy of *Études sur le vin* (1866).[30]

Born in County Cork, Keller was a graduate of (or at least attended) Trinity College, Dublin. He left Ireland for New York in 1832, then went to Texas, where, at the time of the Mexican War, he ventured into Mexico as a merchant. After returning to the United States, he joined the argonauts to California in 1849, and then went south to Los Angeles in 1850. He opened a store there, dealing, as all the stores then did, in general merchandise, including wine; the store's letterhead in 1863 reads: "Groceries, Liquors, Dry Goods, Clothing, Boots, Shoes, etc. Wholesale and Retail." What could the "etc." have stood for?

At some point in the 1850s, perhaps as early as 1851, he acquired a vineyard running along the east side of Alameda Street from Marchessault

Matthew Keller, proprietor of the Los Angeles and Rising Sun Vineyards, where he experimented with 120 varieties of *Vitis vinifera* seeking to "make light wine 'for the million'" (Keller, letter dated February 22, 1871, published in the *Alta California*, February 27, 1871). Courtesy of the Huntington Library.

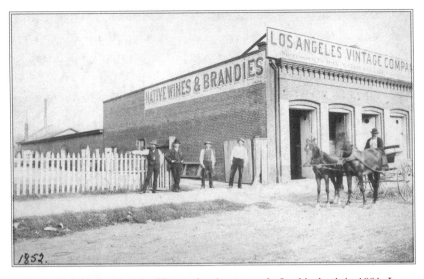

Matthew Keller's Los Angeles Vineyard as it appeared after his death in 1881. It was then operated as the Los Angeles Vintage Company by Keller's former winery superintendent, Henry Stuhr. Courtesy of the Huntington Library.

Street (no longer extant) in the north to Aliso in the south. This was known as the "Los Angeles Vineyard" and is the site now occupied by Union Station. Later, Keller acquired a 150-acre property to the south of the pueblo that he named the Rising Sun Vineyard. In 1857 he bought the huge Malibu ranch, but there is no good evidence that he ever planted grapes on that coastal property.[31] In 1852 he established a winery on the Los Angeles site, and by 1861 he had 100,000 vines planted. He built a house of brick, not adobe, on the vineyard property, which stood until the 1930s, when it was used as the construction headquarters for the building of Union Station and was at last razed to make room for landscaping the approach to the station.[32] The neighborhood had since Keller's day been transformed into Chinatown, before that, in turn, was displaced by the station.

By 1858 Keller had, it is said, twelve different varieties of grapes in his vineyards.[33] This is certainly possible: nurserymen in Santa Clara County had been regularly importing superior grape varieties from France by 1852,[34] so it would be strange if no one in Los Angeles had yet made trial of such new material. Yet Keller himself wrote in 1858 that "various foreign grapes have been tried here, but none succeed so well as that now in cultivation"—that is, the Mission grape. And, he added, "if we ever obtain a better variety, it must be from seeds."[35] This is not the language of a man with a serious commitment to any "foreign grapes."

Keller was for a long time stubbornly loyal to the Mission grape. He told L. J. Rose that it was all right for Rose to experiment with new varieties, since Rose made a great many different sorts of wine for many different markets. But, Keller said, "the Mission grape is good enough for the general grower, because this is a country where we can make wines of generous strength, and sweet wines and brandies, and the Mission has no superior for that purpose."[36] But Keller at last changed his view: in a letter of February 9, 1871, he writes that no "fine light wine" can be made from the Mission, for that grape "makes only a strong wine without bouquet, fit only for sailors to drink, and its further extension ought to be by all means discouraged."[37] Or, as he explained in another letter, the Mission "has no capacity to make light wine 'for the million,' for that is the great desideratum. What I am striving for is to give the people a rational and temperate drink that will become to a great extent a substitute for bread."[38]

Keller had not wholly given up on the Mission grape; in the Industrial Exhibition of the Mechanics' Institute of San Francisco in 1871 he won the diploma awarded for "the best exhibit of Wines and Brandies from Native Grape."[39] But he experimented widely with alternative varieties. In 1871 he had "one hundred and twenty varieties of the grape in cultivation, hoping, after due test, to select therefrom the most appropriate to my locality."[40] But he had turned to the so-called "foreign varieties" even before that; indeed, it appears that even while he was defending the virtues of the Mission he was testing many other varieties of *Vitis vinifera*. As he wrote in 1868, "The Mission Grape is the cause of our not making better wine," and, in consequence, "I have this season planted 30000 foreign vines comprehending all the classes that make the best wines all over the world."[41]

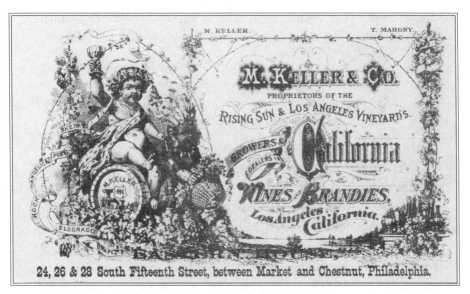

Matthew Keller's business card. Courtesy of the Huntington Library.

In 1872 the newly formed California Vine Growers' and Wine and Brandy Manufacturers' Association held a competitive wine judging during a meeting in San Francisco. Matthew Keller entered a number of wines and brandies, accompanied by notes on their manufacture, as required by the rules of the competition. These notes show that Keller was already using a wide choice of varieties, and had been doing so for the last decade. His 1871 brandy was made from six-year-old vines of Folle Blanche; his El Dorado, a sweet wine, was made from Grizzly Frontignan and Deccan Superbe, whatever that is.[42] El Dorado was described by a contemporary as "an amber-colored wine that was a sort of combination of muscatel and sherry, and had all the excellent qualities of both."[43] The formula for his port included Mission grapes, but, surprisingly, Touriga and Tinta Francesca as well, genuine Douro varieties, and from vines nine years old. The sherry was made from Pedro Ximénez and Macabeo grapes—a thing practically unheard of in California then.[44]

Keller has the distinction of having written the first official report on the winegrowing of Los Angeles.[45] "The Grapes and Wine of Los Angeles" appeared in the annual report for 1858 of the U.S. Patent Office, the agency in charge of agriculture before the formation of the Department of Agriculture in 1862. Keller begins with some surprising statistics:

> The county of Los Angeles has one million five hundred and ten thousand bearing vines, and eight hundred and seventy-five thousand which were not productive last year, while preparations are being made to plant a million cuttings this season.[46]

Taking the usual measure of 1,000 vines to the acre, Los Angeles County, according to Keller's certainly exaggerated figures, then had 2,385 acres in vineyard and another 1,000 acres about to be planted. The State Agricultural Society, also reporting in 1858, put the figure at 1,650 acres, a substantially lower figure, although still a large one.[47] The prudent conclusion about such conflicts is that both sets of figures are wrong, there having been no trustworthy means for arriving at them. One might split the difference and say that the county had around 2,000 acres of vines, an impressive figure for a county that still counted only about 11,000 people.[48]

Keller next reports that, in 1857, Los Angeles shipped 250,000 gallons of wine to San Francisco; in 1858 the figure had risen to 325,000 gallons. The difference is explained by the fact that in 1857 Los Angeles was shipping very large quantities of fresh grapes to San Francisco, but in the next year competition from the vineyards of Northern California meant a falling off of fresh grape sales and a consequent increase in wine production at Los Angeles. This is one of the earliest signs that Northern California was now growing grapes in significant quantity. But it was not yet producing much wine. California was reported as making 385,000 gallons of wine in 1857, of which 350,000 gallons came from Los Angeles.[49]

Yet another surprising figure is in Keller's statement that a "well-kept vineyard" will produce an average of 1 gallon of wine for every vine, and that some vineyards produce 2 gallons per vine. At 1,000 vines to the acre (Keller himself puts the number at 1,100 to the acre), that is 1,000 to 2,000 gallons to the acre, or the yield from around 6.5 to 13 tons of grapes per acre.[50] These are possible figures, but were surely not to be counted on as a regular thing. It is hard not to think that Keller's report was written in a euphoric state by a man keen on boosting his hometown. And certainly the view from a Los Angeles vineyard was highly promising in the late '50s: the population was growing by leaps and bounds; the northern vineyards had barely yet been heard from; there could be no limit to the demand for Los Angeles wine. In the midst of his report Keller suddenly bursts out: "Let us have a railroad, and we will supply the Union with grapes and wine." To his readers in the eastern states, where California wine had been barely heard of and to whom Los Angeles was only a remote and obscure hamlet, the claim to be able to "supply the Union with grapes and wine" must have seemed a fantastic boast.

But California in the 1850s was preparing to make very large quantities of wine. There was in the latter half of the decade a statewide boom in planting vines. Keller's statement that, in 1858, there were plans to add another million vines in Los Angeles alone is no doubt inflated, but the acreage of vines in the county did in fact double between 1856 and 1858. The number of vines more than doubled in the entire state, from 1,540,000 to 3,954,548, and those many vines were planted up and down the state.[51] Sonoma was just beginning to be heard from; Napa hardly at all yet. The county that came next after Los Angeles in number of vines at this time was Santa Clara, with 150,000 in 1856.[52] The confident view from Los Angeles at this time is well expressed by Richard Henry Dana, who, in the summer of 1859, revisited the scene of his labors in the hide trade back in 1835 and wrote about it in *Twenty-Four Years After*. He was taken around the vineyards of Los Angeles, which were, he wrote, "the chief objects in this region. The vintage of last year was estimated at half a million gallons. Every year new square miles of ground are laid down to vineyards, and the Pueblo promises to be the center of one of the largest wine-producing regions in the world."[53] Dana shared Keller's large views, seeing in tiny, remote Los Angeles the beginning of "one of the largest wine-producing regions in the world."

Keller's description of the winemaking process as practiced in Los Angeles shows that, at the bigger and better-equipped wineries at any rate, the days of cowhides and naked Indians were over. Stemming was still performed by hand, but crushing was by means of mechanical crushers with wooden or iron rollers. The crushed grapes and their juice then went into fermenting vats. Pressing was done by a screw press, although, according to one authority, in Los Angeles winemaking the juice from the press was not generally used, only the free-run juice from the initial crushing being fermented into wine. The pomace was, accordingly, richer in juice than if it had gone through the press, and that, it is said, accounts for the superiority of brandy from Los Angeles. Most California brandy was distilled from pomace, not from wine, so a semiliquid pomace yielded a better brandy.[54] New wine was racked three times in the first year. It was Keller's boast that the grapes of Los Angeles were so well balanced that no "extraneous substance" need be added: "The purest and finest wines in the world are made from the juice of the grape alone."[55] This claim for the "purity" of Los Angeles wine, and, implicitly, for the impurity of wines from all other sources, became a tiresome mantra among the local winemakers, who used it for many years, no matter what their actual practices might have been.

Keller presumably followed his own rule of purity in winemaking. In the first two decades of his wine business, he earned a good reputation for his wines; he opened an agency in San Francisco in 1862, and, after the coming of the railroad in 1869, he had agencies in New York and Philadelphia. Before the decade of the 1850s was out, Keller was producing 40,000 gallons of wine annually and a substantial quantity of aguardiente. The wines appear to have been the standard Los Angeles products: port, sherry, Angelica, and white, with perhaps a bit of red as well. But, as we have seen, at least some juice from better varieties than the Mission went into them. Keller's prosperity peaked in 1875, when he entertained the elite of Los Angeles at his "First Annual Vintage Feast and Ball." The menu for this occasion has survived and has been reprinted by the Book Club of California. There were both a dinner at 4:30 p.m. and a supper, presumably around midnight. The wines offered at both dinner and supper were "Claret, Eldorado, Madeira, Angelica, White Wine, Sherry, Port," all no doubt wines of Keller's own manufacture.[56]

Next year the scene had darkened. The delayed effects of the Panic of 1873 were now felt on the remote West Coast. Prices fell and markets shrank. Keller, like every prosperous man in Los Angeles, had made

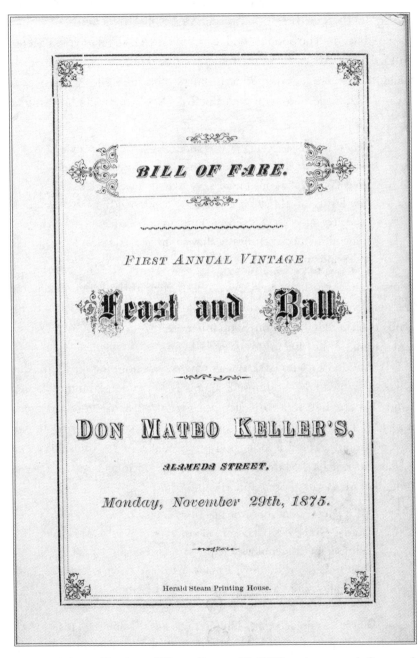

Menu of Keller's "First Annual Vintage Feast and Ball." There is no record of a second. Courtesy of the Huntington Library.

many purchases of land in the city, and some of these were now mortgaged. In 1876 the pressure was such that Keller, reluctantly, went East to see what could be done there. He closed down his Philadelphia agency in October 1876 and sent the manager, one Thomas Mahony, back to California to manage the wine business there in Keller's absence. In April 1877, Keller wrote pathetically from New York to an unidentified recipient:

> My whole object being as you know to sell the wines that I
> have on hand and to pay my debts, to save my property and
> to get out of the wine business—and to do this I have risked
> my life in my old age in N.Y. in the depth of winter to try
> and accomplish it.... The wine business has been a millstone
> around my neck....It has swallowed up all I made on land
> sales and any other way.[57]

More than a year later Keller was still in New York, evidently keeping the agency there alive. "I will struggle on to the end," he wrote to his banker, Isaias Hellman, on September 9, 1878. "I long to return to Cal—I am tired of life in this great Babylon."[58]

Mahony, back at the Los Angeles winery, was not much help. In May 1878, he wrote to defend himself against Keller's complaint that the red wine Mahony had sent to Keller in New York was no good. Mahony replied that it must have been good when he sent it out, since he had had no trouble selling it at a good price locally. As for the sherry that Keller did not like, Mahony reports that he no longer made it, even though he thinks it "a pretty good wine":

> All I know about it now is that it was made of white wine,
> Spirits, Grape syrup, Hickory nut infusion, Quassia, Walnut
> infusion and Bitter aloes, the proportions I could not tell to
> save my life. At the time I made it I noted down on *cards*
> the contents of each vat, so that I could continue to make
> it if it turned out well, but when I received your letter saying it was no account I tore up the cards. At any rate it is
> only a matter of taste. The Hickory nut infusion is needed to
> give it the nutty flavor that all sherries have. If you think the
> Quassia and Aloes are of any use get two 5 Gal kegs[,] make

separate infusions and use them according to your own taste
and judgment.[59]

How much of such synthetic stuff Keller actually sold is not known,
nor do we know how long he had been making it—it could not be more
different from the sherry made of Pedro Ximénez and Macabeo that
Keller exhibited in 1872. That it was made at all is a sad comment on
Keller's earlier boasts about the purity of his wines. Charles Sullivan has
written that he regards Keller as the best of the large-scale winemakers in the Los Angeles of his day, and it may very well be that before
the troubled end his wines were in fact the best.[60] Keller's early use of
foreign varieties in his commercial winemaking, and his quick response
to Pasteur's work, certainly put him among the leaders in progressive
winemaking. The opposite view is forcefully expressed by Keller's fellow
Los Angeles winemaker (and competitor) J. DeBarth Shorb in a letter of
1877. Keller, Shorb declared, "has done more damage to the California
wine trade than any other man in it."[61] He does not explain what he
means by this; perhaps he had tried the sherry.

Before his death in 1881 Keller had managed to leave New York and
return to Los Angeles, where he longed to be. Keller's obituary in the
Los Angeles Express states that Keller had, before his death, succeeded
in restoring his winery to profitability, that he was planting new vines,
and that he was planning to increase production.[62] The statement may
be only the sort of diplomatic untruth allowed to obituaries; or it may
be true, since the wine business was booming at the time. In any case,
Keller's work was at an end. The stock of wines on hand in Los Angeles was bought by Lachman and Jacobi, a big firm of San Francisco
wine merchants, in May of 1881. The agreement for the sale preserved
among the Keller Papers contains this list:

32,000 gals port @ 45c[ents]
5,000 sherry @ 50c
2,000 gals angelica @ 50c
8,000 white @ 20c
1,000 brandy @ 90c

Another list of the wine on hand in Keller's winery at the time of his death includes 20,000 gallons of red wine; evidently Lachman and Jacobi did not care to buy that.[63] I make the sale worth $20,400, an amount Keller would have been glad to have gotten a few years earlier.

Keller's Los Angeles property was taken over by new proprietors, including Henry Stuhr, who had been Keller's winery superintendent. The business operated as the Los Angeles Vintage Company until 1888.[64] After the destruction of his house in 1939, the only remaining memorials of Keller's life and work in Los Angeles are a couple of street names. The short Keller Street—alley, rather—runs next to the river behind Union Station and would once, long ago, have been a part of Keller's Los Angeles Vineyard. So too, probably, was Mateo Street, running north and south between Fourth and Fifth Streets.

KOHLER AND FROHLING

The Sainsevains and Keller deserve much credit for their work in developing the wine interest of Los Angeles, but Kohler and Frohling, the third of the Los Angeles Big Three, did even more. They also introduced the German presence into California winemaking. For the rest of the century, Germans were much the most prominent among the wine men there, as they already were in the other winegrowing regions of America—Missouri and Ohio in particular. The Germans were prominent in Southern California, in large part through the Anaheim Colony, to be discussed in Chapter 5. A representative German in Los Angeles winegrowing was Julius Weyse. A native of Saxony, he had been involved in the rebellion of 1830 and had to flee the country. In 1856 he established his Los Angeles home and a 21-acre vineyard, nostalgically called "Fernheim." Weyse died in 1863, but his son continued the winery until 1880.[65]

Charles Kohler and John Fröhling were both professional musicians, Kohler a violinist, Fröhling a flutist. Fröhling came to America in 1843, Kohler in 1850, and by 1853 they were both in San Francisco. The city, despite its rawness, had a precocious interest in music, and musicians

Fernheim, Julius Weyse's place south of Los Angeles. Illustration from John Albert Wilson, *History of Los Angeles County* (1880). Weyse, a political refugee from Saxony, made wine at his Fernheim property before his death in 1863; the business was continued by his son. Courtesy of the California Historical Society.

were well paid there.[66] Neither Kohler nor Fröhling came from a wine-growing region in Germany, but when they discovered the grapes of Los Angeles, then being shipped in quantity to San Francisco, they were inspired to become winemakers. This was in September 1853. They acted quickly to find backers, and in May 1854, Fröhling traveled to Los Angeles in search of a vineyard. The completeness with which Los Angeles dominated the idea of winemaking in California at that time appears from the fact that Kohler and Fröhling seem never even to have considered the Bay Area as a place where they might operate. As San Francisco's *Alta California* put it,

> Nearly all the wine and brandy made in California comes from Los Angeles County, which is no doubt better fitted, in soil and climate, for the culture of the vine than any other part of the state.[67]

Charles Kohler.
From the author's collection.

In Los Angeles Fröhling bought a 20-acre property from Cristobal Aguilar that lay southwest of the intersection of what is now Central Avenue and Seventh Street, including 12 acres of Mission vines; with that, the firm of Kohler and Frohling was in business.[68] Winemaking began, under Fröhling's direction, in the fall of that year, only a token quantity being produced.

Kohler, meantime, remained in San Francisco, where it was his job to sell the wine that Fröhling made. Kohler continued to perform as a musician, as the infant firm needed his professional earnings besides what he might make selling wine. Nor could Kohler and Fröhling wait until they had wine from their own vineyard. They secured, somehow and somewhere, 500 gallons of wine, rented premises at 102 Merchant Street, and began business as dealers in native wines. The partners' advantage was that no one had yet done this. Los Angeles had been shipping wine to San Francisco for many years, but on an irregular and *ad hoc* basis. Now there would be a steady supply, and, in time, that supply would come from Kohler and Frohling's own production and would be identified as such. This was the model that was soon generally followed in San Francisco, where a number of great wine houses, as they were called, developed to handle the growing production of wine in California. Among them are Lachman and Jacobi; C. Carpy and Co.; Kohler and Van Bergen; S. Lachman and Co.; and C. Schilling and Co. They owned vineyards and wineries, they bought wine from other producers, and they stored, finished, and blended large quantities of wine in their San Francisco premises and sent it to market under their own names. Kohler and Frohling were the first to do this; it was their example that was followed by the rest, and their wine was Los Angeles wine, at least to start with. The catalog issued in 1863 by the New York firm of Perkins, Stern and Co., dealers exclusively in California wines—that is, Los Angeles wines—puts Kohler and Frohling's claim to be first with simple directness: "No particular thought was ever given [in Los Angeles] to the production of wine as a business enterprise till 1854, when Messrs. Kohler & Frohling commenced business." The statement is not strictly true, but it could not have been challenged on the East Coast, where they had never heard of Wolfskill, Vignes, and other pioneers of Los Angeles wine. And there is no doubt that Kohler and Fröhling were more ambitiously enterprising than any of their predecessors.

Fröhling, although he began winemaking without any experience, was a fast learner. We do not know how much he may have made in the first two years of operation at the Pioneer Winery, as their place in Los Angeles was called. But in 1856 he produced 15,000 gallons and took first prize at the State Agricultural Fair for "the best wine from grapes grown in this state."[69] (Keller took second.) The prize was only the first in a long string of prizes to follow.

In 1857 Fröhling made 60,000 gallons; in 1858, 100,000. Production thereafter showed uninterrupted growth. The original 12 acres of vines were expanded to 20, but in order to produce wine in such volume as had already been reached before the end of the 1850s Kohler and Frohling obviously had to have other sources. They bought grapes from growers all over Los Angeles County, and they bought wines in bulk too. Henry Dalton, at the Azusa Ranch, sold some 800 gallons to Fröhling in 1856.[70] In 1859 they are said to have made wine not only at their own relatively small place but at the vineyards of Wolfskill, Antonio

Kohler and Frohling were skillful promoters of their wines, as this undated but early piece of sheet music shows. The song's refrain runs, "There are none anywhere to be found to compare / With the wines of Los Angeles County." Courtesy of the Bancroft Library.

Coronel, and William Workman as well.[71] In 1863 Kohler and Frohling are reported as having used the yield of 400 acres of vines in addition to their own, expecting to make 150,000 gallons of wine and brandy.[72] The success of the firm in selling as well as in making wine was evidently a welcome development for many growers in Los Angeles; if they grew the grapes, they could count on Kohler and Frohling to buy them and relieve the grower of the anxious labor of making wine for sale. The vintage of 1864 is described thus:

> The labor employed in gathering the grapes and in the work of the press is mostly performed by Indians. It is a novel and interesting sight to see them filing up to the press, each one bearing on his head about fifty pounds of the delicious fruit which is soon to be reduced to an unseemly mass, and yield up its purple life-blood for the benefit of man.[73]

The usual claim is made that Kohler and Frohling imported superior varieties of grapes, but as usual no particulars are provided.[74]

Kohler in San Francisco kept pace with Fröhling in Los Angeles. By 1858 the former was able to give up playing the violin by night in order to support his business by day. The firm moved to more spacious premises in the Montgomery Block, first in 1857 and then again in 1862, as Fröhling expanded production in Los Angeles and Kohler matched him with sales in and around San Francisco. The success of the firm seems to have been grounded on the hard work and fair dealing of the two partners, coupled with a flair for promotion and, not least, a better or at least more reliable product than had yet been offered in California. Two officials of the California State Agricultural Society visiting the Los Angeles winery in 1859 reported that Kohler and Frohling

> guarantee all their wines to possess a certain standard. This is effected by introducing a portion of "heavy" wines into casks that are too "light" and *vice versa*, until the desired standard is attained. With the great care, cleanliness, and neatness of everything about this establishment no one, even the most fastidious, could fail to be pleased.[75]

The concern for consistency, and the use of blending to attain that consistency, anticipate the practice of another successful California winemaker. In 1955 the Gallo brothers built a million-gallon blending tank so that, as Julio Gallo put it, "customers can rely upon every bottle of a given type being always identical with the last bottle purchased."[76]

But the real expansion was through increasing sales of California wine outside of California. In this development, Kohler and Frohling was the clear leader, and the firm's success in making California wine known throughout the Union is its main contribution to the story of California wine. The beginning was made in 1858, when, through the agency of a friend named Richard Perkins, Kohler and Frohling shipped about 1,200 gallons of wine to Boston. That venture turned out well and encouraged the next step. Charles Stern, a young man from Mainz, Germany, had joined Kohler and Fröhling at the outset of their business. Now, with financing from Perkins, Stern would go to New York and set up a company devoted to the sale of Kohler and Frohling wines. Perkins and Stern opened for business in 1860 at 180 Broadway. Stern's contribution was of such importance to the success of Kohler and Frohling that, as Charles Sullivan has suggested, the firm was really a triumvirate of Germans: Kohler, Fröhling, and Stern.[77]

From that point on, Kohler and Frohling wines spread throughout the country. As an ad from the firm in 1861 put it, any wines ordered from Perkins and Stern could be sent "to any part of the United States and Europe."[78] The Civil War slowed things but did not stop them: the era of "total war" was not yet. After the war, and after the completion of the transcontinental railroad in 1869, the process was uninterrupted.[79]

John Fröhling died of consumption in 1862, but by that time the firm was solid enough to sustain the loss. The name of the firm remained Kohler and Frohling. By 1876 Charles Kohler could boast that his wines were available in every American city of middle size or more. Those wines now included such varietals as Riesling, muscat, Gutedel, and Zinfandel, as well as the usual sherry, claret, and port. The Mission grape no longer dominated, and there was some movement away from calling all wines after European names and using those of the grape varieties instead.

In a move that prefigured what would happen to the entire California wine trade, Kohler turned more and more northward for the supply of

LET AMERICANS SUPPORT AMERICAN INDUSTRY.

CATALOGUE

OF

GALIFORNIA WINES;

WITH

STATISTICS OF VINES PLANTED, DESCRIPTION
OF VARIETIES, COMMENTS OF
THE PRESS, &c.

PERKINS, STERN & CO.

180 Broadway, New York, 108 Tremont St., Boston.

IMPORTERS AND DEALERS EXCLUSIVELY IN

CALIFORNIA WINES.

Sole Agents for Kohler & Frohling's Celebrated Vintages.

Cover of an 1863 Perkins, Stern and Co. catalog. The "Celebrated Vintages" in the last line had been introduced to New York in 1860, when they were still quite unknown. From the author's collection.

his table wines. The search for a grape that would make an acceptable dry red wine had not succeeded in Los Angeles, and meanwhile the attractions of the Zinfandel had been discovered and promoted in the counties around San Francisco Bay. In 1874 Kohler, who had been buying north-coast grapes and table wines for many years, bought an 800-acre property in Sonoma County, the so-called Tokay Vineyard, and that, henceforth, was where Kohler and Frohling's table wines came from. Since this book is about Los Angeles, we will not follow Kohler any further. He died in 1887 at the rather early age of fifty-seven, prosperous, respected, and admired, one of the pillars of San Francisco's civic and business worlds.

Although Los Angeles at the time of Kohler's death was no longer a main source of table wine for Kohler and Frohling, the winery there was still a substantial and important contributor, producing 200,000 gallons annually. Much of it was sweet wine—port and Angelica—as well as brandy. But, as a visitor in 1886 reported, "Wine of all descriptions is made here. Drank some very fair light red wine."[80] One wonders what the grape was.

4

THE SAN GABRIEL VALLEY

While winemaking flourished in the town of Los Angeles, it also began to grow in a big way outside the town. The San Gabriel Valley, beginning a few miles north and east of Los Angeles, is a vaguely defined region formerly assigned to the San Gabriel Mission. The valley, running along the foothills of the San Gabriel Mountains for some fifteen or twenty miles east from where Pasadena now stands, was, according to all contemporary testimony, the most attractive part of all the Los Angeles Basin. Visitors exhausted their superlatives in attempting to describe its attractions, but perhaps more persuasive is the quiet remark of Benjamin Wilson, who settled in the San Gabriel Valley from Los Angeles in 1855 at what he called "the prettiest and healthiest place in California."[1]

In sparsely populated Southern California, the valley, despite its attractions, remained largely pristine. Young Leonard Rose, Jr., whose family settled in the valley in 1861, describes how, in the early 1870s, he would ride the twelve miles into Los Angeles to attend school; on one stretch of five miles there were only three houses, and on their daily ride Rose and his brother were accompanied by hundreds of brown squirrels, by ground owls that "always ducked their heads in a sort of curtsy at the approach of danger," by roadrunners, and by other sorts of wildlife in a scene in which "one could see for miles" in any direction.[2]

Winegrowing in the valley had been long since established at the San Gabriel Mission, where it all began. Even before the secularization of

1834 it had spread out to other parts of the valley. Hugo Reid, a Scotsman, was perhaps the first of the newcomers to make winegrowing a special interest. Reid's wanderings took him from Scotland to South America, Mexico, the Sandwich Islands, and China before he settled in Los Angeles in 1834. There he married an Indian woman from the neophytes of the San Gabriel Mission. In 1839 he petitioned for the grant of Rancho Santa Anita and, even before receiving title to the property, set out a vineyard there. By 1843 he could boast that his vineyard, now walled around, had 22,000 vines, and he is reported in that year as having loaded a ship with his wines and brandies and embarked on a sales trip to San Diego, Santa Barbara, and Monterey.[3] "I consider myself a first-rate wine maker," Reid boasted.[4] Since his Santa Anita vineyard was then only in its third year, Reid must have had his grapes from other sources, possibly from the still-extant vineyard of the San Gabriel Mission, or from the property called the Huerta de Cuati, belonging to his wife, Victoria. He had built an adobe house near the Mission—"Uva Espina," he called it: "Gooseberry House"—and he continued to live there even after obtaining the Santa Anita grant.[5]

In 1847, in financial difficulties, Reid sold the Santa Anita ranch to an Englishman named Henry Dalton, who, after many years as a merchant in Peru, had come to Los Angeles in 1843. Dalton acquired the Azusa ranch at the east end of the San Gabriel Valley by purchase in 1844 and there, as has been noted in Chapter 2, he planted a vineyard on a small part of his 4,000 acres of grazing land and was producing wine before the time of the American occupation in 1847. He does not appear to have maintained Reid's vineyard at Santa Anita, which he kept only a few years, but he continued to make wine on Rancho Azusa de Dalton into the 1860s. So far as I know, Hugo Reid was the pioneer winemaker in the San Gabriel Valley after the Franciscan priests at the mission.

BENJAMIN D. WILSON AND THE LAKE VINEYARD

The catalyst for the expansive development of what Reid and Dalton had well started was Benjamin D. Wilson, whose Lake Vineyard, besides producing a large quantity of wine, enjoyed a reputation up and down California as a model enterprise, attracting to the region many growers and many winemakers, large and small. Wilson, originally from Tennessee, had had a rough and danger-filled life before becoming the respected patriarch of the San Gabriel Valley. As a young man he had made his way to Santa Fe, where he worked as a trapper and a trader. On one occasion his party was massacred by Apaches. Wilson was about to be put to death when he escaped, nearly naked, managed to evade his mounted pursuers, and struggled barefoot the hundred miles back to Santa Fe. In 1841, moved by the growing hostility to *gringos* in Mexican New Mexico (following the Texas revolution of 1835–36), Wilson joined

B. D. Wilson and his wife, Margaret. Courtesy of the Huntington Library.

a party of Yankees, including John Rowland and William Workman—afterwards fellow winegrowers in Los Angeles—who were leaving Santa Fe for Los Angeles. Wilson had an idea that he would find a ship there to take him to China, but when no such ship appeared, he remained in California. There Wilson soon managed to acquire both a wife and a ranch from the Californios. His adventures continued even after he had exchanged a mountain man's life for a domestic one: he was mauled and nearly killed by a grizzly bear; he was shot by a poisoned arrow; he pursued predatory Indians and demanded—and was presented with—their heads. In the Mexican War he, as an American, was imprisoned by the Californios, at one time under threat of death. It is perhaps no wonder that after the war he left his ranch (now the site of Riverside, California) and settled in Los Angeles.

Despite his rough and adventurous past, Wilson presented a calm and polite persona; he chose to appear as a Southern gentleman, in ruffled shirt and flowing black tie. He was a Southern sympathizer during the Civil War and was, of course, a Democrat. He was universally respected and, I think, generally well liked. William Brewer, who met him in 1860, called him "uneducated but of strong character."[6] William Hutton, who knew him in 1849, called him "a quiet, kind man, who has spent much of his life in the mountains and has done a great deal for us."[7] Hutton's description is borne out by other testimony that Wilson was a civil and generous man, despite having had his education in the hard school of the mountains and deserts of the west, among hostile Indians and half-savage mountain men.

In Los Angeles he operated a store and showed a marked talent for the acquisition of land. Wilson's name is found, at one time or another, all over the map of Los Angeles County as a landowner.[8] He also had a 10-acre vineyard at his Los Angeles place and made wine, probably for sale at his store.[9] According to Captain E. D. Townsend's journal of his visit to Los Angeles in 1855, Wilson's was then one of the three "most famous" of Los Angeles vineyards, along with those of Vignes and Wolfskill.[10]

Wilson showed a willingness to experiment in winemaking by attempting to produce a sparkling wine: "How comes on the Champagne?"

one of his friends asked. "I am very curious to learn how you have succeeded in that matter."[11] That year, 1855, Wilson exhibited a sparkling
wine at the California State Fair, so the project did not wholly fail.[12]
The *Alta California* was led even to pronounce it of the "first quality."[13]
A fellow Los Angeles winemaker, Dr. T. J. White, declared that Wilson's
champagne, "manufactured at his beautiful and picturesque vineyard
near the old mission of San Gabriel," was a wine of "excellent quality."[14] But sparkling wine was never destined for success in Southern
California: the Mission grape is far too low in acid to make a tolera-
ble sparkler, and although Wilson and others continued to make the
attempt, no one, so far as I know, succeeded, unless one allows the Sainsevains to have succeeded. If so, it was a Pyrrhic victory.

Among the many properties that Wilson acquired, one—among the
smallest of them—stood out beyond the rest. This was the Huerta de
Cuati (the Twin's Garden, or the Buddy's Garden, in Mexican Spanish),
a tract of 127 acres in the San Gabriel Valley on hilly ground that is now
shared between the towns of Pasadena and San Marino, although when
Wilson bought it in 1854 no town was to be seen. It belonged to Victoria Reid, Hugo Reid's widow (Reid died in 1852), who had it in virtue
of her long service to the San Gabriel Mission. The Huerta included
a vineyard and the winemaking equipment belonging to Reid.[15] For his
$8,000 Wilson received, among other things, "all the wine vats, pipes,
barrels, and all other vessels for wine and distilling purposes, excepting
the stills."[16] Why the stills were excepted I have no idea. I do not know
whether Wilson made brandy at his Los Angeles place, but he certainly
would do so now.

Although he felt satisfaction in his Los Angeles residence—it was,
as one of his friends wrote, a "beautiful cottage and garden"—he was
greatly smitten by the charms of the Huerta de Cuati. To his brother
he described the Huerta as "one of the most beautiful places that heart
could desire," and he soon determined to leave Los Angeles and settle
on this most beautiful place in the San Gabriel Valley.[17]

It took some time to prepare the way. He had to arrange for the
sale of his Los Angeles place, and he chose to send his children and his
wife (his second, Margaret; his first wife, Ramona, died in 1849) away

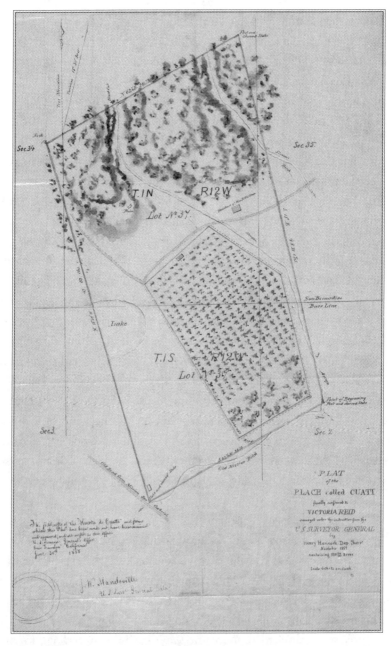

Map of the Huerta de Cuati in 1854, the year before B. D. Wilson bought it from
Hugo Reid's widow, Victoria; it was already a working vineyard. Courtesy of the
Huntington Library.

for a long visit to her family in St. Louis while he built a new house. The house, long and rambling, stood over a capacious cellar and commanded a view of the lake—a pond, some would call it—formed below the old mill built by the San Gabriel mission. Wilson accordingly named his new property the Lake Vineyard.[18] By the fall of 1856 Wilson had settled permanently at the Lake Vineyard and made his first vintage there that year: some 12,000 gallons from the vineyard already established on the site. It was, he wrote his wife, "a fine crop of grapes."[19] And when the vintage was over, Wilson, not a demonstrative man, made a bold vow to her: "I feel so well pleased with the place here that I feel disposed to make it all that money will make out of it. I intend if my life is spared and no bad luck befalls to have the finest and best place in the State."[20]

New planting went on steadily at the Lake Vineyard, and by 1860 Wilson's production was up to 20,000 gallons and rising. He had an agent in San Francisco, and we hear not only of a substantial domestic trade but of small and irregular shipments to Oregon, Boston, and Japan.[21] As Wilson's San Francisco agents wrote him, "The reputation of B.D. Wilson's wine, Los Angeles, is becoming more popular every day."[22] There is no record of any other grape than the Mission being used for the wine of Los Angeles at this time, although perhaps a small quantity of muscat was produced from vines obtained originally at Mission San Gabriel.[23] So-called port was still, as it had been in earlier years, the main product; it sold in San Francisco for $1 a gallon.[24] White wine, or "hock," as it was often called, came next, then Angelica, and last, dry red wine or "claret," a hierarchy that would endure as long as the Mission grape was the chief source of Los Angeles wine, although most winemakers of the region also offered a sherry.

Not all was idyllic at Lake Vineyard. Wilson, like everyone else in isolated Los Angeles, had trouble finding competent help. When Captain E. D. Townsend visited the Lake Vineyard in October 1855 he noted that Wilson had "an old German, who has learned the art [of winemaking] in Europe, to superintend the work for him." Townsend and his friends, who had been invited by Wilson to help themselves from his vines, gathered some fruit and were "accosted" by the German.

B. D. Wilson's Lake Vineyard house in 1880. From John Albert Wilson, *History of Los Angeles County* (1880). Courtesy of the Huntington Library.

"I see you got some grapes!" "Yes, we are friends of Mr. Wilson who told us to help ourselves." "Well, you do not come every day, but I keep a gun to drive away the Spaniards when they go into the vineyard to steal grapes." "Well, we are not stealing, for Mr. Wilson gave us permission yesterday to take as many as we wanted, and we have only a few." "That is good, but suppose every one does the same, all the grapes will be taken; then how will Wilson pay us?"[25]

The question, Townsend says, was unanswerable.

A few months later, in January 1856, Dr. Henry Myles, one of Wilson's neighbors and a fellow vineyardist, called at the Lake Vineyard in Wilson's absence (Wilson had been elected a state senator and was doing his duty in Sacramento) and reported that there he found an old man drunk. This must be the German winemaker. A few weeks later Myles wrote again to say, "I do not believe the old man will be able to do anything in the way of Champagne, and any one can make as good white wine as he can, and *I* think better. If the Vineyard was mine I would not keep him for his board and liquor." Wilson evidently was still experimenting with a sparkling wine, as he had done before moving to the Lake Vineyard. Late in February Myles wrote again: "He [the old man] has been pottering at the Sparkling wine since you left, none ready yet....The truth is that he never will make any thing of it, and even though he should make the best sparkling wine in the world it would bring you in debt the way he is going on with it, but I believe him to be a *humbug.*"[26] Myles must have been right; some sparkling wine was produced, but Wilson did not go on with the venture. I do not know what became of the old man.

The problem of finding trustworthy help never went away. In April 1868, Wilson complained that for three years the winery had been without a good man and had suffered much loss in consequence. A year later we hear that "the Dutchman" now in charge has brought everything into confusion. "The Dutchman I would not trust beyond doing work when watched," Wilson wrote, and added, "He is a snarly disagreeable man." A month later we learn that one Myers, "a drunken, coarse fellow," is leaving. "The man that is to take his place will be more civil and respectful and not feel it is his duty to let every one drink who goes into the cellar," wrote Wilson.[27] Later, in 1872, we learn that the cellar man at the Lake Vineyard was a Mr. Meletta, and that the man in charge of the winery was a Mr. Schliefer; evidently Los Angeles continued to draw a cosmopolitan influx.[28] As commercial winemaking increased in Los Angeles County, experienced people were increasingly attracted to it, and the local supply would naturally develop too. Bela Haraszthy, one of Agoston Haraszthy's sons and thus a man trained up in wine from childhood, is said to have served as Wilson's winery superintendent for eight years in the 1870s.[29] But the pool of capable workers could never have been large.[30] At that time, the only way to learn how to make wine in California—and in the rest of the country—was to do it.

Another difficulty came from a local peculiarity: earthquakes. The San Gabriel River, which drains the San Gabriel Valley, was sometimes known by the Spaniards as the "Rio San Gabriel de los Temblores," the river of earthquakes. The region still lived up to that name. Dr. Myles wrote to Wilson in Sacramento on January 28, 1857, that he was then engaged in racking the new wine from the first vintage of 1856. It was not very clear, Myles wrote, because they had had "about fifty earthquakes in the last two weeks."[31]

Despite such troubles, Wilson steadily increased the size of his vineyards and the volume of his winemaking. One acquisition was the Mound Vineyard, on high ground above the Lake Vineyard, later to be the site of Henry Huntington's mansion and the Huntington Library. After Dr. Myles was killed in 1863 when the small steamer *Ada Hancock* was swamped and exploded in San Pedro Bay—"among the worst tragedies in the early annals of Los Angeles," according to Harris Newmark—Wilson acquired a large part of the Myles vineyard near his own Lake Vineyard.[32] About this time, too, he began to import Chinese labor to harvest his grapes in the fall.[33]

The Mound Vineyard was the source of a Wilson specialty, called simply "Mound Vineyard" wine. This was introduced in 1863 and was described as a "natural sherry" made from very ripe grapes that did not ferment to dryness—what variety of grape was used is not said, nor are we told how the difficult business of keeping an unfortified sweet wine in sound condition was managed.[34] In 1864, hoping, so it is said, to find timber suitable for wine barrels, Wilson opened a burro path to the top of the main peak behind his property and collected some sixty burros for the purpose. But the pine, live oak, and cedar on the mountain were worthless for wine barrels. Wilson's only reward for his efforts was to have the mountain named for him.[35]

Wilson was not notably active in introducing new varieties, but his papers at least provide some particulars in this matter. On February 23, 1864, Wilson's agent in San Francisco wrote that he was sending "a thousand white wine cuttings from the vineyard of Comandante Vallejo in Sonoma beside a bundle of another sort of white vines called the St. Peter."[36] The cuttings from Vallejo are not identified, and there were, according to Charles Sullivan, "many vines with 'St. Peter' in their names" among the vines distributed by New England nurserymen.[37] But the document is evidence that new varieties were being sought. In

1866 Wilson Flint, the distinguished Sacramento nurseryman, sent Wilson cuttings of Muscat of Alexandria sufficient to graft 2,000 or 3,000 vines, a supply that, Flint said, "will give you a good start in this most valuable of all the grapes."[38] Experienced wine drinkers today are not likely to agree with Flint's estimate, the Muscat of Alexandria being the source of wines regarded as "strong, sweet, and unsubtle," with an aroma "vaguely grapey."[39] California still had almost everything to learn about the character and qualities of the bewildering number of commercial varieties in cultivation. Muscat or muscatel wine figures in the records of the Lake Vineyard after 1873; in 1875 there were 1,500 gallons of it on hand there.[40]

In January 1869, Wilson's son-in-law, James DeBarth Shorb, wrote from San Francisco, "I send down by steamer 10,000 cuttings of the Frontiniac variety. For white wine I think it the very best grape…[;] the wine from it of one year old is certainly superior to any wine I have seen of California production."[41] Three years later Shorb wrote Wilson at planting time to suggest that they should order a stock of Malvoisie for replanting a part of the vineyard.[42] Shorb probably means the grape then called Black Malvoisie in California, which is now identified as the old French variety Cinsaut.[43] Otherwise, as Jancis Robinson explains, "malvoisie" is not the name of any particular variety but a generic term "for a wide range of, usually white-berried, grape varieties producing full-bodied, aromatic whites."[44] The muscat vines were for sweet wines. Wilson had in his vineyard such varieties as Burger and Blaue Elba for making dry white table wines, but the main interest apparently lay elsewhere. Dry red wine was not wholly neglected—Shorb reported in 1870 that he had "lately received a good lot of claret grape cuttings from Napa"—but such wine never figured very importantly in the Lake Vineyard's production.[45] Wilson showed a wine called "Sultana" at the annual Mechanics' Institute Exhibition in San Francisco in 1870, but I have no information about its varietal origin. The name is that of the grape also called Sultanina and Thompson's Seedless in California, but according to Charles Sullivan that variety did not come to California until 1872.[46]

Like the Sainsevains, Kohler and Frohling, and Matthew Keller, Wilson depended on the San Francisco market for the sale of his wines. Doing business as B. D. Wilson and Son—his only son, John, supplied the "Son"—Wilson worked through an agent in San Francisco from around 1860. The still-unspecialized character of the trade appears from the fact that their agent—Hobbs, Gilmore and Co.—had as its main business a planing and saw mill that also manufactured boxes and other wood products. The connection between Hobbs, Gilmore and Co. and B. D. Wilson and Son apparently came about because Wilson bought barrels and other items from Hobbs, Gilmore, and paid for them in wine; from this kind of transaction Hobbs, Gilmore's role as Wilson's agent developed. Wilson could not expect, therefore, to be served so efficiently as Kohler and Frohling, who sold nothing but their own wines; in addition to the trade in barrels, Hobbs, Gilmore also

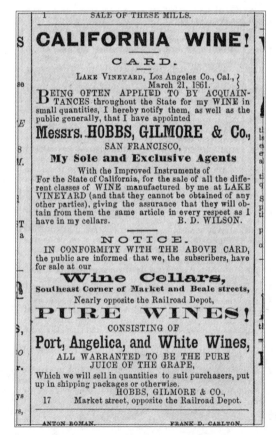

Ad announcing the appointment of Hobbs, Gilmore and Co. as agents for B. D. Wilson's Los Angeles wines. From *California Farmer*, August 2, 1861. Courtesy of the Huntington Library.

supplied Wilson with such items as candles, sewing machines, and wheel-barrows; in return, Wilson sent them on commission not only wine but oranges, lemons, and other fruits from his Lake Vineyard estate. Wilson also managed somehow to secure an agent in New York and to supply him by the difficult route around Cape Horn. Whereas Kohler and Frohling had, in Charles Stern, a full-time representative of their own in New York; Wilson was not so lucky. He had a succession of more or less unsatisfactory agents, and at one time sent his son, John, to the city to act for him.[47]

If wine was a sideline for Hobbs, Gilmore and Co., it was nevertheless a fairly substantial trade. When Wilson decided to appoint a new San Francisco agent in 1864, the statement of sales from between 1860 and January 1, 1864, drawn up by Hobbs, Gilmore and Co. as a final accounting, makes an interesting record.[48] They received from Wilson in those four years 28,757 gallons of port, 27,980 gallons of white wine, 11,052 of Angelica, and a mere 684 gallons of "Red Sweet Wine," a total of 68,473 gallons of wine, for which Wilson received $62,493. The prices that Wilson received were 85 cents a gallon for port, 65 cents for white and Angelica, and 50 cents for red wine.[49] These sales were achieved in the face of sometimes cutthroat competition from the other big Los Angeles producers—the Sainsevains, Matthew Keller, and Kohler and Frohling—who, with Wilson, dominated the market. As Hobbs, Gilmore and Co. advised Wilson in 1863, he had to compete only against the Los Angeles people, since "the Anaheim and Sonoma wines are not as good as the Wine from Los Angeles."[50] This seems to have been the general view at the time. As a newspaper writer put it in 1864,

> Los Angeles County may justly be considered the leading wine manufacturing county in the State. We undoubtedly produce better wine, and more of it, than any other county in the State, not excepting Sonoma, which county may be considered our rival in the wine manufacture.[51]

Wilson appeared to be tiring of the wine trade after a decade at the Lake Vineyard, and was even thinking of selling "the finest and best place in the State" in 1866. As his wife, Margaret, wrote to a friend,

"The heavy duties on the wine and the expense of making it leaves very little profit." The problem was the expense of shipping and of maintaining an agency in San Francisco. "We could do well," she wrote, "if he could only manage to sell his wine here."[52] But Los Angeles in 1866 had only about 5,000 people and grew but slowly—to 5,728 in 1870, hardly enough to make a difference. The town could not possibly drink up the growing production of the Los Angeles winemakers.

The situation was transformed by the entrance upon the scene of James DeBarth Shorb, who infused a wholly new energy, ambition, and confidence into Wilson's affairs. Shorb, originally from Maryland, had come to Southern California in 1864 looking for oil. This he did not find, but in 1867 he found and married Wilson's daughter, Maria de Jesus Wilson, always called Sue. Shorb was a man full of projects; in the course of his rather brief life he prospected for oil, made wine in partnership with his father-in-law, built the "world's biggest winery," promoted several land and water companies, laid out new towns, invested in a concentrated grape-must venture, founded the first citrus growers

J. DeBarth Shorb.
Courtesy of the
Huntington Library.

cooperative, speculated in Arizona land and in mines, served on the Board of State Viticultural Commissioners, was elected treasurer of the city of Los Angeles, and was active in Democratic politics and in all political movements touching agriculture. And that is only a selection from his multifarious activities.

Unlike his father-in-law, who, despite his very active life, was given to a resigned melancholy,[53] Shorb was euphoric, aggressive, quick to take offense, and eager to have a part in whatever was going on. He was, a contemporary remembered, tall, handsome, well-dressed, articulate—"one always realized his presence."[54] Or, as it was stated in the *Pacific Wine and Spirit Review*, "By his associates he is considered one of the finest, if not the finest looking man in California."[55] He married Sue Wilson in June 1867; in December he took over Benjamin Wilson's wine business on a ten-year lease. B. D. Wilson and Co., as the new enterprise was first called, was run by Shorb; Wilson retired as an interested but passive observer of the business, having no responsibility for its affairs. Shorb at once left for San Francisco, where he had set up an agency for the sale of Wilson's wines in partnership with Carlton Curtis. Two months later he was boasting to Wilson that within a year, and despite the competition, "I will sell more wine than the whole of them put together."[56] That was the style of the man: the boasts were often unfulfilled, but no matter.

Through B. D. Wilson and Co., Wine and Commission Merchants, as the San Francisco agency was styled, Shorb could reach out in all directions, and did so at once. "I think we may get the handling of all the brandy made by Sam Brannan this year," Shorb wrote to Wilson in January 1868. In March he reported that "we have some agencies promised already, for Sonoma wines and brandies" and that he expected to do a "considerable trade from other vineyards beside our own." There was the prospect of a large trade to Lima, and elsewhere in South America, "where we think a large market can be found." A trial shipment of port and white wine was made to Glasgow in another search for new markets, and the New York house (Shorb had found a new agency there) wanted 5,000 gallons of brandy "as soon as possible. Our brandy takes well in New York." After a year in business, Shorb

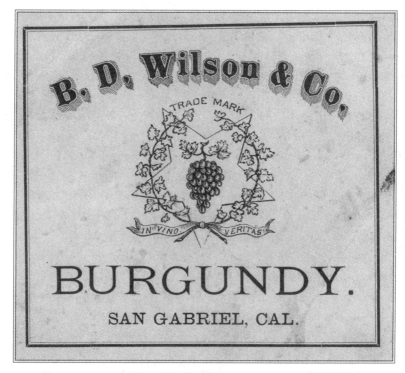

The label for wines from the vineyards of B. D. Wilson and J. DeBarth Shorb from some time between 1867 and 1869, when the company name was changed to Lake Vineyard Wine Co. Courtesy of the Huntington Library.

blandly declared in January 1869 that we "stand today at the head of the wine trade of the State."[57]

Such restless activity evidently made Wilson uneasy. He consulted a lawyer to learn whether the use of his name for Shorb's company made him, Wilson, liable for the firm's debts. The answer was yes, it did. Wilson at once demanded that Shorb change the name of the company, and so in April 1869, B. D. Wilson and Co. became the Lake Vineyard Wine Co.[58]

Shorb could not keep up the pace at which he had begun, and after some months of strenuous activity he began to have doubts about the wine business. On a trip to New York in 1869 (by the newly completed transcontinental railroad) he wrote to Wilson that Morrow and Chamberlin, their agents in the city,

have a double fight before them: first to introduce a new
article which all importers are fighting against, and secondly
to remove the bad effects and strong prejudices against all
California wines, created by the horrible stuff offered here
as Cal wines on this market. Out of one hundred and ten
dealers in Cal wines on this market alone, there are but four
or five who even buy a gallon—they manufacture it here in
their cellars.[59]

A few weeks later, Shorb, still in the East, writes that he is exhausted,
out of patience with the wine business, and thinking of some other
way to make a living.[60] This fit of annoyance passed, but a change had
occurred. Shorb now determined to return to the Lake Vineyard and
to make that his permanent base. He would manage the wine business
at the source, although the new arrangement took some time to set up.
In 1873 Shorb and Wilson formed an equal partnership to run the wine
business, once again using the name B. D. Wilson and Co. Wilson had
made a gift to Shorb of the Mound Vineyard, behind and above the
Lake Vineyard; the two vineyards, now under separate ownership, continued to supply B. D. Wilson and Co.

Under this name, and under Shorb's management, the winery at Lake
Vineyard prospered for the next few years. To mark his success—and to
accommodate his growing family (James and Sue ultimately had eleven
surviving children)—Shorb built, in 1877, a big house in the midst of
his vineyard and named it San Marino, after the Shorb family estate
in Maryland. Most of the wine trade was carried on through agencies
in San Francisco and in New York. According to Shorb, B. D. Wilson
and Co. shipped more than 500 pipes of 150-gallon capacity annually
(mostly by sailing vessel) to New York—at least 75,000 gallons of wine.[61]
Wine was also sent from San Gabriel direct to customers in Baltimore,
New York, Cleveland, Detroit, Chicago, and Montreal, among other
places. Shorb confidently assured his customers, "We make the best
wines of California."[62] To a new customer in 1875 Shorb wrote:

We are the largest wine manufacturers on the Pacific Coast
and I think enjoy the best reputation for the high qualities
of our wine. We manufacture all classes [of wine] and our

usual crop is about 150,000 gals. per year and about 11,000 gals. brandy.

Our vineyards young and old comprise about 200,000 vines—representing over 50 varieties of the best European grapes.[63]

The statement about fifty varieties is a surprise, but perhaps something like that number had been tried experimentally without ever becoming a significant part of the winemaking.

On the same day Shorb wrote that B. D. Wilson and Co. enjoyed "the best reputation for the high qualities of our wine," he also wrote to Samuel Lachman, a prominent wine merchant in San Francisco, proposing that B. D. Wilson and Co. should supply Lachman's "large and growing trade" in port and Angelica, and even that Lachman should take over B. D. Wilson's entire production of those wines. Wilson himself had now retired, and Shorb was so busy with outside interests that

"San Marino," the house built by J. DeBarth Shorb in 1877, and afterward the site of Henry Huntington's mansion, now the Huntington Art Gallery. The town of San Marino takes its name from Shorb's house. From John Albert Wilson, *History of Los Angeles County* (1880). Courtesy of the California Historical Society.

he wanted some relief. Hence, he told Lachman, he would be "glad to retire from all the commercial part of this business and merely manufacture for other firms."[64] Lachman evidently did not take up the offer.

A distaste for the sort of men he knew in the wine business also contributed to Shorb's wish to "retire" into a peaceful life of making wine without having to sell it. As he wrote to a friend who had dropped out of the wine trade, "My strong predilection even in business is to deal with gentlemen, and God knows our wine business has been handled almost exclusively by another class."[65] But Shorb was to stay in the business for the rest of his life.

Benjamin Wilson died in 1878, and with his death the first phase of winemaking in the San Gabriel Valley may be said to have come to an end; after that, there would be many changes. A word may be said here about Wilson's many public services. He was the second mayor of Los Angeles (1851–52), not a burdensome job at that time, and in 1852 he was appointed Indian Agent for Southern California, a position in which he attempted to protect the native peoples against the unchecked exploitation they suffered. He was elected a state senator in 1856 and again in 1869, when he served as chairman of the Senate Committee on the Culture of the Grape. Perhaps more important than his work in elective office were his unpaid contributions as a lobbyist for Los Angeles interests in Sacramento and Washington. In that position he lobbied for the development of a Los Angeles harbor at San Pedro; for bringing the Southern Pacific Railroad to Los Angeles; and for lifting a tax on California brandy. He spent long months in work of this kind, with notable success, for which he modestly refused all recognition.

L. J. ROSE AND SUNNY SLOPE

Only a few years after Wilson had settled in the San Gabriel Valley he was joined by a newcomer who would build a winemaking operation even grander than the Lake Vineyard's. This was Leonard J. Rose, a German-born merchant from Iowa who cared more for blooded horses than for wine, but who nevertheless made a great deal of wine in the high-flying days of the San Gabriel Valley. He had set out for California from Iowa in 1858 with a carefully prepared and well-supplied wagon train. This had encountered disaster at the Colorado River crossing, where an attack by Mojave Indians killed several of the train and forced the survivors to retreat to Albuquerque with the loss of all their goods. Rose, a resilient man, went to Santa Fe, took over the La Fonda inn, prospered through the inn's bar and gambling rooms, and before a couple of years had passed was ready to resume his trek to California. He made it to Los Angeles County at the end of 1860.

After visiting a number of sites up and down California, Rose bought from B. D. Wilson, for little more than a dollar an acre, 1,300 acres of the San Pasqual rancho, to the east of what is now Pasadena, only a short distance from Wilson at the Lake Vineyard. Rose later expanded the property by adding 640 acres from the Santa Anita rancho.[66] He named his place Sunny Slope and immediately began to plant vines—60 acres in the first year, 360 acres after three years. The land had never been planted before, and, as Rose's son described it, the soil was "over-

Leonard J. Rose, owner of the Sunny Slope Vineyard and Winery. Courtesy of the Huntington Library.

grown with cactus, sage brush, grease wood, large weeds and occasional elder [alder?] trees. All of this had to be grubbed out by the roots, collected and burned."[67] Always thinking of expansion, and accordingly always in debt, Rose aimed at a thousand acres of vines; by 1879 he had reached that figure. His winemaking capacity paralleled the expansion of his vineyard. As Rose's son has written, the winery in that year, 1879, produced a half-million gallons of wine and 125,000 gallons of brandy. He thought that they were then "using at least 75% of all the grapes raised in Los Angeles County."[68] That is certainly an exaggeration, but no one else in Los Angeles then was making wine on such a scale. In addition to the harvest from his own vineyard Rose bought grapes from growers all over the county; he had a standing promise "to buy all grapes delivered at the winery."[69]

Rose's first vintage, in 1864, had been a much more modest affair. When the grapes were brought in they were dumped into a wooden box with a slatted bottom laid over a wooden fermenting vat. Barefooted workers then climbed into the box and trampled out the juice into the vat. The method, somewhat more sophisticated than the leathern bag and sweating Indian of earlier years, but more primitive than the use of mechanical crushers such as we know Keller, Wilson, and others to have been using at least two decades earlier, seems to have persisted for some time yet. The old Sunny Slope method was still being followed at the Workman winery on Boyle Heights in the 1870s.[70] In what may be the best known illustration of the vintage in California from the nineteenth century—a scene drawn by Paul Frenzeny for *Harper's Weekly* (October 5, 1878) fourteen years after Rose's first vintage—Chinese workers are shown treading out the grapes just as was done at Sunny Slope in 1864: they march around in a wooden box laid over a large fermenting vat. Things were very different at Sunny Slope by 1879, when, as young Rose put it, "we had the most complete and capacious wine-making establishment in southern California, if not the state."[71] Several big brick buildings housed the steam-driven machinery, the fermenting vats, the storage casks, the stills, and all the other apparatus of large-scale commercial winemaking. Rose had his own cooperage to provide casks and barrels.[72]

Top: Sunny Slope winery. Bottom: The first harvest at Sunny Slope, 1864. L. J. Rose is seated just left of center in hat and vest. Courtesy of the Huntington Library.

At the outset of his work Rose had followed the usual practice and planted Mission grapes. He determined, however, on the unusual practice of doing without irrigation. His neighbors thought this a foolhardy thing to do. He was able to show them, however, that the vines did very well and the fruit was of a better color and a higher sugar than the fruit from irrigated vines. Rose also differed from his neighbors in refusing to accept passively the unsatisfactory Mission grape; instead, he tried to find something better. According to his son, Rose had at one time thirty-five different varieties of grape on trial from which he made experimental wines. From this lot Rose narrowed his choices down to three: Zinfandel for dry red wine, and Blaue Elba and Burger for white.[73] The Mission remained as the source of his staple fortified wines, port and Angelica especially. He soon discovered that his Zinfandel, although it produced a wine much superior to that of the Mission, nevertheless could not compete against the Zinfandel from Napa and Sonoma Counties, where by now it was being made in substantial quantities. Rose accordingly confined his Zinfandel production to serve a local trade, bought Zinfandel from the north to supply his eastern markets, and continued the unrewarding effort to find "a new variety to replace it."[74] Ludwig Louis Salvator, the Austrian archduke, however, wrote of Rose's table wines that "a fine product made from Blue Elba grapes, and Zinfandel claret are highly prized."[75] Rose had some hope that blending might be the way to go after finding blends he liked in Napa Valley: one was an unidentified blend from William Scheffler, another from H. W. Crabb "consisting of *Malbeck*, *Pied de Perdrix*, *Gamay*, *Teinturier*, *Lenoir*, and *Petit Pinot*."[76] But he remained cautious: "What the red wine of the future will be is yet in doubt."[77]

There was at this time in California, as more and more untried European varieties were brought into the state, a widespread experimenting with blends. There were dozens of hopeful new blends exhibited at the State Viticultural Convention in 1884, apparently made by the purest guesswork. One was of Zinfandel, Burger, Mataro, and Carignane; another, of Mataro, Charbono, Chauché noir, and West's White Prolific (French Colombard).[78] Most of them failed to impress the judges.

The wines that Rose made were of the usual Los Angeles types: port, dry white wine or "hock," Angelica, muscat, sherry. By this time, the production of these wines in Southern California was standard: port, from the Mission grape, was fortified to 20 percent alcohol and gave general satisfaction; Rose's dry white wine, from Blaue Elba and Burger grapes, was no doubt a slight improvement upon white wine from the Mission. In either case, it was a usual practice to add a little muscat to lift the otherwise flat taste. Muscat by itself was also a standard item. Achieving an acceptable dry red wine was, as has been said, a goal never quite reached in Los Angeles. It is certainly possible to do so, but encouragement and determination were both lacking, not to speak of an inadequate knowledge of possible varieties and suitable methods in the vineyard.

A decent equivalent for sherry was also a special difficulty. Matthew Keller's strange compound called "sherry" has already been described. Rose did no better. In an effort to capture the "nutty" flavor of true Sherry, Rose took unripe English walnuts, leached them in high-proof spirits, and added a dash of the resulting extract to each barrel of sweet white wine destined to be called sherry. "This process," his son concluded, "was but a makeshift."[79] Brandy, as it had been since the beginnings of California winemaking, was well liked. Rose made it in large quantities. By 1882 he was described as "much the largest distiller in California."[80]

The summary so far given of a seemingly smooth progress in steady prosperity omits to mention that Rose, at the outset, had much hard work to do in doubtful circumstances. Writing in 1892 of his early struggles at Sunny Slope, Rose recalled that after buying the property

> my life was covered by the darkest clouds, and my wife's lot was, I believe, one of the hardest. We struggled on in the very teeth of adversity, scraping, and economizing, pawning and borrowing, till the estate, which was very large, became productive. Finally [c. 1864?], with a quantity of wine which I had made, and a supply of provisions, I started, deep in debt but high in hope, for Prescott, Arizona.[81] Bad roads deterred others from starting, and I had a monopoly, reaping thereby

heavy returns. This is the history of the first important load
of wines which left the now famous Sunny Slope vineyards.[82]

With the example of Kohler and Frohling, the Sainsevains, and Benjamin Wilson before him, Rose made shipments of wine to New York as early as 1867, by the tedious route from Los Angeles to San Francisco, and from San Francisco by sailing ship around the Horn—a six months' journey. Rose also undertook to sell wine in the largely untouched Midwest, and to do it himself rather than through an agent, a move made possible by the completion of the transcontinental railway in 1869.[83] His first venture was in 1870, when he called on wholesale druggists, wholesale liquor dealers, and wholesale grocers in such raw places as Omaha and Kansas City before moving on to Chicago, Detroit, Cleveland, and the eastern cities. The effort paid off, and Rose repeated it in each of the next five years. By 1875 he was glad to make a deal with Perkins, Stern and Co. in New York, the firm originally set up as agents for Kohler and Frohling.[84] They had dealt in other native wines as well—Rose's Sunny Slope wines among them; now they would be agents for all sales of Rose's wine in the East. Perkins died in 1877, and the firm was then reorganized as Stern and Rose. Rose himself now arranged to stand back a little from the wine trade and devote himself more to his horses. Charles Stern took care of the sales end; the winemaking was in the hands of a German, William Schoelgens.[85]

Rose remained an active businessman and an important figure in the California wine trade. When the Board of State Viticultural Commissioners was formed in 1880, Rose was appointed commissioner for the Los Angeles District and served until 1892. But his heart was in his splendid stables.[86] Rose was distinguished as a leader in the California wine trade, as the owner of a great estate, and as a prominent citizen of Los Angeles County, but it was as an expert in horse flesh that he was best known and admired: "Rose was always the center of a group of men, for he was an authority on horses."[87] Another of his accomplishments, we are told, was that "he could play on any instrument, the banjo being his favorite."[88]

The prosperity achieved by California winemakers at the end of the 1870s continued into the early '80s. These were the years in which the

PERKINS, STERN & CO.

STANDARD

CALIFORNIA WINES

AND

GRAPE BRANDIES.

The Purest! The Cheapest! The Best!

HAVING formed a copartnership with Mr. L. J. ROSE of Los Angeles, California, we now have the entire Crop of Wines and Brandies, from his celebrated "Sunny Slope Vineyard." The Wines and Brandies made in this Vineyard, are, without doubt, the finest of any made in California, and as we are now the producers of these Wines, parties purchasing from us, are dealing DIRECTLY with the Makers of these Wines, which is an advantage too obvious to need comment.

A modest announcement ("The Purest! The Cheapest! The Best!") of the new partnership between Perkins, Stern and L. J. Rose, 1875. Courtesy of Cal Poly Pomona University Library Special Collections.

production of wine in Europe was falling catastrophically through the ravages of phylloxera in the vineyards. In consequence, there was an intense search for alternative sources of wine, and a keen interest in California as an attractive possibility. Rose was approached by English investors in 1882, and after prolonged negotiations he sold Sunny Slope to them in 1887 for $1,035,000.[89] Now identified as the L. J. Rose Company, Ltd., the business did not reward its investors as they had hoped, considering the extravagant description of the property and its assured profits that they had been given.[90] The wines were now made under the management of E. C. Bichowsky, who also succeeded Rose as a member of the Board of State Viticultural Commissioners. Sunny Slope wines continued to be among the best known of California wines. But the company, rather than paying dividends, reported losses, and the stockholders soon grew restless. The winery continued to operate, but with diminishing success. In 1898 it was described as "idle"; in 1901 it was offered for sale at the distress price of $40,000 but found no takers.[91] The land, according to L. J. Rose, Jr., "was peddled about...for $250 and $300 per acre to local people, and all traces of the English syndicate vanished."[92]

Rose, too, ran out of luck. He entered political life and was elected a state senator in 1887; at the same time, always in debt, he began to suffer catastrophic losses. He had taken part payment from the sale of Sunny Slope to the English syndicate in the form of stock. When the company failed to prosper, Rose, according to Harris Newmark, lost $500,000 and was "almost penniless."[93] Desperate for money, and yet unable to find any, Rose took an overdose of morphine and was found dying in the chicken yard behind his house in Los Angeles on May 17, 1899.

The Lake Vineyard and the Sunny Slope winery were the giants of San Gabriel Valley winemaking, but their splendor attracted many others to the region and to the business. In 1861, E. J. C. Kewen, a noisy and contentious lawyer in Los Angeles, acquired (as a gift from his father-in-law, Dr. T. J. White) the Old Mill property just west of Wilson and made wine there from 50 acres of grapes. Another lawyer, Volney Howard, a neighbor of Wilson's to the south, had 20 acres of vines by 1863.[94]

No additions to this group appear in the next few years, which were a time of great economic distress in Los Angeles County. Prolonged drought, from 1862 through 1864, had devastated the ranch owners and all who depended on them. Cattle and sheep died in uncounted thousands, and their owners, now impoverished, could no longer maintain their vast holdings. It was in these years that the traditional ranch life of Southern California is said to have come to an end. The big pastoral estates were divided up and put on the market. Newcomers, of whom there were many following the end of the Civil War, could now buy smaller properties and engage in farming based on livestock, grain, orchards—and vines. The Los Angeles winemakers saw this development as a pure gain. In 1863 prices for wine had been so low that they would not pay for the cost of cultivating the vineyards. But since the dying of the cattle, wine "has already become the leading staple of Southern California, but more especially of Los Angeles County... new vineyards are constantly coming into bearing."[95] Three years later this had become the received view of things. As Matthew Keller wrote in 1867, the years of drought had been good to California because now the big landowners, facing ruin,

> will open their large domains to the tillers of the soil at fair rates and will introduce a better class of animals. Some large landholders will hold on to their immense domains with a deadly grasp, but taxation and Californian interests will soon rank them among the played out institutions of the nineteenth century.[96]

By the end of the 1860s the hard times had been left behind and Los Angeles, although still a small town, now enjoyed something of a boom. Real estate prices soared as housing was hastily put up for the newcomers. Some of old winemaking Los Angeles was lost in the surge:

> Recent enterprises have placed a large number of lots, situated upon First, Aliso, Sainsevaine, and other streets on sale. That productive vines fifty years old or upwards should be taken up, wine cellars removed, and bearing orange trees in considerable numbers be uprooted for the purpose of making room for those who must have houses to live in, and lots

George Stoneman, Civil War general and governor of California (1883–87). He planted 200 acres of vines and built a winery at his Los Robles estate, on land purchased from B. D. Wilson. Courtesy of the Library of Congress.

upon which to build them, is an evidence that enterprise, so long slumbering in Los Angeles, is now awake.[97]

The San Gabriel Valley shared modestly in the boom. Benjamin Eaton, yet another lawyer, acquired the Fair Oaks property on the San Pasqual ranch, to the north of Wilson's Lake Vineyard, in 1865 and began planting vines in unirrigated land; by 1870 he had 30,000 of them, although they suffered much from the depredations of coyotes and bears from the nearby foothills.[98] In 1871 George Stoneman, a general in the Union Army and later a governor of California, retired (temporarily) to a property he named "Los Robles," next to Kewen's Old Mill place. The land was sold to him by Benjamin Wilson, who had known Stoneman as a young officer with General Kearny's force at Los

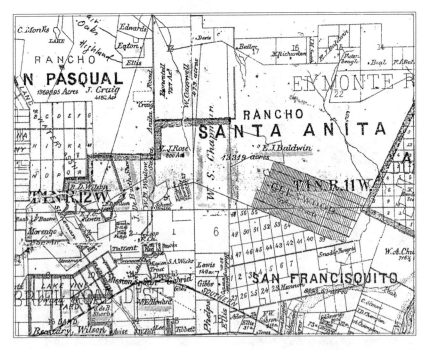

The San Gabriel Valley, showing vineyard properties in 1877. L. J. Rose's property is approximately in the center, Shorb's and Wilson's are to the west, and Lucky Baldwin's is to the east. Other vineyard owners named here include Kewen, Chapman, Bacon, Stoneman, and, to the north, Eaton. "Winslow," adjoining Rose on the west, is a misprint for "Winston." The Indiana Colony at the upper left later became Pasadena. Detail of a map of Los Angeles County by J. J. Wildy. Courtesy of the Library of Congress.

Angeles in 1846–47. At that time Stoneman camped on the site of Los Robles and was so smitten by its attractions that he determined it should some day be his home.[99] When he succeeded in buying the property, Stoneman began planting vines at once and had more than 100 acres of them within two years. He had 200 acres by 1879 and made 40,000 gallons of wine that year in a steam-powered, gravity-flow winery he had built from scratch. He did not, so far as I know, undertake to market his wine but sold it in bulk to such buyers as B. D. Wilson and Co., L. J. Rose, or Kohler and Frohling. Another army man—in this case a Confederate—to whom Wilson sold land was Colonel W. H. Winston, "a dyed-in-the-wool southerner...still fighting the war at his death."[100] The Colonel planted a vineyard but did not make wine. His place flanked Rose's Sunny Slope on the west. On the east Sunny Slope was flanked by the property of Albert B. Chapman, a graduate of West Point but now yet another Los Angeles lawyer, who developed a vineyard there on a part of the Santa Anita ranch.

The flashiest of these new proprietors was Elias J. "Lucky" Baldwin—"Lucky" because of his fabulous successes as a speculator in mining shares.[101] Baldwin came to Los Angeles in 1875, bought the Santa Anita ranch, and immediately began to extend the planting of vines, oranges, and other fruits that were already on the property in considerable quantity. In 1876, only a year after he took over the ranch, he is reported as having "two or three hundred acres of vineyards" and having spent $30,000 to build "a wine and brandy manufactory."[102] As his neighbor L. J. Rose was doing, Baldwin also set about building a great establishment for racehorses. Today's Santa Anita racetrack is successor to the track that Baldwin built on his estate. In a few years after his purchase of Santa Anita, Baldwin had 200 acres of vines and a substantial winery and distillery; brandy was a prominent item in his production and remained so for the life of the winery. According to Ben Truman, by 1887 Baldwin had 1,200 acres of vines producing 300,000 gallons of wine and 50,000 gallons of "very fine brandy" annually.[103]

In 1874 a large part of the San Pasqual grant, then owned jointly by Dr. John Griffin and B. D. Wilson, was sold to a group calling themselves the San Gabriel Orange Grove Association, who then subdivided

E. J. "Lucky" Baldwin, of Rancho Santa Anita. Courtesy of the Huntington Library.

the property, laid on water, and planted oranges and grapes so that prospective buyers were offered something more than bare land. The town that grew up there was first known as the Indiana Colony (although there were only a few Hoosiers among the early settlers) and then later as Pasadena, a made-up name alleged to mean in Chippewa "Crown of the [San Gabriel] Valley."[104] The sale of the property had been made in January 1874; by June 1874, 100,000 vine cuttings had been set out, and in the next year there were 150,000.[105] The vineyards in and around Pasadena supplied grapes to the San Gabriel Valley wineries for many years, as well as to several wineries in the town itself: the Marengo Vineyard, the Highland Vineyard, the Lamanda Park Winery, the Sphinx Winery. Pasadena, dominated as it was by Protestant Midwesterners devoted to the struggle against Demon Rum, passed an anti-saloon law in 1886, the year of the town's incorporation. But grapes continued to be grown and wine continued to be made for many years in nominally dry Pasadena.

5

ANAHEIM AND THE GROWTH
OF THE INDUSTRY, 1860-90

At the very moment that Benjamin Wilson was starting to develop the Lake Vineyard in the San Gabriel Valley, another, different winemaking enterprise was taking shape to the southeast of Los Angeles. This was the settlement called Anaheim, lying about twenty-five miles from the city, in what was then Los Angeles County but is now Orange County (created in 1889). Who first had the idea for Anaheim is not certainly known. Maybe it came from Los Angeles, where Kohler and Fröhling were early actors in the story; maybe it came from San Francisco, where the Germans who were to be the citizens of Anaheim were gathered. In any case, its history may be traced from the moment in 1855 that Fröhling, accompanied by the Austrian-born George Hansen, a surveyor practicing in Los Angeles, traveled to San Francisco to meet with Charles Kohler and Otto Weyse, publisher of the German-language *San Francisco Demokrat*. I imagine that Fröhling, the winemaker, and Kohler, the merchant, who together were making Kohler and Frohling the leading winemaking firm in all of California, were the energizing elements among the four men. Hansen provided the practical knowledge of a civil engineer and surveyor who knew the Los Angeles region well. Weyse, the publisher, had the means to advertise whatever might be decided.

The ideas discussed in that meeting took shape as a plan to found a colony of German émigrés in Southern California, where they would devote themselves to grape growing and winemaking. Kohler and Frohling,

Seal of the organization that created Anaheim in 1857. Orange County had not yet
been separated from Los Angeles County. From the author's collection.

who had great confidence in their prospects, would buy what Anaheim
grew or made. The plan was soon being promoted both among the Germans of San Francisco and among those of Los Angeles as well.[1]

Early in 1857 the plan was acted upon. A company called the Los
Angeles Vineyard Society was formed, and prospective settlers in the
community that was to be laid out were invited to purchase one or more
of the fifty shares to be issued by the Society. Each $750 share entitled
the buyer to a 20-acre tract, 8 acres of which were to be planted to
vines. The plan was to make all the essential preparations in advance;
land would be bought, the lots surveyed and laid out, the irrigation
works built, the vines planted, and the property fenced. Meantime, the
shareholders would remain at work, thus enabling them to pay for their
shares. By this method, the rigors of pioneering would be lessened, and,
more important, the investors would be able to earn the means to pay
for their shares.

The Germans who joined in this scheme were, like so many pioneers in American winegrowing, without any experience in that line at all; they included "several carpenters, a gunsmith, an engraver, three watch-makers, four blacksmiths, a brewer, a teacher, a shoe-maker, a miller, several merchants, a book-binder, a poet, four or five musicians, a hatter, some teamsters, a hotel-keeper, and others." Of this group, it is said that "only one had ever made wine."[2] Practical ignorance did not seem to matter. There was already a great deal of winemaking experience accumulated in Los Angeles, city and county, so the Anaheim novices could certainly get help when they needed it. They could lean especially on Charles Kohler, who was vice president of the Society, and on John Fröhling, who was a member of the Society's Auditing Committee in Los Angeles. Kohler and Fröhling knew wine, and the wine trade, as few others in California did.

There was a hitch in the proceedings at first, when George Hansen, who was entrusted with the work, had trouble finding a suitable tract of land. At last Charles Kohler was sent down to Los Angeles to advise in the matter, and it was Kohler who decided to purchase more than 1,000 acres at $2 an acre from the Rancho Cajón de Santa Ana, belonging to Pacifico Ontiveros.[3] This was bare, semiarid land, not even fit to pasture goats, according to Ontiveros. But it included a strip leading from the Santa Ana River, three miles distant, from which the land would be irrigated, and the land itself was part of an alluvial fan laid down by the river. It looked bleak, but water would transform it.[4]

Hansen now set to work on the formidable job of converting the thousand acres of sand, brush, and cactus into a site fit for habitation. He recruited a small working army—"eighty-seven men, ten women, eighty-four horses, seven plows and seventeen wagons"—whose first job was to dig a canal 5 miles long to bring water to the property, which was then distributed through some 346 miles of lateral ditches.[5] The direction of flow from the river was northeast to southwest, and that is how the streets of Anaheim were originally laid out and how they remain today—not square to the points of the compass but tilted at an angle dictated by the slope of the land.

After Hansen's Mexican and Indian laborers had dug the irrigation canal, they laid out the streets, a public park, and a 40-acre townsite in the center of things. They planted each lot with 8,000 Mission grape cuttings obtained from Santa Ana Valley and Los Angeles vineyards, including William Wolfskill's, and then fenced the whole with 40,000 eight-foot poles of willow, alder, and sycamore, planted two feet deep and eighteen inches apart.[6] These soon grew into a live fence, five and a half miles long, and impenetrable, it was hoped, by livestock and the wild animals that still abounded in that undeveloped country.[7] By the end of 1859, slightly more than two years after Hansen had begun the work, the first shareholders arrived to occupy their property. Before that, a meeting had been held to give the new community a name. "Anna-heim," meaning "home by the Santa Ana River," narrowly won over "Annagau," meaning "Santa Ana River District." The German "Anna" soon yielded to the Spanish "Ana," and so it has remained. Hansen was credited at the time with "one of the greatest agricultural achievements ever performed in California."[8]

George Hansen, the Los Angeles surveyor who laid out the site of Anaheim, built the irrigation system, and planted the grape vines before the town was settled. Courtesy of the Anaheim Public Library.

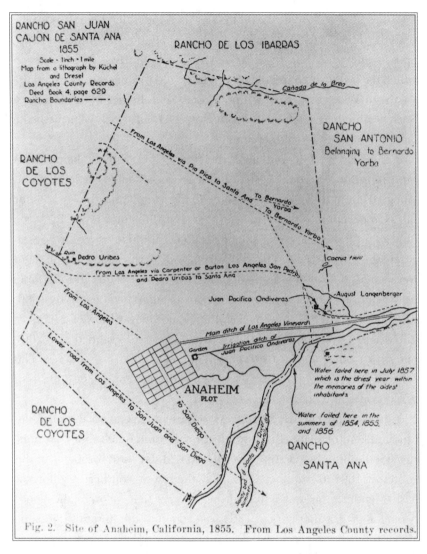

Fig. 2. Site of Anaheim, California, 1855. From Los Angeles County records.

Original plan of Anaheim, showing the main irrigation ditch and the tilt of the property. Courtesy of the Anaheim Public Library.

The Society had provided the means of irrigation and had planted vineyards, but now the further necessities—as, for example, a house to live in—would have to be provided by the individual owners themselves. By the end of the year twenty houses had been built or were being built. Only then was the property distributed by lottery. The lots were assessed at around $1,200 each, more or less. If a shareholder drew a lot assessed at less than $1,200 he was paid the difference; if more, he paid the difference. The Anaheim colony is often referred to as a cooperative enterprise, but it was so only in getting started. The Society in which they were all shareholders was later sold to a new entity called the Anaheim Water Co., at which point each shareholder in the Vineyard Society now had stock in the company, and that stock went with the land; it could not be sold separately.[9]

Things did not long remain as they had begun, with all the residents on a more or less equal basis. Almost at once, some people acquired vineyards from their neighbors, some made wine, some grew grapes for sale, some went into the businesses that served the new town. By 1863, only about three years after the first settlement, there were thirty-seven Anaheim vineyards listed in the Perkins and Stern catalog; six of them were rated at 16,000 vines, twice the original measure, and a couple were at 12,000. Rearrangement and consolidation had begun. By 1880, roughly twenty years from the beginning, one vineyard was of 240 acres (the original 1,165 acres of the colony had been expanded to 3,200), one of 70 acres, and a scattering of others from 20 to 45 acres. The original arrangement of fifty 8-acre vineyards had entirely disappeared, as, no doubt, it was expected to happen.

Early accounts of Anaheim tend to present it as an ideal, not to say utopian, kind of place. But it went through some rough times. A monster flood on the Santa Ana River inundated the entire property in the winter of 1861–62, and Anaheim, like the rest of Southern California, had to endure the devastating drought years that followed the flood. A plague of grasshoppers in 1863 was added to the unremitting damages caused by the local wildlife—squirrels, gophers, hawks, coyotes. A severe frost in 1873 cut the production of wine that year by more than half. Some vineyards went uncultivated and reverted to weeds and brush. The vineyards that were cared for, however, unlike the poor cattle belonging to the ranchers, managed not just to survive but to grow productively. Despite the early vicissitudes, it is said that only one of the original investors left the colony in the first years.[10]

Winemaking was largely an individual enterprise at the outset, and to a considerable degree it remained that way. The operations varied in size, some larger, some smaller, and one, at least—that of Benjamin Dreyfus—growing to be genuinely big. But as long as Anaheim made wine, a number of small proprietors persisted.[11] The original vines at Anaheim had been planted in the spring of 1858; the first, small vintage of 2,000 gallons was made in 1860, when the vines were in their third leaf. Production from that point on zoomed as the vines matured and new plantings were made. In 1861, 75,000 gallons were produced; in 1862, 125,000 gallons; in 1863, 300,000; and so on in increasing quantity, year after year. The peak year was 1884, when the vineyards of Anaheim yielded 1.25 million gallons of wine.

That first substantial vintage in 1861 was made under the supervision of John Fröhling, who bought all of it for his firm.[12] The connection between Anaheim and Kohler and Frohling, so important in the creation of the colony, did not last. Fröhling died on September 21,

Benjamin Dreyfus, the biggest grower of Anaheim wine, and the leader in its distribution. Courtesy of the Anaheim Public Library.

1862, just at the time of a vintage that he could not now supervise, and with his death the special relationship seems to have ended. Anaheim was lucky to have another marketing resource in the person of Benjamin Dreyfus, a Bavarian Jew who had come to Los Angeles in 1854 and set up as a merchant. In 1858, while the site of Anaheim was still being prepared, Dreyfus, in partnership with August Langenberger, a shareholder, built a general store in the center of the Anaheim acreage in anticipation of the arrival of the shareholders. When they did arrive, they found Dreyfus ready for them.

He proved to be immensely useful. The Anaheim people, no doubt aware that they could not depend solely on Kohler and Frohling as a market for their wines, formed the Anaheim Wine Growers' Association at the end of 1859 to consolidate their individual productions. In 1863, when the colony had 200,000 gallons to sell, Dreyfus went to San Francisco to manage the Association's agency there, and from that point he went on to open outlets under his own name in San Francisco and New York to sell

The house and winery of Theodore Reiser at Anaheim. From John Albert Wilson, *History of Los Angeles County* (1880). Courtesy of the Huntington Library.

Anaheim wines. Dreyfus was also producing kosher wine for sale in San Francisco as early as 1864.[13] The Anaheim Wine Growers' Association was described in 1871 as the "chief wine establishment of the state," owning no vineyards but making wine for its individual shareholders.[14]

One of the more successful of the individual winemakers in Anaheim was Theodore Reiser, a cooper and brewer from Baden, and therefore one of the few who knew anything about the mysteries of fermentation. Reiser claimed to have "organized" the Los Angeles Vineyard Society. He also claimed to have produced in 1860 "the first wine made at Anaheim" from grapes purchased from Thomas Scully, who had a vineyard in Santa Ana.[15] The first claim is more than doubtful, although Reiser may have been a helpful promoter; the second is impossible to prove or disprove. Reiser's winery, never very large, was still operating in 1884 and is said to have persisted nearly to the time of Prohibition.[16] He evidently prospered. Early Anaheim, in common with other Southern California settlements, was built of adobe. Reiser, however, managed to build a house of brick and was always afterward jokingly known as the "Graf von Brickenstein."[17]

Another notable name among the early commercial winemakers was Henry Kroeger, who was trained as a cooper in his native Germany and who continued to practice the craft after he had immigrated to San Francisco. He was one of the original shareholders in the Los Angeles Vineyard Society, buying not one but two shares. He did not arrive in Anaheim until 1862, where, according to his own account of things, he "accumulated considerable property by energy and prudent management."[18] He built a winery at once, to process the yield of his two vineyards, which, by 1880, had grown to 40 acres of vines, including a few acres of Muscats as well as the standard Missions. Kroeger came from Holstein, in the remote north of Germany, far from any vineyards, and so, as he put it, he "was entirely inexperienced in viniculture and winemaking, and has paid dearly for the knowledge he now possesses."[19] Most of his neighbors could have said the same thing. Kroeger might stand for the Anaheim Germans as a whole: a trained craftsman, hardworking and prudent, inexperienced but ready to learn, and rewarded by a solid prosperity.

Not every citizen of Anaheim would achieve prosperity, but even the poor of Anaheim drank wine, "for this is the least expensive drink here."[20] That was the observation of the Polish writer Henry Sienkiewicz, the author of *Quo Vadis*; he had come to the region with the famous Polish actress Helena Modjeska in 1876, attracted by a more or less Utopian colony near Anaheim. The colony did not work out, and Sienkiewicz soon left. The Modjeska, however, thought enough of the place to build a house there and to remain in this country. Orange County now contains a Modjeska Canyon and a Modjeska Peak in memory of this distinguished resident.

By 1880, some twenty years after winemaking began in Anaheim, there were sixty winemakers in Anaheim Township, according to the U.S. Census of that year. German names continued to dominate: Boege, Hartung, Koenig, Korn, Luedke, Meyerholz, Schneider, Wehmeyer, and Zeyn, to give a sample. Although Anaheim was exclusively German at the outset, it did not jealously guard its German identity but was open to settlers of different origin. Names such as Adams, Brackett, Kelley, and Lee soon began to appear among the lists of the town's winemakers.[21]

The king of Anaheim winemakers was Benjamin Dreyfus, whose ambitious enterprise set him apart from all the others. Dreyfus, as we have seen, was living in Anaheim even before it was a town. Sent to San Francisco in 1863 to sell Anaheim wine there, he developed one of the major wine houses of the city: Benjamin Dreyfus and Company. Dreyfus remained loyal to Anaheim, building the largest winery in the town,

Letterhead of B. Dreyfus and Co. Courtesy of the Huntington Library.

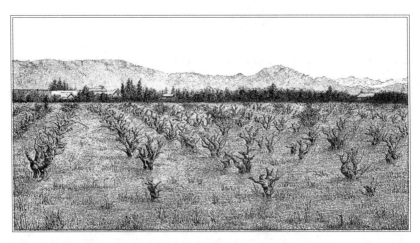

Dead vineyard in Anaheim. From Newton B. Pierce, *The California Vine Disease* (1892). From the author's collection.

but to meet his growing needs he eventually acquired vineyard properties in Cucamonga, the San Gabriel Valley, and Napa Valley as well as in Anaheim. By 1874 he was making 175,000 gallons and selling it to the eastern trade. When his company was absorbed into the California Wine Association in 1894, a million gallons of wine lay in Dreyfus's Wine Vaults in San Francisco.

In 1884 Dreyfus erected a big stone wine cellar two hundred feet long and three stories high in Anaheim, a bold monument to the town's success. And then disaster struck. Not all at once, although it seemed that way at the time. There had been some warning; in 1885 men noticed diseased vines here and there in the vineyards, although production was not affected. In the next year, the disease was everywhere and could not be ignored, and by the end of the decade winegrowing in and around Anaheim was finished.[22] The vineyards were dead, and no one knew why or how. There was no name for the thing; it was called "The Mysterious Disease," "The New Disease," "The Los Angeles Rot," "The California Disease," "The Anaheim Disease." The disease did not appear at the beginning of a season but only after it was in progress, so growers were mocked by vines seemingly in good health at the outset. Then the leaves began to show red or yellow discoloration around the edges; next, the edges turned brown and the leaves fell from the vine. Without the support of the leaves, the fruit dropped, the canes failed to ripen and died back, the root system declined, and the wood dried out. It might take several years before an individual vine died. Some varieties appeared to resist a little longer than others—the Mission, the most widely planted variety, was especially vulnerable—but all were equally doomed. It was "only a question of time."[23]

Every possible cause was suggested, and every one was rejected: it was not the soil, not the atmospheric conditions, not the irrigation water, not sunburn, not excessive rainfall, not climate change, not cultivation methods, not any form of the familiar diseases and pests. What was it? In response to the appeals of the Anaheim growers, the U.S. Department of Agriculture sent an investigator to the Santa Ana Valley in 1887; he was of no help, although he suggested that, since the disease

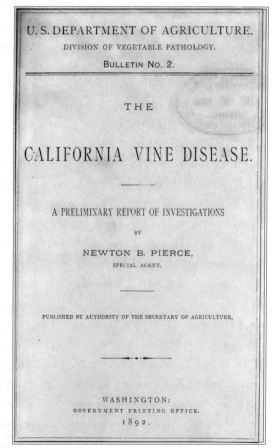

U.S. DEPARTMENT OF AGRICULTURE.
DIVISION OF VEGETABLE PATHOLOGY.

BULLETIN No. 2.

THE

CALIFORNIA VINE DISEASE.

A PRELIMINARY REPORT OF INVESTIGATIONS

BY

NEWTON B. PIERCE,
SPECIAL AGENT.

PUBLISHED BY AUTHORITY OF THE SECRETARY OF AGRICULTURE.

WASHINGTON:
GOVERNMENT PRINTING OFFICE.
1892.

Title page of *The California Vine Disease* by Newton B. Pierce, the man for whom the disease is now named. From the author's collection.

came mysteriously, perhaps it would mysteriously disappear.[24] A second investigator, Newton B. Pierce, was sent out from the department in 1891 to conduct what was essentially a post mortem; by that time 25,000 acres of vineyard were dead, not just in Anaheim but in the San Gabriel Valley and east into San Bernardino County and what is now Riverside County. After conducting a careful survey, Pierce concluded, correctly, that the disease was different from anything known and that there was no remedy for it. His findings were published in 1892 in a bulletin titled *The California Vine Disease: A Preliminary Report of Investigations*, setting forth his negative findings. The one positive result of the investigations was that the California disease was named Pierce's disease, although not until 1935. Pierce did suspect what ultimately proved to be true, but he had no means to confirm the suspicion at the time. "The observed phenomena," he wrote, "would be in the main explained if there were a form of micro-organism within the vine capable of altering the normal physiological relations of the plant at the heat [*sic*] of the season, and which organism began to spread in the Santa Ana Valley about the year 1884."[25]

It has since been observed that the Muscadine grape, native to the Gulf South, shows resistance to Pierce's disease, and so it is supposed that it came from that part of the country and had somehow made its way to Southern California. Today it is still the case that only Muscadines can be safely grown along the Gulf Coast. The best guess for many years was that the disease was caused by a virus, more or less as Pierce had speculated. In 1974 scientists at the University of California, Davis, determined that the cause of Pierce's disease was a bacterium with the elegant name of *Xylella fastidiosa* and that it was typically transmitted by the insects called leafhoppers. The bacterium, which lives on a variety of host plants besides the grape, kills the infected vine by shutting down its circulatory system. Although the disease is now better understood, there is still no remedy for it; the only effective measure so far known is to control the insects that carry it. There is also work going on to develop a resistant vine using genes from the Muscadine. Sporadic outbreaks of Pierce's disease have appeared up and down California since the Anaheim disaster, although never with such devastating effect as in that first outbreak.[26] Controlling the vector has been made more difficult by the introduction into the state in recent years of a leafhopper called the glassy-winged sharpshooter, which has a greater range than the indigenous grape leafhoppers and so spreads the infection more widely. When Pierce's disease strikes a vineyard today, the grower is pretty much in the same situation as the bewildered Anaheim grower in the 1880s; the modern grower now knows how the disease got there, but not when or how it will go away. He can only hope.

Some people in Anaheim did continue to hope. When a reporter for the Anaheim paper visited the big Dreyfus winery in October 1888 he found the place busily at work, although it was importing grapes from Los Angeles and San Gabriel.

> With regard to the blight prevailing among vineyards in this portion of the State, Mr. Weglein [the manager] is of the opinion that it is caused by climate influences, is purely temporary and will die out in short order, when vineyards will again resume their favored place.[27]

As for some of the small growers, "They expected," writes one historian, "to replant the holdings to vineyards as soon as the disease

The big Dreyfus winery building at Anaheim, with a storage capacity of a million gallons. It was erected in 1884, just before Pierce's disease struck. Courtesy of the Anaheim Public Library.

waned."[28] In the event, few did.[29] Growers turned to oranges, walnuts, and other tree crops, and did so well with them that to try again with grapes did not seem worth the risk. Anaheim and the Santa Ana Valley found their special role in growing Valencia oranges, as the San Gabriel Valley did with the Washington navel orange. The two valleys could combine harmoniously, since the navel is in season in the first half of the year, the Valencia in the second. For a time, wineless Anaheim was notorious for its breweries and beer gardens, the last surviving vestige of its German origins. The Dreyfus winery operated as a property of the California Wine Association after 1894, making wine from grapes brought in from other parts of Southern California, and when Prohibition put an end to further winemaking, the building was used at various times as a warehouse, a factory for chicken-feeding equipment, and the winter quarters for a circus. It was not demolished until 1973.

The winemaking history of Anaheim having come to an abrupt and decisive end, what can be said about its achievement? Although it made a lot of wine, Anaheim does not appear to have done anything new or creative or superior in that line. It is true that by the end of the affair a great many new varieties of grape had been introduced. Newton Pierce, the special agent sent by the Department of Agriculture to study the Anaheim disease, found, not just in Anaheim but in other parts of the Santa Ana River valley to which winegrowing had spread, Almeria, Black Hamburg, Black Malvoisie, Blaue Elba, Burger, Charbono, Chasselas, Klaeber, Malaga, Muscat, Riesling, Traminer, Trousseau, and Zinfandel. Most prominent in the mixture, after the Mission, was Muscat, which was planted not so much for wine as for raisins; apart from those in Anaheim, the vineyards along the Santa Ana were largely given over to raisin production. Besides these vinifera vines, people were also growing such native American vines as Catawba, Concord, Delaware, Isabella, Ives, and Lenoir.[30] The highly miscellaneous character of this list, which might have been duplicated in other parts of the state, shows that the search for the right variety was still in progress. No one of these grapes did much to affect the continued dominance of the Mission. Nor could one expect wine of any distinction from most of them when planted in Southern California.[31]

As for the wine of Anaheim, winemakers there followed the already established path. They could hardly do otherwise, given the dependence on the Mission grape: port and other sweet wines dominated from the beginning. The list of Anaheim wines offered by a New York agent in 1869, after the usual white, red, port, Angelica, and sherry, has a few surprises: a sparkling Angelica, something called "Santa Ana," and a wine bitters.[32] Sparkling Angelica seems to be an impossibility, since there can be no second fermentation in a wine that has already had its first fermentation stopped by the addition of brandy; a "sparkling" Angelica could for that reason have been an Angelica in name only. As to what actually went into it I have no information.

And was the wine any good? Who can say? Early in Anaheim's history Benjamin Wilson, as we have seen, was assured that he need not fear competition from Anaheim wines, since they weren't much good. But Charles Brace, in 1867, found Anaheim wine "unusually pleasant and light....It cannot be stronger than ordinary Rhine wine." Probably Brace had mostly tasted the fortified wines that dominated California's production and was pleasantly surprised to encounter a light table wine—a Zinfandel, perhaps, or a Black Malvoisie (Cinsaut)?[33] He adds that Anaheim wine could be found throughout the state: "I found it even in the Sierras, where it was sold at $1.00 a bottle."[34]

The winegrowing origin of Anaheim has now been so overlaid by later developments having nothing to do with agriculture—Disneyland and the Angels baseball team chief among them—that it is a surprise to most people to learn about it. But there was a time when the name Anaheim was synonymous with wine.

THE INDUSTRY TRANSFORMED, 1860–90

Between the early 1860s, when Anaheim got started, and the late 1880s, when winegrowing at Anaheim came to an end, the California wine trade grew to a new order of magnitude. Production in the state as a whole in 1866, a year for which fairly reliable statistics are available, was 2.5 million gallons of wine; in 1887 it was 15 million gallons.[35] The latter figure was not reached by a smooth, regular progression but through a series of ups and downs, as weather and the state of the economy might dictate. California produced 10.2 million gallons in 1880, for example, but 8 million the next year; 18 million in 1886, but 15 million the next year. The general direction, however, was up, and it remained so until Prohibition put a stop to things in 1920.

Among the ups and downs of these years, especially in Southern California, the drought of 1862–64 has already been mentioned. The modest boom that followed the end of the Civil War was dampened by the Panic of 1873, which was felt in the West as in the rest of the country. Markets shrank and prices fell: at the low point in 1876, prices for a ton of grapes varied from $2 to $10.[36] The number of wineries in California fell from 139 in 1870 to 45 in 1880.[37] From that low point of the market in 1876 an upward climb began, so that by 1880 the wine business in California was prosperous as it had never been before. A new surge of planting began then, although it ended, by the mid-1880s, in the collapse of prices through overplanting. The distress was compounded for wine people in the south by the scourge of Pierce's disease in the latter half of the decade. Phylloxera, incidentally, never became a problem in Southern California, although it devastated the north after it had been first noted in the state in 1873. Through all this, the production of wine in the state as a whole continued to grow, although, for various reasons, not in Los Angeles County.

The growing scale of California production meant that California wine had a growing presence nationally. But Eastern wines—from New York, New Jersey, Ohio, Missouri, and North Carolina—had, relatively, a much stronger role then than they have had since. Just how unknown California wine remained to most of the country is suggested by the annual *Report* on agriculture for 1861 published by the U.S. Patent Office, the agency in charge of American agriculture at that time. The *Report* begins by describing a program in the chemical analysis of native grapes being carried out at the United States Propagating Garden (established in 1858) in Washington, D.C. The aim of the program was to determine objectively which varieties were best for wine, "to the end that pure domestic wines may supplant the vile and poisonous adulterations, foreign and domestic, now in use."[38] The section devoted to grapes and wine opens with a detailed account of the planting and training of grapes on Kelley's Island, Ohio. This is followed by a report from New York on trials of grape cuttings received from the Patent Office. Next is a description of "The Grapes of North America" by Samuel Buckley, a distinguished botanist, who notes that the European grape "is a positive failure in nearly every portion of the United States" and who does not mention California. He does, however, include a description of *V. californica* and quotes from an official report recommending trials of this grape.[39] Then follow an illustrated article on the cultivation of grapes under glass, an account of grape growing and winemaking in Hammondsport, New York, and an article on the grapes of Afghanistan (the Kishmish and others) "with a view to the introduction of the grapevine of that region into the central climate of the United States."[40] Nearly seventy pages devoted to grapes and wine in America and not a single mention of the vineyards and wines of California—and this when California had already been one of the United States for eleven years, was producing a good deal more wine than any other state, and was the unique source of vinifera wine in America. Yet Afghanistan got some attention and California precisely none. One could hardly imagine better evidence of how remote and unknown California remained to the rest of the country—except, no doubt, as a place to find gold.

Such ignorance was unaltered six years later when Peter B. Mead published his very thorough *Elementary Treatise on American Grape Culture and Wine Making*, a work of some 476 pages without one word about California. The state as a source of grapes and wine seems not to have had any place in Eastern heads, even though Los Angeles County alone was then producing more than a million gallons of wine annually.

But if California wines were unknown for most of the 1860s, they dominated the market by the next decade and thereafter. The big San Francisco wine houses, of which Kohler and Frohling were the originals, grew as wine production grew. They combined large-scale storage facilities with sales and distribution, and effectively controlled the trade in California wine outside of California.

A change just as important as the increase in size was the rise of the Bay Area counties as sources of wine, particularly of table wine. Los Angeles County, going back to the Mission era, had been practically the sole source of California wine until the gold rush. It continued to dominate wine production through the 1860s, but by the 1870s the south was playing second fiddle.[41] The advantages of the Bay Area counties, especially Sonoma, Napa, and Santa Clara, were clear: closeness to the market; a cooler, less arid climate suited to grapes for table wine; and many and more varied sites. It is possible to make good table wine in Southern California, and it is easy to imagine that, given modern understanding of viticulture and winemaking, the foothills of the San Gabriel Mountains and some favored sites near the Pacific might today be the sources of some of the finest, most celebrated, dry wines in the country.

That didn't happen. The south was for too long too dependent upon the inferior Mission grape and upon the production of the sweet fortified wines that were the best the Mission could give. The destruction made by the Anaheim disease was a heavy blow to the Southern California industry, both in its immediate effects and, perhaps more important, in the loss of confidence in the future that it produced. There are other reasons for the relative decline of the "Southern Vineyard" after 1870, including urbanization and a turn to alternative crops. Here it is enough to say that the lead in winemaking had passed from south to north by the 1870s. But winegrowing in Los Angeles County after that date continued to be a substantial and important business. Ben Truman, in 1874, could coolly assert that "Los Angeles is the oldest and the best grape-growing district in the state."[42] The first part of that statement could not be disputed, but the second could. Best or not, the persistence of substantial winemaking in Los Angeles was a fact, and it took a while before it was recognized that Los Angeles no longer had the lead it had held for so long. Ludwig Louis Salvator, the Austrian archduke who paid a long visit to Los Angeles in 1876 and wrote sympathetically about what he had seen, declared, "Los Angeles…is the best grape district of the state" and it "will produce more wine no doubt than is now made in the entire state."[43] The prophecy was not fulfilled, but it is interesting to know how things looked to an intelligent observer at the time.

The growing importance of the wine trade to the economy of the state as a whole began to be officially recognized in 1859, when the legislature passed a bill exempting newly planted vineyards from taxation for the first four years.[44] In 1861 the legislature established a commission to promote grape growing; it was as one of these commissioners that Agoston Haraszthy made his much-publicized European tour in search of new varieties. In 1869 a special committee of the legislature on grapes and wine was formed with Benjamin Wilson as its chairman. Its main work, as seems to have been true for most other official or commercial bodies formed to assist the wine trade, was to protest federal taxation. There was an increasing professionalism in the trade as production grew. The California Wine Growers' Association of 1862, the first statewide group, was formed to protest the wartime tax laid on wine, the first such tax in American history.[45] A revived Wine Growers' Association in 1866 aimed at instruction and improvement as well as protest, although it did that too. Its main object was to reduce the newly laid tax of $2 per gallon on brandy. But the association was also reported as "at work gathering information, which they propose to publish and distribute among their members, and great good may be anticipated as a result of their labors."[46] At the same time, the Los Angeles Grape-Growers' and Wine-Makers' Society was formed, with Benjamin Wilson as president and Matthew Keller as vice president. This, with other county organizations formed at the same time, was really a satellite of the state association devoted to the same ends.[47] In 1872 a statewide society with the ponderous name of California Vine-Growers' and Wine and Brandy Manufacturers' Association (soon shortened to California State Vinicultural Association) was formed with Wilson as president—a sign that the Los Angeles winemakers were still prominent in the trade. This organization endured for some years, and as well as protesting taxes, it did some work in promotion.[48] The names of its original committees give an idea of the level of sophistication reached since Spanish days: "cultivation of the grape and pruning of the vine," "wine making and the clarification of wine," "manufacture of brandy from grapes," "casks, vessels, presses, and machinery," "statistics," "memorials to

Congress," "best varieties of grapes for general use," and "classification of grapes."[49]

A development of great importance was the introduction of new
varieties. From an early time there was much talk about the need for
this; as we have seen, Jean Louis Vignes, Matthew Keller, Kohler and
Frohling, and others have each been credited with being the first to bring
in new varieties, having at once recognized the defects of the Mission
grape. But if they did, they did so, as has been repeatedly said, to little
or no effect. Agoston Haraszthy has long been credited with introducing
most of California's European varieties through his trip to Europe in
1861. He did, in fact, bring back a large miscellany of *Vitis vinifera* vines,
but not a single one of the established wine grapes in California comes
from Haraszthy's importations. They had either all been here before
Haraszthy or were not part of his collection. His net contribution to the
varietal stock of the state was thus less than negligible. It is necessary to
insist on this point because the claims made for Haraszthy have become
legend by force of repetition; but they are claims that Haraszthy himself
never made.

The conventional perception by the end of the 1850s in California
was, as the *Alta California* put it, that "we have but one variety."[50] That
was technically false—there were already other varieties in the state—
but practically it was true. How unsatisfactory that one variety was is
shown in "Report on Native Wines," published in 1859 by a committee
of the California State Agricultural Society.[51] Troubled by the low quality of the California dry wines entered for judging at that year's state
fair, the committee had one of those wines analyzed. They found that
it contained a heroic 15 percent alcohol and a minuscule 0.28 percent
of tartaric acid—in short, that it was grotesquely imbalanced.[52] The
conclusion from this analysis was clear:

> Your committee believe they are authorized to call the seri-
> ous attention of our wine growers to the necessity of an early
> introduction into this country of varieties of foreign grapes
> which appear to possess those qualities which are wanting
> in our own, or, in other words, which contain less sugar, and
> more free acid.[53]

But when it came to naming any "foreign grapes" that would fill the bill, the committee was frankly embarrassed. It was clear that better varieties were needed, but who knew what they were? Anything that the committee could suggest would, "for want of experience," be "of doubtful value." After this confession, the report goes on to name, haphazardly, a "white and red muscat" much cultivated in the south of France, the "Verdot" of Bordeaux, and the "Kleinberger" of Germany, "which would probably do well on our hillsides."[54] In short, no one had any knowledge of varieties, and even less knowledge of how they might be expected to do when brought to a new region. That, no doubt, is one big reason why there was so much talk about the desperate need for new varieties and so little done about it.

Yet all the while behind this clamor for new varieties, a few people in California were in fact importing such things, and had been doing so since 1852, when Antoine Delmas, a nurseryman in San Jose, brought in Cabernet, Merlot, Folle Blanche, and other French varieties. In the same year, Frederick W. Macondray brought in as part of a group of table varieties from New England nurseries the first Zinfandel in California. Jacob Knauth imported the Orleans Riesling in 1853. Others, especially in Northern California, were soon actively importing different varieties to add to the available stock. The great source of this supply were nurseries on the East Coast, especially in Massachusetts, which furnished vines to amateur growers of hothouse grapes.[55] By the end of the 1850s a grower who wanted to try something different had a wide range of choices, although perhaps that fact was not generally known to the growers themselves. A decade later, in 1868, a writer in the report of the Industrial Exhibition sponsored by the San Francisco Mechanics' Institute, an important showcase and competition for California wines, claimed that "the greater part of the vines being planted at present are of foreign varieties [i.e., other than Mission] while many wine growers are grafting the same on bearing Mission stocks with a view of ultimately dispensing with the latter entirely."[56]

It was one thing to have a choice; it was quite another to know how to choose. Practically no one in the state had any experience using the new varieties. What kinds of soils suited them? How should they be trained and pruned? How much would they yield? How should they be handled in the winery? What were the qualities of their wines? Who would buy them, and for how much? Since no one could answer such questions, the obvious thing to do was try as many varieties as possible. That, I think, explains the curious mélange of varieties one encounters in the record. In Los Angeles County alone in the 1870s and '80s one could find, in addition to the fifteen varieties named earlier in this chapter from the Santa Ana Valley, the following from the San Gabriel Valley: Carignane, Folle Blanche, Frontignac, Grenache, Lenoir, Malbec, Mataró (Mourvèdre), and Sauvignon vert, as well as all of those to be found at Anaheim.[57] When a writer in the *Pacific Wine and Spirit Review*, the leading trade journal for the wine business in California, scolded the Los Angeles growers for their stubborn insistence on planting Mission vines even as late as 1885, L. J. Rose sent in a firm correction:

> We [growers in Los Angeles County] have planted more foreign vines in the last two years than any county in this State. Mr. Nadeau, some few years since, planted very largely of Mission vines, but since then has planted 500 acres of foreign. Mr. Shorb has planted 500 acres. I have 650 acres. Messrs. Mayberry, Dreyfus, Monroe, Stillman, Langenberger, Johnson, Dr. Griffin and hundreds of others have planted from ten to a hundred acres or over, and all foreign varieties.

But, Rose had to add, "whether we have planted the 'proper varieties' time can only tell."[58]

The main guide to choice was quantity. Those varieties that were big producers became the favorites. Burger, a greenish-yellow and robustly productive grape, was popular among the white varieties; L. J. Rose thought that it made "the most pleasant white wine in California."[59] Another popular choice was the heavy-yielding Chasselas (Palomino), providing a neutral wine that could, with the addition of a little Muscat of Alexandria, go to market as "hock." Zinfandel among the reds was widely planted, and so was the Mission, stubbornly persisting in the Los Angeles vineyards despite its many defects. The reason for planting such vines was, according to L. J. Rose, quite simple: "Blaue Elba, Zinfandel, and Berger [*sic*] will make at least fifty per cent. more wine to the acre than the Mission grape," and their wines got twice the price. The money argument settled the question of what varieties to plant.

To a contemporary reader, the absence of today's most-favored varieties must be immediately apparent: where are Cabernet Sauvignon, Merlot, Chardonnay, Sauvignon blanc? The answer is, Nowhere. They were all among the early importations but failed to catch on. The virtues that we find in them were at first unrecognized in most of California, and, so far as I know, they never appeared in Los Angeles. L. J. Rose, among the leaders in Los Angeles County winemaking, wrote in 1885 that the "Cabernet, the Shirraz and Malbec are grapes which in Europe make the finest of all wines." But where he had seen them in the Napa Valley they were shy bearers and he could recommend them "for experiment only."[60] By the end of the 1880s their qualities had been recognized in Napa and Sonoma Counties, but even there the hard times impeded their spread.[61]

The somewhat limited advance in the cultivation of better varieties does not seem to have made any difference to general vineyard practices in Los Angeles. Vines were still head-pruned, and spaced at a thousand vines to the acre, and I have not learned that any experiment in these matters was carried on in Southern California, although it might well have been. L. J. Rose, beginning in the 1860s, had shown that vines would grow in the lower foothills without irrigation, but I have no reliable information to determine how widely that example was followed. My guess is that irrigation continued to be the standard practice.[62]

There was some advance in the technical understanding of winemaking. Louis Pasteur's explanation of the role of yeast in fermentation (*Études sur le vin*, 1866) was a crucial first step toward the understanding and control of that process. The means of pasteurizing wine were available in California not long after Pasteur first described the process in 1866. Matthew Keller undertook to translate extracts from Pasteur's work "for the benefit of my fellow wine-makers of California." In November 1866, pasteurization, or "heating wine" or "conserving wine," was discussed at the state convention of California Wine Growers. By 1869 Keller could write that "Pasteur is as popular amongst the vituculteurs of California as the President of the United States, and if he were here they would elect him to high office." Keller adds, "As soon as I received a copy of his 'Etudes sur le vin,' to do him honor I heated 20,000 gallons of wine in one lot, according to his process, which verified all he predicted for it."[63] Pasteurizing is no longer regarded as a desirable step in winemaking, but it must have saved a lot of doubtful wines in the nineteenth century.[64]

Another step toward scientific understanding was made in 1880 in response to the threat of phylloxera in California. The legislature created a Board of State Viticultural Commissioners in that year, charged to study and to disseminate information not only about phylloxera but about viticultural and winemaking practices in general. The Board published many bulletins and papers, mostly translations of European work, on all of the questions about growing grapes and making wine.

Eugene W. Hilgard, dean of the College of Agriculture at the University of California. Hilgard presided over the university's research work on grapes and wines for many years. Courtesy of the Bancroft Library.

The same bill that created the Board also funded work in viticulture in the College of Agriculture of the University of California. A cellar in which to carry on experimental work at the University was built on the Berkeley campus and the work was put in charge of the distinguished scientist Eugene W. Hilgard. Phylloxera was never a threat to the vineyards of Southern California, but the University's research must have been useful there in a variety of ways. Wines from all over the state were analyzed in the University laboratory, providing an objective account of their virtues and defects. Hilgard's special interests were on the control of phylloxera, on varietal character, and on fermentation, but he and his assistants published a steady stream of original work on the whole range of winemaking questions. The list of Hilgard's bulletins and reports on these matters takes up four pages in James Gabler's bibliography of wine books in the English language.[65]

Serious study of viticulture and enology was also carried on by others besides those on the Board of State Viticultural Commissioners or at the University of California. The wish to advance beyond the merely empirical winegrowing procedures that had been good enough in California from the beginning was embodied in books that now began to appear, the first of which was T. Hart Hyatt's *Hand-Book of Grape Culture* (1867), a practical manual written by a California vineyardist.[66]

6

GREAT EXPECTATIONS

"The present outlook for the wine and grape interest," L. J. Rose wrote in 1880, "is very bright, brighter than at any other period of California's history."[1] Three years later this euphoric view was undisturbed. Writing at the end of 1883, in his official report on Southern California to the Board of State Viticultural Commissioners, Rose saw nothing but prosperity around him:

> All is busy, happy, content, yet two years have slipped by, years that have added much to the viticulture of California, have doubled the acreage of vines, have added to the knowledge of wine-making, have added very much the varieties of grapes and opportunities for testing their adaptability and to the making of improved kinds of wine. More has been accomplished in these ways in the last two years than in ten years previous, and yet the work has only begun.[2]

In fact, a boom in planting new vineyards had spread all over the state; California had 36,000 acres of wine grapes in 1880, and by 1885, when overplanting ended the boom, there were nearly 66,000 acres.[3] It took a bit longer for the increase in wine production to match the increase in acreage, since the vines needed time to grow, but the 10 million gallons of the 1880 vintage (an unusually large one) soared to 18 million in 1886.[4] The result of the expansion was, predictably, a severe depression in the California wine industry that lasted for years, but that is to get ahead of the story.

Southern California made a substantial contribution to the general expansion. The figures are not reliable, but they show the trend clearly. Los Angeles County had around 5,000 acres of vines in 1880, in which year it was planned to set out an additional 1,200 acres.[5] In 1883 the county assessor's report put the acreage at 22,500. That is certainly much too high; it probably reflects the way that people were excitedly talking about the explosion of planting (and the casualness with which the assessor's work was done). L. J. Rose, in his official report as a member of the Board of State Viticultural Commissioners, estimated more soberly that in the years from 1880 to 1883 "vineyard planting has tripled the acreage of our [Southern California] vineyards."[6] Estimated figures for wine production in Los Angeles County parallel those for acreage: around 2 million gallons in 1880 and around 5 million in 1885. N. W. Griswold, writing about Los Angeles in 1883 in his promotional booklet *Beauties of California*, summed up the general feeling: "The fruit and wine business is assuming vast proportions, engaging millions of capital, with the prospect of large profits."[7]

The great expansion of vineyards up and down the state called for a great expansion of winemaking capacity. This was in part provided by a new thing in California: big winemaking establishments established by large-capital sources. The industrial-scale winery had arrived. There had been big winery operations already: in Los Angeles, L. J. Rose's Sunny Slope reached a capacity of half a million gallons from 1,000 acres of vineyards. But this was the outcome of a slow growth, sustained by the hard work of an individual proprietor. The new gigantism was an affair of the very rich, or of corporations that could create an instant enterprise, comparatively speaking, on a grand scale.

In 1881 Leland Stanford, he of the Big Four of the Central Pacific Railroad, determined to go into the wine business on a scale not seen before. He began buying property in Tehama County, in the Sacramento Valley, and by 1885 he had 55,000 acres there. Vineyards went in at once, and by 1887 he had 3,575 acres of these. A winery built to handle the deluge of grapes from Stanford's vineyards had a capacity of 2 million gallons. There was nothing else to match Stanford's Vina Ranch, as it was called; it was more extravagant and costly than anything else of that sort in California. But it wasn't the only big new winemaking business. In the same year that Stanford started as a winemaker, Robert Barton, an English mining engineer, built big in Fresno. By 1884 he had 500 acres of vines and a winery to match; the Barton vineyards ultimately reached 700 acres, and the Barton winery a capacity of half a million gallons. In 1884 Juan Gallegos, whose fortune came from the coffee trade in Costa Rica, built a million-gallon winery at Irvington, in Alameda County, that was the "largest in the world" until Stanford overtook him. In Sonoma County, the Italian Swiss Colony, not originally intended to be a winemaker at all, found itself in 1886 unable to sell its grapes and so built a winery at Asti that, ultimately, reached a capacity of 4 million gallons.[8] Southern California had its own giant: the San Gabriel Wine Company.

THE SAN GABRIEL WINE COMPANY

When Benjamin Wilson died in 1878 his estate went to his ambitious son-in-law, J. DeBarth Shorb, who was then free to let loose his expansionist energies. Speculation in land and water was one major occupation. Shorb had platted the town of Alhambra in 1871 (his life-size statue now stands in a downtown courtyard there), and in 1875 he and Wilson had formed the Lake Vineyard Land and Water Company, developing a water supply for irrigation and domestic use and selling off 6,000 acres made valuable by the water.[9] Later, in the boom year of 1886, Shorb promoted another new San Gabriel Valley town, this one south of Alhambra, called Ramona. (Helen Hunt Jackson's wildly popular romance of that name had been published in 1884.[10]) The wine business was not neglected; on the contrary, Shorb had the biggest plans of all for that one of his many interests.

The origin of the idea lay some years back. As early as 1875 Shorb was writing of his hopes to form a company to plant large vineyards and produce wines that would be held for maturity, a thing that the American market so far had not allowed. "What is required is a company of sufficient capital," Shorb wrote, and he hoped to find investors in

New York when he visited there that year.[11] By 1881 Shorb had found his investors and was busily at work organizing what was intended to be the world's biggest winery. He had some backing from Isaias Hellman, the head of the Farmers and Merchants Bank, the leading bank in Los Angeles, and in San Francisco, Senators William Sharon, F. G. Newlands, and William M. Gwin were shareholders. Evan J. Coleman, a San Francisco businessman, the son-in-law of Senator Gwin, and a large shareholder, was also the means whereby a group of English investors was brought into the San Gabriel Wine Company, as the new venture was called. The English shareholders were perhaps more symbolic than financially important, for Shorb had foreign markets in mind, and in particular the English market.

His plan was quite splendid. On undeveloped land between the Lake Vineyard and Alhambra he would build a winery with a capacity of

J. DeBarth Shorb on the steps of San Marino with some of his large family. This photo is probably from the early 1880s, when he still hoped to supply Europe with wine from California. Courtesy of the Huntington Library.

(Photos by Robert Schlosser)
The largest winery in the world in 1883 was heralded as a scientific wonder. Built by James De Barth Shorb, it was a unique, self-contained complex of several buildings with a capacity of 1,500,000 gallons (see Chapter IV). Located in what is today the western end of Alhambra, California, it was sold after the turn of the century to the Standard Felt Company, but nothing of it remains today. The last of the three major brick buildings (inset) was demolished to make way for a shopping mall as this book went to press.

The building originally built to serve as the storage cellar of Shorb's San Gabriel Wine Company, as it appeared after being sold to the Standard Felt Company in 1903. It was demolished in the 1980s. The inset figures show the fermenting cellar and the storage cellar in their original forms. Courtesy of Special Collections, Charles E. Young Research Library, UCLA.

1.5 million gallons. The main work would be carried on in three big brick buildings: a fermenting cellar 260 feet long with a 900,000-gallon capacity; a storage cellar 217 feet long containing seventy-seven 2,200 gallon tanks, seventy upright tanks of 4,000 gallons capacity each, and a sherry room of 50,000 gallons capacity; and a distillery with four steam-heated stills. In the fermenting cellar two steam-powered crushers would handle 250 tons of grapes a day. The grapes would move from crusher to fermenting vats, and from fermenting vats to storage by the smooth power of gravity. The bricks for the buildings would be made from clay on the grounds. Two warehouses, a cooper's shop, stables, boarding-houses, and a superintendent's residence would complete the establishment. The property was already served by a spur of the Southern Pacific Railroad (the junction was called Shorb Station). And all around it, on 1,500 acres, there was to be a vineyard capable of supplying the giant winery. The whole operation thus would be self-contained.[12]

Shorb always had big ideas, but what could have persuaded moneyed San Franciscans and far-off Englishmen to invest in such a grandiose scheme? One reason was the growing market for wine in America, itself the result of a growing immigration of Europeans from wine-drinking countries. Without such immigration it is unlikely that wine consumption would have made much advance, since the established American was not then a wine-drinking creature. Another reason was phylloxera, the root louse that was even then devastating the vineyards of France and the rest of winegrowing Europe. Phylloxera (*Daktulosphaira vitifoliae*)[13] is native to North America and had much to do with the failure to grow vinifera grapes in the eastern United States, despite uncounted thousands of efforts to do so. As long as ships crossing the Atlantic depended on sail, phylloxera was unable to reach Europe, but the introduction of steam, making a relatively rapid crossing possible, gave phylloxera its chance. It was first observed in England in 1863, in France in 1866. The English had nothing to worry about, having no vineyards; France was obviously different. By the 1870s the destructive effects of phylloxera in the vineyards of France were impossible to ignore, and they continued to grow unchecked. In 1875, before phylloxera had done its worst, France made 2,200 million gallons of wine; by 1880, wine production had fallen by half, and by the end of the 1880s the figure had collapsed to 23.4 million gallons.[14]

The destruction was at last halted by grafting the vulnerable vinifera vines onto resistant American rootstocks, but it took years of controversy and experiment to determine that plan, and more years to carry it out. Meantime, how was Europe to be supplied with wine? To observers like Shorb—and to his English investors—one of the answers was California, the Golden State, the one favored region of the United States where the vinifera vine flourished. Europe would need a lot of wine; California would make a lot of wine. And the San Gabriel Wine Company would lead the way. Shorb was not the only California grower to see the opportunity, but he was certainly among the most ambitious—and boastful. California, he had declared back in 1876, would "in the next decade...produce the best wines of the world."[15] That decade had now arrived, and Shorb was eager to show what he could do.

Shorb, who held 40 percent of the shares in the San Gabriel Wine Company, was to have absolute control of the business: if it prospered, the wealth was his; if it failed, the burden was his. But what could go wrong? The land was there, the experience was there, the market was there. Construction began early in 1882 and was feverishly rushed in order to be ready for the vintage of that year. Planting the new vineyard began at the same time, and carload lots of cuttings of Burger, Zinfandel, and Black Malvoisie (Cinsaut) were bought from such sources as Benjamin Dreyfus of Anaheim, who was also one of the investors in the new company. The company would not depend on the Mission grape, but since sweet wines like port and Angelica would be a large part of the production, there would be plenty of Missions as well as other varieties.[16] The company vineyard could not provide any grapes for several years yet, so Shorb planned to buy 4,000 tons of grapes from Los Angeles sources to feed his crushers in the vintage of 1882.[17] That would be enough to make 600,000 gallons of wine, and that, according to the plan, would be just the beginning.

Troubles came at once. There was competition for grapes—it was suspected that L. J. Rose and others were conspiring to raise prices[18]— so that the San Gabriel Wine Company got only just under 2,000 tons for its first vintage.[19] Planting the vineyard did not go as it should have either. Shorb reported a new 200 acres planted in 1883, but hopes to plant 400 more acres in the next year were defeated by wet weather, and only 200 acres were managed.[20] As late as October 1886, the time of the fifth vintage of the San Gabriel Wine Company, the expectation was for only 500 tons from the company's own vineyard, nothing like the yield from the planned 1,500 acres.[21]

The fact was that the company's holdings of land now seemed more valuable as real estate for immediate sale than as potential vineyard; this was the period of the 1880s boom in Los Angeles when selling land was all the rage—and when the overplanting of the first half of the decade was beginning to be felt in the shape of falling prices. The vineyard that had been planned for 1,500 acres never came close to that size, and the proposed advantage that the winery would have over its competition by growing its own grapes was never gained. The San Gabriel Wine

Company was in a constant scramble for money. It was undercapitalized—the full number of shares had not been sold—and overbuilt. "A
great mistake was made in the beginning in building on such a grand
scale," Evan Coleman wrote in early 1884.

> We should have built a winery and cellars of not over one
> half the capacity of that constructed and had $40,000 more
> by that means on hand, instead of in buildings which we
> cannot use to their full capacity for ten years to come.[22]

That may be how things appeared in hindsight, but, given the plan
to feed the European market, production on a large scale was absolutely
necessary. To the heavy costs of building was added the expense of
holding the wine for two years before sending it to market. The result
was a serious lack of funds. For the first two years the company had constant expenses and, with nothing to sell, no income at all. The money
pinch was so sharply felt that Coleman traveled to London in the summer of 1883 hoping to find new investors. "The object of new capital,"
he wrote, "is to enable us to carry our wines etc. and not be forced to sell
them prematurely."[23] He had little or no luck.

The harried search for money went on without ceasing for the life of
the company. Coleman, who had at the beginning written, "My whole
heart is in our enterprise," came, after only a few years, to doubt that
the wine business would ever pay. Writing from New York, where he had
visited the wine company's local agents, Coleman broke out disgustedly:
"The more I see of the wine business the less I like it, it seems impossible
to do an honest, straightforward business, and compete with others all
of whom are lying, adulterating, etc. etc."[24] It was probably some relief
to blame their troubles on the chicanery of others rather than on their
own missteps. No doubt both were to blame.

By 1885, when prices were sinking, the idea of selling the business
was seriously discussed. Nothing came of it then, or later, although the
fortunes of the company were so parlous that the thought was always
present. But who would buy? Coleman, again in London in 1888 with
the express purpose of selling the company, found no interest whatever. California wine no longer had any allure for investors, who knew
about the Anaheim disease and knew that the English syndicate that

had bought L. J. Rose's Sunny Slope had been badly burned by the deal. Like it or not, Shorb and his associates were stuck with the San Gabriel Wine Company.

Shorb was still full of resource. In 1885, when the pinch of falling prices was felt and when vineyard owners in the San Gabriel Valley were thinking about selling out, Shorb outlined a plan of expansion. He wrote as though the prospect were entirely untroubled. "My efforts in producing high grade wines from my vineyard planted with the noble varieties of grapes imported from France and Germany are completely successful," he said. "Soon we will be able to turn out clarets and white wines which will astonish America and are bound to bring high prices."[25] But until that happy day arrived he thought that buying the productive vineyards of General George Stoneman, Henry D. Bacon of the Marengo Ranch, and Edward Mayberry, all San Gabriel Valley neighbors, would be a good plan, and he hoped to form a "syndicate" of New York investors to swing the deal. That didn't happen.

When a Dr. Ferdinand Springmuhl came to California in May 1887 to demonstrate his new method of making grape concentrate, Shorb seized on that as a sure moneymaker. He at once bought Springmuhl's patent, organized the American Concentrated Must Company, set up machinery at Healdsburg, in Sonoma County, and arranged to ship the concentrate to Springmuhl in London, where it would supply the trade in "British Wines." The business would, Shorb announced with his usual certainty, "inevitably make the whole State the greatest wine country in the world."[26]

Making such wine was an established business in Britain. It depended on importing grape concentrate, which, being unfermented, paid no duty, and then fermenting it as a domestic wine that undersold imported wine, which did pay a duty. Springmuhl himself was operating just such a company in London, using concentrate from Italy.[27] Some California concentrate was produced and shipped to England, but Springmuhl proved an unreliable agent (Shorb called him much worse than that), and Shorb was glad to rid himself of the business in 1889, just two years after it had been founded.

Despite all the failures and disappointments that plagued the San

Gabriel Wine Company, it did make and sell wine in large quantities, although nothing like the quantities that Shorb had projected: 107,000 gallons in 1882, the first vintage; 101,000 gallons in 1883; 76,500 in 1884, and so on. Production seems to have hovered around the 100,000-gallon mark through the decade of the '80s. By 1893, when the winery was in terminal decline, it made 43,000 gallons of sweet wine, 5,200 gallons of brandy, and no table wine at all.[28]

The wine types were the usual ones in Southern California; they were, as listed in 1888, the two staples, port and Angelica, followed by sweet muscat, hock, sherry, claret, Mound Vineyard (carried over from the Lake Vineyard days), Riesling, Gutedel, Zinfandel, malaga, madeira, burgundy, and brandy.[29] These wines came from a highly mixed assortment of vines; by the 1880s so-called foreign vines were distributed all over California, without, however, any clear understanding of their qualities or of their suitability to different sites. Shorb had Trousseau, Chasselas (Palomino), Charbono, Burger, various Muscats (including Frontignac), Zinfandel, Gutedel, Riesling (so-called; the name was loosely applied), Blaue Elba, and doubtless others. How the winemaker chose to distribute and identify the wines from this mix does not appear. What was the basis of sherry? Of hock? Of claret? Palomino no doubt went into sherry, Burger into California hock, and Zinfandel into claret. But what was done with the yields from those other varieties?

Shorb took special pains to produce an acceptable claret, by which is meant a good, dry red table wine. In the north this was provided by the Zinfandel, but Zinfandel in the vineyard and winemaking condition in Shorb's day was not a success in Los Angeles County. (It could have been, but that is another story.) In 1883 Shorb boasted to a New York correspondent that "in a few more years we will turn out the best claret in the State this I am assured of."[30] The boast was hollow. In the next year we learn that a shipment of San Gabriel claret to New York was rejected by the customer as "too acid." It must have been from some grape other than the Mission, a low-acid grape—or perhaps acetic acid (vinegar) is meant. The company secretary, reporting this to Shorb, suggested that "in this matter of clarets" they should simply buy the stuff from up north.[31] In the next year Shorb's winemaker thought that they

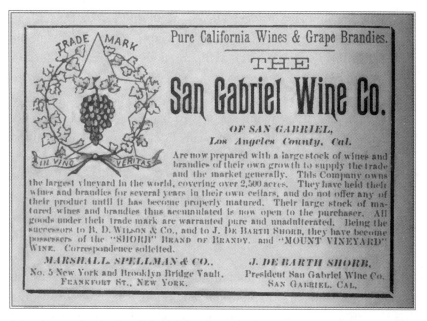

Advertisement for the San Gabriel Wine Company in the *Pacific Wine and Spirit Review*, February 28, 1891. Shorb retained the trademark design of B. D. Wilson and Co. From the author's collection.

might make a claret by "picking out good varieties" from other vine-yards in the San Gabriel Valley.[32]

The San Gabriel Wine Company did on occasion make a Zinfandel in substantial quantity, good enough so that it was accepted in the New York market. But it could hardly claim to be "the best claret in the state."[33] In 1891, when a London agent was sent samples of San Gabriel wine, he found the port, sherry, Angelica, and Riesling better than he expected, but he could not say the same for the red wine: it was "not satisfactory."[34] Yet Major Ben Truman, writing in the *New York Times* in March 1887, affirmed that "the most exquisite claret I have ever drank (although not yet for sale) was made by the San Gabriel Vineyard Company of Los Angeles County."[35] *De gustibus*…Or perhaps Truman, a shameless California booster, just invented that wine "not yet for sale." As Julia Child would say, "Who's to know?"

The agency for the San Gabriel Wine Company for the entire country east of the Rockies was the New York firm of Marschall, Spellman and Co., operating from a three-story Manhattan building under the arches of the Brooklyn Bridge. The connection began in 1884 when, according to the original plan for the San Gabriel Wine Company, the wines of its first vintage would have matured for two years. Besides selling through the New York agency, the winery also shipped directly to customers all over the country—Philadelphia, Chicago, St. Louis, Kansas City, Omaha. If the planned vineyard had ever been fully planted, and if it had yielded 2,000 tons annually (a modest estimate), then the San Gabriel Winery could easily have produced some 300,000 gallons of wine at every vintage. But it never came close to that; the land surrounding the winery was only partly planted, and much of it was sold off piecemeal. Shorb more and more depended for his supply of grapes upon what he already had at the Lake and Mound Vineyards and upon purchases from his neighbors.

As he wrote to Evan Coleman in August 1885, Isaias Hellman of the Farmers and Merchants Bank would lend Shorb no money against the coming vintage, and so "we cannot proceed with the vintage beyond our own grape crop and that of Stoneman's."[36] They might obtain some crops on credit, but he was not even sure of that. He seemed to be locked in a vicious circle: without money he could not plant his vineyard or buy grapes in sufficient quantity; without grapes he could not make much wine; without much wine he could not possibly supply the big markets that he had originally aimed at; and that left him without money.

Letterhead of Marschall, Spellman and Co., New York agents for Shorb's San Gabriel Wine Company. Courtesy of the Huntington Library.

The winery made 107,000 gallons in 1882, the first year; 101,000 in 1883; 76,500 in 1884; and 79,400 in 1885.[37] For those four years the gross sales amounted to $180,523.[38] So far, then, the business was a losing proposition, and would continue to be because of the inadequate production—and because of the low prices that plagued the whole wine business, north and south, from 1885 onward. Shorb may have had the "world's biggest winery," but it did not make as much wine as many other California wineries.[39]

Paul Garrett, the North Carolina winemaker who invented the "Virginia Dare" brand, never had enough wine to satisfy his needs, for he was a master salesman. In his unpublished memoir he says that in 1888, seeking new supplies, he ventured to California to find them. He rejected the Napa Valley wines, "practically all of them being known as 'Dago Red' wines." Instead, he says that he bought from the San Gabriel Winery "about 300,000 gallons of wine, chiefly of old Port and Sherry."[40] The wines could not have been old, and it seems doubtful that the winery could have had so much as 300,000 gallons to sell, even if Garrett had bought the entire inventory. But Garrett was writing many years after the fact and might easily have stretched the size of the deal. In fact, the San Gabriel Winery regularly bought wines from other wineries in order to fill its orders—Chasselas from August Langenberger in Anaheim, sherry from the Los Angeles Vintage Company and from Stern and Rose at Sunny Slope; Riesling from Isaac De Turk in Sonoma County; and dry muscat from Kohler and Frohling.[41] Other wineries did this too, and so they continue to do in California, but the practice had not been in the original plan for the San Gabriel Winery.

Shipping wine to distant markets was always full of difficulties. Often the wine arrived in cloudy condition, even though it may have left the winery bright and clear. E. L. Watkins, the winemaker, after a long struggle with this problem, enlisted the help of Professor Hilgard of the University of California, who recommended a process of "aeration" that seemed to do the trick.[42] Sometimes shipments were simply refused by the customer, as did a Mr. Webster in Chicago, who wrote "savagely" about some spoiled port on the same day that a Philadelphia customer refused a shipment worth $5,500: "these," the besieged secretary wrote to Shorb, "are simply some of what come every day."[43] A hint of the hazards involved in selling doubtful wine appears in a report from Milwaukee by a Marschall, Spellman salesman. He wrote that he had "bluffed" a Milwaukee customer into taking back the wine that the customer had earlier refused. When the salesman called the next day, a Mr. Bergenthall of Bergenthall and Co. "followed him to the street, knocked him down and only stopped when Lury [the salesman] drew a pistol—then had Lury arrested and fined $10."[44]

A basic aim of the San Gabriel Wine Company at its founding was to hold its wines until they had matured for at least two years, but it was not long before the desperate pressure for money compelled the company to send out to market wines that were not ready—one of the reasons that they got so many rejections.[45] And, as it happened, the design of the storage cellar was defective; the building was too hot, so that wines kept in long storage there would be damaged.[46] There were also some very dubious winemaking procedures that probably had more to do with inferior grapes than with any wish to cheat. One of them was the addition of "cherry juice" to color and sweeten wine, particularly the port that was the mainstay of the trade. The first mention of it is in June 1884, when F. W. Wood, after bringing up the subject, adds: "If we have to go into the doctoring business in order to meet the market can we not find some book that will give us the necessary formulae and suggestions so as to avoid the delay and expense of experiments?"[47] I do not know if they found such a book, but they continued to use cherry juice. The winery people had it sent in unmarked containers or in ordinary wine puncheons "so that we can avoid advertising the fact that we use it."[48]

This practice was evidently not confined to the San Gabriel Wine Company. In 1886 Wood sent to Shorb a clipping from the *San Francisco Chronicle* containing a letter from prominent California wine man Charles Wetmore, the founder of the Cresta Blanca Winery and the head of the Board of State Viticultural Commissioners. The letter, addressed to the secretary of the treasury, explained that so-called cherry juice was being used in California to adulterate wine by giving it "intense color, fruit taste, and alcohol." It is in fact an imported cordial, Wetmore said, no more "fruit juice" than Port is; its only use is for fraud, and it should, he advised the secretary, be taxed as a fortified wine.[49] Wetmore's language suggests that the practice was frequent in California; perhaps he suspected Shorb, his fellow commissioner on the State Board.

There were some other unpermitted additions to the pure juice of the grape in use at San Gabriel, although none of them deleterious. When they had trouble getting a satisfactory taste to their wine called "sherry," we hear that "Mr. Watkins has been using the Walnut colouring and flavouring—making it here."[50] The added phrase was no doubt meant to assure Shorb that the walnut juice was strictly secret. So too was the addition of molasses as a sweetener. Benjamin Dreyfus was suspected of using that as well as cherry juice, and so did the San Gabriel winemaker, with "good results."[51]

The failure of the San Gabriel Wine Company to meet any of the goals that Shorb had originally set for it was pretty clear only a few years from the beginning of operations in 1882. The great vineyard that was to supply all the needs of the winery was only a fraction of what had been planned; instead of crushing inexpensive grapes from their own vines, they had to compete with hostile others for the local crops; they never found sufficient capital that would allow wines to be held until properly matured; only a small part of the capacity of the "world's biggest winery" had ever been used; and no foreign markets at all had been established, despite talk about England, France, Canada, and Mexico.

No serious investigation of foreign markets seems to have been made. Writing to Senator Leland Stanford in 1885, Shorb declared that the great need of California was to send a competent man to France to "make a close examination into the bulk of the wines sold on the Bordeaux market, and if such examination and personal inspection…establishes the fact that our wines can be sold at fair prices then immediately get together the suitable wines and make a trial shipment." Shorb himself, he wrote, was "willing to risk $10,000 worth of wines and brandies" in a trial shipment, and if no competent man could be found to make the necessary investigations, he, Shorb would go, for expenses only, as soon as the vintage was over.[52] Stanford was not interested in the proposition; his experience at Vina would not have inspired confidence in any further wine business.

Yet hope persisted. The general manager, F. W. Wood, the most able and intelligent of Shorb's lieutenants, outlined an ambitious plan for the vintage of 1886. For the next spring's trade they would need, Wood calculated, 80,000 gallons of port, 30,000 of Angelica, 80,000 of sherry, and so on through the whole list—a total of 620,000 gallons, as well as brandy. They would have to have 5,680 tons for the vintage, which would yield wines worth $167,000 at prices varying from 40 cents for port to 15 cents for claret and hock. As he contemplated this scheme, Wood concluded that if they could hold out for the next two seasons they should do well.[53]

It was all fantasy. Two weeks later Wood reported that the winery owed $17,000 and that they were out of money. Hellman the banker would lend no more: what should they do?[54] Shorb contrived to patch up things for the moment, but, when the vintage season of 1886 came around, the San Gabriel Winery could buy no grapes and depended entirely on the crop from Shorb's own vineyards. At this point Wood resigned, and when Shorb tried to tempt him back by offering to make him head of the whole enterprise, Wood politely refused. He had a high regard for Shorb, he wrote, and although he liked the business, it would be too much work. Instead, he urged Shorb to manage it himself and to give it his best personal attention—then success would be assured![55]

The winery continued to struggle on, but something even worse than anything that it had so far endured lay just ahead. The Anaheim disease, not content with annihilating the Anaheim vineyards, was now in the vineyards of Los Angeles and the San Gabriel Valley. On September 2, 1889, Evan Coleman wrote from San Francisco to Shorb asking, "Do you consider it a fixed fact that our vineyard (and others down there) is doomed?"[56] Shorb had evidently written dramatically about the situation before, but this time he did not exaggerate. The disease, against which there was no defense, was at work; by April of the next year the San Gabriel Winery's vineyards had been effectively destroyed.[57]

Shorb did not passively suffer this attack: he was a big proprietor; he was a member of the State Board of Viticultural Commissioners; he was a man of decision—he would do something about the Anaheim disease. As it happened, he received a letter on September 6, 1888, sent from a Los Angeles hotel by one Ethelbert Dowlen, a man unknown to Shorb, or to anyone else in Los Angeles. Dowlen, an Englishman who had studied with the great biologist Thomas Henry Huxley at the Royal Institution, explained that he had heard of Shorb's concern over the Anaheim disease and wanted to offer his services. "I should be pleased to conduct," Dowlen wrote in his stiff style, "under proper auspices, an investigation into the causes referred to."[58]

Shorb lost no time in setting Dowlen to work: he brought him to San Marino, built a hot house for him there in which to conduct his experiments, and arranged an appointment for him on the State Board of Viticultural Commissioners as "Special Agent to Investigate Vine Diseases in Southern California." Dowlen was nothing if not dutiful. He almost immediately began a series of weekly reports on his work, explaining in detail what he had done and would do next; there were forty-five of these reports in all. There is no reason to doubt that Dowlen was competent, but he got nowhere. On the first of December, 1890, after nearly two years of fruitless experiment, Dowlen handed in his last report to Shorb. He continues to be heard of as an investigator in Southern California but apparently was no longer supported by Shorb.[59]

Poor Coleman wrote after learning of this disaster that the wine business would certainly have succeeded if it had not been for the disease.[60] But one may doubt that. The onslaught of the disease coincided with the collapse of prices brought about in 1885 by the overplanting frenzy of the first half of the decade. The lean and difficult years that followed were profitless for most growers and winemakers, and there were many business failures. Prices were not restored until the creation of the near-monopoly power of the California Wine Association in 1894, and by that time the affairs of the San Gabriel Winery were in so dangerous a state that there was no chance of recovery. As it was, the company managed to keep breathing for as long as it did largely owing to sales of land and from Shorb's income from the sale of oranges, lemons, apricots, and other fruits from his and B. D. Wilson's estates.

Efforts to sell the winery in 1890 got nowhere, for the depressed condition of the California wine trade was obvious to the most naive observer. Since the wine business made no profit, and since the company could not be sold, it should, logically, have gone out of business. Shorb would not do that. Watkins, the winemaker, announced in August 1890 that "the disease has run its course" and that the San Gabriel Winery would buy all the grapes it could get from that season's small crop, reduced as it was by the ravages of the disease.[61] A form letter dated March 1, 1892, and addressed to "Our Patrons and the Trade" explained that because the depressed market for wine made it impossible to earn anything, the San Gabriel Winery would cease to sell wine and would make brandy exclusively.[62] This change of course was of no avail. Leland Stanford had already diverted much of the harvest from his huge property at Vina to the production of brandy, Lucky Baldwin at Santa Anita was more and more concentrating on brandy, and there were other big players in the field. The market was already well supplied.

Shorb then tried large-scale planting of oranges on the winery's land, not a move that could produce quick income, although he may have intended the young orange trees to render the land more attractive to prospective buyers of home lots. When Isaias Hellman heard of this development he exploded. "It is all nonsense," he wrote to Coleman. "I insist that the San Gabriel Wine Co. must go out of business as other similar corporations have done down South [Hellman had moved to San Francisco in 1890]; pay our debts and divide the land and property amongst the shareholders."[63] Time was running out for Shorb. His health was failing, his San Gabriel vineyard was destroyed, his debts were mounting, and his personal estate was mortgaged to Hellman. By the end of 1895 he was seriously ill from rheumatic causes complicated by heart problems. In April 1896, he died at the age of fifty-four. Hellman appears to have taken over the direction of the San Gabriel Wine Company, or of such remnants of it as still survived. He is said to have had a "controlling interest" in the company in 1897, and his biographer writes that he sought to help Shorb's widow, Sue, by "taking over as president" of the winery.[64]

As for the widow, she tried by desperate means to repudiate the mortgage to Hellman. In 1899 the Superior Court of California declared against her, and in the next year the Shorb estate was taken over by Hellman's bank. The widow and her family retreated to San Francisco, and so ended the Wilson-Shorb era in the San Gabriel Valley. Some connection remained, however. Ruth Wilson, one of Benjamin Wilson's daughters by his second wife, married an up-and-coming Los Angeles lawyer named George Patton. The couple lived at the Lake Vineyard, where they remained after Benjamin Wilson's death in 1878. Patton, a more astute businessman than his brother-in-law Shorb, successfully developed the city of San Marino and prospered. He and his wife had a son, also George, who grew up at the Lake Vineyard before going off to West Point and then to notoriety as the flamboyant General George C. Patton.

In 1903 Henry E. Huntington, who had recently come to Southern California and was looking for an attractive place to live, bought Shorb's mortgaged property from Isaias Hellman's bank, razed the big house Shorb had built in 1877 and had christened "San Marino," and on that site erected his own mansion, now the Huntington Art Gallery, in what is now George Patton's town of San Marino, California. The Huntington Library, Art Galleries, and Gardens occupy the ground that had been J. DeBarth Shorb's Mound Vineyard.[65]

Henry Huntington's mansion, now the Huntington Art Gallery. The building sits squarely on the site formerly occupied by J. DeBarth Shorb's "San Marino" house (see Chapter 4). From the author's collection.

After Shorb's death the San Gabriel Wine Company still somehow managed to operate, although it no longer had any connection to its origins; I suppose that the mere size of the establishment compelled men to make some use of it. At one point it was known as the Ramona and San Gabriel Wine Company, and it probably had other aliases as well.[66] In 1901 we learn that a substantial quantity of wine was made there by the San Gabriel winemaker Jacob Rudel and that all of it was sold to Edward Germain, a wholesale dealer in wines and brandy in Los Angeles.[67] In the next year, 1902, some wine was made there, and when the vintage was finished the winery attended to "the trade of tourists, many of whom visit the winery as it is noted afar."[68]

In 1903 it went to Huntington as part of his purchase of the Shorb estate. The last wine was made there in the season of 1903, and that, with all the remaining wines and brandy from earlier vintages, was sold to Charles Stern and Sons (descendants of the company that originally represented Kohler and Frohling in 1860). Some of the cooperage—200,000 gallons of oak oval casks—was bought by Secondo Guasti, just then developing the Italian Vineyard Company winery at Cucamonga.[69] It was Huntington's idea that a series of model communities, each dedicated to one kind of manufacturing, should be founded around Los Angeles. He determined to make the San Gabriel Wine Company property the center of one such community, to be based on the manufacture of felt (for such things as piano hammers) in the big winery storage cellar. Huntington entered partnership with a man named Alfred Dolge to operate the factory, and so the town was then called Dolgeville.[70] The felt business operated until late in the century; the town was absorbed into Alhambra. Nothing now remains of Shorb's big, unhappy winemaking establishment.

When the Board of State Viticultural Commissioners met in December 1888, Commissioner Shorb reported that "thousands of acres were being destroyed by this [Anaheim] disease, and if it was not checked, that all of the vineyards of the south were doomed."[71] This was said in Shorb's usual style of exaggeration, but the destruction of Shorb's and the Anaheim vineyards was a disaster, widely shared. The Workman Winery on Boyle Heights, for example, where Andrew Boyle's vineyard, which went back to Mexican days, had been greatly expanded by his son-in-law William H. Workman, was smitten in 1888: the vines were destroyed "so completely that the vineyards looked as though they had been swept by fire."[72] The disease was also destructive in vineyards at Glendale, at Pomona, and as far east as San Bernardino and Redlands.[73]

As it had in and around Anaheim, the disease not only destroyed vines, it destroyed confidence. One grower wrote from Pasadena at vintage time in 1889, "The vineyards will be turned into orange groves as soon as their owners are able to convert them....Hundreds of small vineyards, family vineyards, were left unpruned this year and the poorest stocks used for fuel."[74]

The fate of the great Nadeau Vineyard and Winery was especially discouraging for the prospects of winegrowing in the region, although there was already discouragement enough. Remi Nadeau had come to Los Angeles from Quebec in the 1860s and prospered as a teamster, hauling silver from the Cerro Gordo Mines to San Pedro for shipment and then taking supplies back to the miners. He built the big Nadeau Hotel in downtown Los Angeles, by which his name is now best known. Before that, in 1876, he bought 3,400 acres just south of the city in the area known as Florence. There he planted a vineyard that grew to 2,700 acres of Mission, Zinfandel, Blaue Elba, Trousseau, and Black Malvoisie grapes. In 1883 he built a winery, "an immense affair" according to Frona Eunice Wait, with a fermenting capacity of 450,000 gallons of wine and two brandy stills capable of converting 10,000 gallons of wine daily into 2,000 gallons of brandy.[75] The next year, according to Ernest Peninou, the entire crop was ruined by insects—what kind of insects not stated.[76] Then the Anaheim disease struck the vineyard, and by 1889 the thousands of acres were no longer productive. Nadeau had died in 1887, so he escaped the worst; the property was sold to General Edward Bouton, a Civil War veteran, in that year, and then, in 1893, sold again to the meatpacking Cudahy brothers of Chicago. At the time the Cudahys bought their 2,700 acres, the vines were all dead; "the place is overgrown with weeds and underbrush and the buildings are in wreck and ruin."[77] Some of the property is now a part of the small, still independent town of Cudahy, surrounded by South Los Angeles.

The death of Nadeau and then the death of his vineyard put the affairs of the winery in confusion. According to E. L. Watkins of the San Gabriel Wine Company, creditors were besieging Nadeau's heirs, who had been forced to dispose of 4,000 barrels of brandy to New York buyers at the distress price of 45 cents a gallon, a transaction that killed the brandy market for everyone else in California that year.[78] The Nadeau vineyard and winery was quickly and thoroughly effaced, hardly an encouraging example to anyone who thought of making an investment in the future of Los Angeles wine.[79]

There were other discouragements, a notable one being provided at Lucky Baldwin's Santa Anita Ranch. The Anaheim disease did not show up there until the 1890s, but that was more disturbing than if it had arrived earlier, for it showed that it had not really gone away.

THE BOOM AND WHAT IT DID

Bold enterprises such as those of Rose and Stern, the San Gabriel Winery, and the Nadeau Vineyard showed that Los Angeles could think big. But while it was possible to imagine and to develop such ambitious things there, the town and the county remained isolated backwaters. The population of the county was 15,309 in 1870 and 33,381 in 1880; for the city, the figures were 5,728 and 11,183. These were relatively huge increases, but absolutely Los Angeles was still a small town, difficult of access, without a secure and efficient port, without industry, and without any of those things that ornament a community: no institution of higher learning, no musical organization, no galleries or museums, to say nothing of such grosser amenities as paved streets and attractive buildings. Los Angeles was the metropolis of Southern California, but Southern California, to the sophisticates of the north, was familiarly known as "the cow counties."

The doubling of the small population between 1870 and 1880 was due in large part to the extension of the Southern Pacific Railroad from San Francisco to Los Angeles in 1876. The city had been held at gunpoint by the railroad, which had threatened to bypass Los Angeles far to the east. Before it would lay tracks to Los Angeles, the Southern Pacific demanded a $600,000 subsidy, a gift of land for rail yards, and ownership of the short line railroad running to the port at San Pedro.[80] The voters meekly followed the railroad's orders and were not ashamed to celebrate when the first train arrived. Charles Crocker and Leland Stanford, the construction master and the lobbying master of the Southern Pacific, were feted at a monster civic rally. At the reception and banquet at the end of the day the local products were exhibited in an elaborate display under a banner proclaiming the Masonic trinity of "Corn, Wine, and Oil." Prominently on show were wines from Anaheim, from Matthew Keller's Los Angeles Vineyard, from the Lake Vineyard, and from Sunny Slope. J. DeBarth Shorb was on the celebration committee and had seen to it that Los Angeles wine was properly recognized.[81]

The Southern Pacific connection opened up north-south traffic, but to reach Los Angeles from the east one still had to go to San Francisco and then some 400 miles to the south. Direct access to Los Angeles from the east was finally opened when the Santa Fe Railway reached

The Santa Fe Railway heading toward Los Angeles, crossing the Arroyo Seco south of Pasadena, 1885. Courtesy of the California Historical Society at the University of Southern California.

town over the Mojave Desert and down the Cajon Pass in March 1885. A furious rate war then took place between the rival railroads. This brought in thousands of tourists, some merely curious, others prepared to invest in Southern California. The crowds touched off a real estate boom—now become legendary as "The Boom of the Eighties"—and although the boom subsided almost as quickly as it arose, the character of Los Angeles, city and county, was decisively changed in the brief span from 1885 to 1888.

An estimated two thousand real estate agents, taking advantage of eager innocents, sold lots at auctions featuring excursion trains, picnics, brass bands, and hoopla exalting the beauties and wealth of Southern California. New towns sprang up like mushrooms after rain, and many lasted only as long. In 1887, the year of the greatest excitement, there were twenty-five new towns laid out along the line of the Santa Fe from Los Angeles to San Bernardino through the San Gabriel Valley. Some of them—Monrovia, Duarte, Glendora, Claremont—flourished; many more did not. There are countless stories about the frauds practiced: towns were laid out and lots were sold in riverbeds, on mountaintops, in swamps; hotels, churches, college buildings, and schools were hastily run up to demonstrate successful settlement, although there was nothing to sustain them.[82] As Harris Newmark put it, "During the height of the infection, two-thirds of our population were, in a sense, more insane than sane."[83]

The real estate frenzy had its destructive effect on the vineyards. The pioneer names attached to vineyards and wineries were now used to identify the new tracts from which the vines had been uprooted. Among those in the town were the Vignes Tract ("ideal for parties desiring a home"); the Wolfskill Orchard Tract, entirely cut up into tiny twenty-five-foot frontage lots,[84] and the Kohler and Frohling Tract. The Stoneman Tract, the Santa Anita Tract, and the Azusa Tract were in the San Gabriel Valley, where the real estate fever was especially virulent and where many other vineyard properties were no doubt converted into tracts for projected new towns.[85] Another loss owing to the boom was the formation of Orange County. The swelling population in the Santa Ana Valley, aided by the developers, succeeded in passing the bill creating the new county in March 1889.[86] By that time the devastations of Pierce's disease had made the vineyards of the Santa Ana Valley hardly worth hanging on to. From this point on, Anaheim and its neighbors no longer figure in the story of Los Angeles wine.

The boom subsided, but the changes that it had made did not go away.[87] Despite the loss of the 780 square miles of Orange County, the population of Los Angeles County had nearly tripled to 100,000 in 1890; the city had grown at an even greater rate, from 11,000 to 50,000. This process of growth has never been interrupted since: the population of Los Angeles was 102,479 in 1900; 310,198 in 1910; 576,673 in 1920; and so on and on. Whatever vestiges of Spanish and Mexican Los Angeles remained were overwhelmed by the newcomers; they were typically Protestant, middle-class, middle-western, and, often, retired. Their mass movement into Southern California has been called the "Protestant migration," or the "Pullman migration."[88] The favored style of life was suburban—a bungalow, an acre or two for oranges and independence, and unalloyed enjoyment of mild winters and uninterrupted sunshine. Pioneering ambition and enterprise were not part of the picture. Nevertheless, as the next chapter will show, some of the newcomers were drawn to the wine business and did very well at it.

The attractions of California, especially Southern California, had not been suddenly discovered at the moment when the Santa Fe arrived in town. The region had been promoted for years before as a winter retreat, as a place for health-seekers, and as a dazzling combination of mountains, desert, ocean, fruits, and flowers, attractions all summed up in the title of Charles Nordhoff's *California for Health, Pleasure, and Residence* (1872), a highly successful promotional piece commissioned by the Southern Pacific Railroad. Another effective promotion, *Semi-Tropical California: Its Climate, Healthfulness, Productiveness, and Scenery* (1874), was written by the veteran Los Angeles flack Major Ben C. Truman; like Nordhoff's book, it was commissioned by the Southern Pacific. Another author who contributed to advertising Los Angeles could not be suspected of a commercial motive. This was Ludwig Louis Salvator, Archduke of Austria, who made a lengthy visit to Los Angeles in 1876 and wrote enthusiastically about it in *Los Angeles in Südcalifornien: Eine Blume aus dem goldenen Lande* (*Los Angeles in Southern California: A Flower from the Golden Land,* 1878). This was not translated into English until 1929 but had its effect in Europe.

Thus, when the railroad opened the way in 1885, there were a lot of curious people eager to see this wonderland for themselves. Many of them stayed, and, as has been said, Los Angeles was not the same place thereafter. It had first been a Spanish colony at the remote margin of the empire; it was then a Mexican village; after the American conquest it was expanded on American lines with a diminishing but still distinct flavor of the Latin. Now what was it? Hostile critics have said that it became bourgeois, without imagination or enterprise but looking only for a comfortable, conventional life. Sympathetic observers might call it law-abiding, conscientious, decent—as different as it could be from the dusty adobe village with its daily murder in the 1850s, at the beginning of American control.

Los Angeles in 1887. This view looks southeast toward the river and shows the sharp contrast between the burgeoning city and the cultivated fields now being overtaken by commercial development. Detail of "Los Angeles, 1887" by W. W. Elliott. Courtesy of the Huntington Library.

One thing was clear: the population was now made up of newcomers, people whose minds and tastes had been formed elsewhere and who now found themselves in an alien scene. The consequent feeling of uncertainty and dislocation, it is said, explains the notorious vulnerability of these new Southern Californians to flashy evangelists like Aimee Semple McPherson, or to crackpot political schemes like "Ham 'n' Eggs," or to synthetic cults led by bogus prophets, or to pseudoscientific health programs.[89] They responded to such things because they needed reassurance and direction. Maybe so. Down to quite recent years, it continued to be true that most of the people in the state came originally from someplace else, whatever that might mean to the local culture.

At the same time that the character of the population was changing, so too were the prevailing ideas about Southern California's past. It was now that Southern California history began to be idealized, romanticized, sentimentalized. The missions, which had been entirely neglected as of no importance whatever, were now imagined as havens of simple spirituality, where the priests (always called "the good padres") ministered devotedly to pious Indian neophytes. The Indians got their share of idealization too, most sensationally in Helen Hunt Jackson's romance *Ramona* (1884), which represents the Indian as virtuous victim rather than as hostile savage. And the era of the Mexican rancheros was transformed into a golden age of the Californios, a time peopled by aristocratic dons and elegant señoras living in splendid and dignified idleness.

What all this meant, as it always does when the past is so glamorized, is that the things so glamorized were now dead. The present felt no living connection with that past—what idea, after all, would an accountant newly arrived in Los Angeles from Peoria, Illinois, have about California's history?—and so could make of it whatever it wanted. The realities of that past no longer threatened, no longer pressed on anyone as hostile, or unpleasant, or oppressive. The Yankee intruders no longer had to compete with the Mexican ranchers, the white man no longer had to fight the Indians, and the Protestants had overwhelmed the Catholics, so all of those things could be recreated in a comfortable unreality. However one looked at it, it was clear that Los Angeles had changed. The pioneer past was now over for the wine business too.

The 1880s, which began with the promise of great prosperity for winegrowing in Los Angeles, had not brought prosperity but, instead, a succession of disappointments, not to say catastrophes. Anaheim had been destroyed by the unknown disease against which there was no defense and which went on spreading unchecked in the San Gabriel Valley and beyond; the big investments in the Sunny Slope Winery, the San Gabriel Winery, and the Nadeau Vineyard were lost, and so was the confidence that had created them; new crops, oranges and walnuts especially, were taking over what had been vineyards, and they dominated the new plantings; and finally, the coming of the transcontinental railroads and the turbulent boom years of the '80s had set Los Angeles in new directions, away from agriculture. In a highly symbolic move, the zanja system for delivering water to gardens and farms in Los Angeles was abandoned in 1888, there being no more agriculture in the city to irrigate (and because underground pipes were a better system). The vineyards in the City of Vineyards were now home lots or commercial sites.

The year 1887 may be said, with considerable plausibility, to mark both the high point and the turning point in the fortunes of Los Angeles wine. That was the year of the frenzied boom following the arrival of the railroad from the east, a boom that decisively turned Los Angeles in the direction of the city it has become. That was the year in which the overplanting of the first half of the decade produced a glut of grapes and the collapse of prices—a collapse that took years to overcome. Finally, that was the year of the greatest devastation of the Anaheim disease—Pierce's disease—which, besides destroying vineyards, made men turn away from the risks of grape growing and opened the way for the triumph of the orange in Southern California. But the decade, difficult and destructive as it had been, did by no means put an end to grapes and wine in Los Angeles.

7

FROM 1890 TO PROHIBITION

No one in Los Angeles at the beginning of the 1890s would project a winery to be "the largest in the world," as Shorb had done just a short decade before. Nevertheless, much remained of the winemaking establishment in the region, and new things continued to appear, some of them on a big scale after all.

In 1890—to take that year as the beginning of a new chapter in Los Angeles winegrowing following the tempests of the 1880s—Los Angeles County produced 1,342,800 gallons of wine, by no means a negligible figure. (The rest of the state produced 13,283,200 gallons, to give an idea of scale.) To provide the grapes to make all that wine, there were then, according to the enumeration by the Board of State Viticultural Commissioners in 1891 (the 1890 federal census does not give the relevant figures), 122 grape growers in Los Angeles County, mostly in the San Gabriel Valley and its neighbors. The figure for growers in 1891 is almost certainly much too low. The Board, in its survey of grape growers and winemakers in 1888, had listed 531 names in Los Angeles County, and it is not conceivable that more than 400 of these people dropped out between 1888 and 1891. But from the highly erratic statistical record from the nineteenth century, one must take what one is given. The 1891 record gives a total of 4,695 acres of vines in the county— a plausible figure, after deducting the loss of the Orange County vines and the depredations of Pierce's disease. The production of wine in 1891 is not stated, but at a modest estimate 4,695 acres would easily yield at least as much as the 1,342,800 gallons of the 1890 vintage.

Further analysis of the 1891 survey yields a few more items to add to this sketch of a deflated Los Angeles after the boom. The varietal mix appears to be more or less settled; not all of the growers reported the varieties they grew, but those that did showed a clear preference for Zinfandel, the grape most frequently named, over the Mission; the score was 32 to 13. Pasadena and its neighborhood—La Cañada, Lamanda Park, and San Gabriel—were the leading producers by a long shot: 3,506 acres of vines out of the county total of 4,695. The L. J. Rose estate, with 640 acres, was the largest property listed; a handful were of 2 or 3 acres only, and between those extremes were vineyards of almost every size. The shape the wine business in Los Angeles County had now taken, centered on the eastern side of Pasadena, was the shape it retained until the turn of the century.

The 1891 survey lists only four names of growers and winemakers in the city of Los Angeles itself, certainly a gross underestimate. (The 1888 survey listed 365, a gross overestimate achieved by lumping together different communities into the category "Los Angeles.") Whatever the correct number might be, traditional winegrowing in the city was rapidly declining under urban pressures. The railroads, their yards, and their associated industries now occupied the fields along the river that had long been planted in vines. New housing covered many old vineyards immediately south of the old town. But there were still wineries operating in the city, some of them substantial.

Los Angeles winegrowing, as soon as it ceased to be wholly Spanish or Mexican, was in the hands of men with English names (Chapman, Wilson, Baldwin, Stoneman, Dalton), or German (Kohler, Fröhling, Shorb, and everyone in Anaheim), or French (Bauchet, Clement, Vignes, Beaudry, Sainsevain), as well as many men with Spanish names. By 1890 some significant changes might be noted. The Spanish names had virtually disappeared, and some exotics now first appeared: Ah Sam and Ah Sing, for example, or Kerchaff.[1]

The surveys made by the Board of State Viticultural Commissioners do not show another new development, but it is readily apparent from other sources: the Italians were now arriving in force. Italian immigration had not been at all significant before the end of the nineteenth century, when it suddenly swelled to a great size. In the decade of the 1860s Italian immigration was one half of one percent of the total immigration to the United States. It increased ten times in the decade of the '80s, and tripled again in the '90s. This was the period in which Italian names began to be prominent in the winemaking of Northern California—Sbarboro, Rossi, Seghesio, Cribari. And they appear in Southern California too—Bessolo, Borioli, Demateis, Grangetto, and so on.

The Italians kept up the tradition of winemaking in the city itself long after it had mostly migrated elsewhere. Some of these operations were small, essentially supplying a neighborhood with wine rather than shipping out wholesale lots. Louis Carbone, for example, had a small winery on San Fernando Street from 1899; the Italian-American Vineyard Co. of Giovanni Demateis[2] stood on what is now the north end of Olvera Street, across Alameda Street from what had been Benjamin Wilson's house and vineyard in the early 1850s. One of the earliest Italians making wine in Los Angeles was Antonio Pelancoli, whose winery was also on Olvera Street, or, as it was then, the Calle de los Vinos—Vine Street, in allusion to its main business.[3] An account of Pelancoli's winemaking from the 1870s makes it appear remarkably primitive, although it may have been usual among the small wineries. The reporter found at Pelancoli's large vats over which slatted boxes were laid and then filled with grapes. These were then trodden by barefooted and barelegged Indians. When the "cap" of skins, seeds, and pulp rose to the top of the fermenting vats, it was punched down into the fermenting juice by a simple method. A large man, clad only in a shirt, climbs into the vat, clinging to a stout pole laid across the top of the vat, and sinks by his weight into the mass and so immerses it in the must.[4]

Yet another on Olvera Street was the winery and distillery of Antonio Valla and Giacomo Tononi, founded in 1870. Valla is said to have been the first Italian in the wine business of Los Angeles, with what authority I do not know.[5] He and Tononi figure in the account books of Matthew Keller as large purchasers of wine in 1876–77.[6] In the latter year they bought Pelancoli's winery.[7] Taken all together, the small Italian wineries in the city, at vintage time, were said to "utilize many carloads of grapes,

Interior of the Pelancoli winery on Olvera Street sometime between 1901 and 1910, when it was being rented by Giovanni Demateis (left). The primitive winemaking methods of earlier years no longer applied. Courtesy of El Pueblo Historical Monument.

beside those that are delivered to them by wagon, from nearby vineyards."[8] I count at least twenty Italian names among the winemakers of Los Angeles in the years between 1890 and the coming of Prohibition in 1920, and doubtless some others have escaped my survey.[9] They are clustered in that part of Los Angeles just north of the plaza, on Olvera Street and in what is now Chinatown: Alpine Street, Ord Street, Cleveland Street, Yale Street. "Wine country" in Los Angeles at any time around the turn of the century was here in this efflorescence of small Italian-American wineries.

Not all the Italian wineries were small neighborhood affairs. Ferdinando Bessolo, whose winery, founded in 1899, stood on Ord Street, was described as having "a good city trade" for table wines and grappa, making "a large quantity each year to meet its demands."[10] But the big man among the city Italians was Secondo Guasti. Indeed, before he was through, his was the biggest winemaking operation in Southern California, fed by the "biggest vineyard in the world." That will be seen later.

Guasti came to Los Angeles in 1878 and, it is said, first made wine around 1883, to supply his father-in-law's restaurant. In 1886 he built a small winery on Aliso Street and then, at some time before 1891, he joined John Bernard, whose offices were in Los Angeles but whose vineyard and winery were in unincorporated space between West Glendale and the now-vanished Tropico, which stood on the east bank of the Los Angeles River (both places now parts of Glendale).[11]

In 1894 Guasti and Bernard built a big new winery, not out by West Glendale but in Los Angeles itself, in the riverside region of the city being progressively taken over by railroad yards and heavy industry, at Palmetto and Matteo Streets (the latter named for Matthew Keller). The railroads were no doubt welcome, since Guasti and Bernard were supplying a large trade in the eastern United States, where their main business lay. How large that was may be seen from some early figures. In 1895, the second year of operation for the new winery, Guasti had arranged for the purchase of 3,000 tons of grapes and had installed 100,000 gallons worth of new cooperage in addition to the considerable capacity that he already had.[12] Bringing in those grapes was another service provided by the railroad: the grapes from the loaded cars were fed

Secondo Guasti, who became the biggest of all winemakers in Southern California. Courtesy of the Wine Institute.

SECONDO GUASTI

⌒◦GROWER AND DISTILLER OF◦⌒

Pure California Wines and Brandies

Winery, Cor. Palmetto & Matteo Sts.

Office and Wine Vaults, Cor. Third & Alameda Sts.

LOS ANGELES, CAL.

LARGE PRODUCER OF SWEET WINES.   Send for Price List and Samples

The first appearance of the name "Secondo Guasti" alone on a label. From *Pacific Wine and Spirit Review*, August 25, 1897.

directly to the crushers. Three years later Guasti was making 330,000 gallons of wine and 40,000 of brandy from 3,500 tons of grapes.[13] How far he had to reach in order to get all those grapes I do not know, but certainly everywhere in Southern California and no doubt some Central Valley vineyards as well. But the wine was being made in Los Angeles. In 1897 Guasti bought out his partner Bernard; the firm was thereafter called simply "Secondo Guasti."

The kinds of wines that Guasti was making, and the kinds of grapes that he made them from, are spelled out in the report of a visit to the big Los Angeles premises in 1898. There were two locations: the original office at Third and Alameda, a building that also incorporated extensive storage space for wine, and the new winery at Palmetto and Matteo Streets. These were identified as "Winery No. 1" and "Winery No. 2." The 3,500 tons of grapes brought in by rail were, according to the report, "Zinfandel, Riesling, Burger, Mission, Muscat, Carignan, Black Malvoisie, Blue Alva [Elba], Marie Blanche and Monteraux."[14] The wines produced were divided thus:

Sweet muscatel	20,000 gals.
Port	65,000
Claret	120,000
Sherry	125,000
White wines	10,000

The prominence of sherry is not surprising, but that of claret is, as is the relatively minor role of port. The report adds that "the greater portion of this is consumed in the East,"[15] and this no doubt accounts for all that claret. The people who drank Guasti's wines in eastern cities were largely Italians, who wanted a dry red table wine. Guasti would have had an adequate local supply of Zinfandel grapes by this time.[16]

Italians were not the only people still to be found making wine in the city. Henry Baer opened a "cut-rate wine house" on Spring Street in 1897 as the Los Angeles Wine Company.[17] That does not sound very promising, but it was a legitimate winemaking business. One source of grapes for his winemaking was Charles Pironi, of West Glendale, whose 60 acres of vineyard apparently gave him more grapes than he could use in his own winery.[18] Pironi died in 1901; two years later Baer and his partner and winemaker, Bert Lytle, bought Pironi's West Glendale winery and incorporated it into the Los Angeles Wine Co. The Pironi winery, at the time Baer and Lytle bought it, had a storage capacity of 100,000 gallons; the new owners planned to expand, bought new machinery and by the next year were shipping wine by the carload to Ohio and other eastern markets.[19] Baer kept his Los Angeles winery, but then sold it to a San Francisco firm in 1912 and planned to retire. The *Pacific Wine and Spirit Review* on that occasion called Baer "one of the pioneers of the wine business in Los Angeles County."[20] That is probably merely the sort of thing that is said conventionally, but if it was seriously meant, it was an error of perspective. We have seen that many generations of pioneers lay behind him.

Henry Meyer, an Alsatian, came to Los Angeles in 1881 and set up as a cooper, making large tanks and vats for the local wine industry. He built a winery and a distillery in addition to his cooperage on the flatlands below Boyle Heights on the east side of the Los Angeles River.

One of several brands belonging to the Goldschmidt brothers' Southern California Wine Co. From *Pasadena City Directory 1902/3*. Courtesy of the Huntington Library.

At some later time—not given in my authorities—he owned a winery in the more usual location of south Alameda Street. Here, according to a local historian, he "engages in winemaking for the wholesale trade; raises grapes and buys large amounts to make into wine, which finds a market here and elsewhere."[21] Meyer is listed among the makers of sweet wines in Los Angeles in 1898;[22] after that I have found no further record of him.

Much more ambitious were the Goldschmidt brothers, Hugo and Marcus. I have no information about their origins, but they were in Los Angeles not later than 1892, when they were operating as the Sunset Wine Company, dealers in wine and, to some extent, makers of wine at their premises on Aliso Street, just across the river to the east.[23] They also owned the Southern California Wine Company in Los Angeles, which did not make wine but marketed "the produce of a number of immense vineyards in Southern California."[24] The Southern California Wine Company ads offered, at various times, the "famous Gold Medal Wines," the "Good Samaritan" wines and brandies, and the "Peerless Brand" of ditto—all of them probably house brands.[25]

The brothers added to their winemaking by buying the Hillside Winery of Paul Wack in 1902. Wack, a German from the Rhineland and the son of a winemaker, had lived in St. Louis before coming to Los Angeles in 1885. He had a small vineyard on his property on North Main Street, but most of his grapes came from a vineyard in Azusa. For the Goldschmidts this purchase was an interim step, for they operated the Hillside Winery for just two years. At the same time that they bought the Hillside Winery they also bought a much bigger enterprise, the California Star Winery at Lyon and Macy Streets, and this is where they concentrated their production as the Sunset Wine Company.[26] The California Star Winery was itself no mean operation. Founded in 1881 by two Italians, Giuseppe Sormano and G. Borioli, it had, at the time of Sormano's death in 1902 (no doubt the reason for the sale to the Goldschmidts), a storage capacity of 200,000 gallons and had made 150,000 gallons of fortified wines in the preceding year's vintage.[27]

The California Star Winery—or the Sunset Wine Company as it was after 1902—was probably second only to Secondo Guasti among the wineries actually making wine in the city of Los Angeles. The Gold-schmidts announced in the year after their purchase that they intended to make wine "on a large scale." They had a vineyard near San Gabriel and presumably bought grapes from other growers if they were in fact to produce "on a large scale"—that is, several hundreds of thousands of gallons of wine.[28] They continued down to Prohibition.

Rather surprisingly, Los Angeles had two wineries at this time making retsina, the Greek-style white or rosé wine flavored with pine resin. One was operated by the Chicos brothers on Twentieth Avenue; the other, the Retsina Wine Company, on Anderson (later Mission) Road, was where a Mr. Julius made retsina largely for the Chicago trade. The traditional method is to add small pieces of resin to the must before fermentation and then remove them at the first racking. The *Oxford Companion to Wine* states that retsina is "rarely made outside Greece and southern Cyprus," but it has long had a small place in Los Angeles winemaking. Neither the Chicos nor the Julius operations survived Prohibition, but after Repeal retsina was produced in Los Angeles by the Alexakis Retsina Winery and, in Glendale, by Nicholas Verry.

LEAVING THE CITY

A large quantity of wine was made in the city of Los Angeles after 1890, but not much of it from grapes grown there. The rising pressures of urban development meant that Los Angeles wine was, increasingly, wine from the county, not the city. To the south of Los Angeles the town of Downey was a minor center of winemaking. John Downey, governor of California from 1860 to 1862, in 1865 had subdivided the Santa Gertrudis Ranch and named the town for himself. He also grew grapes and made wine—an estimated 50,000 gallons in 1868.[29] So the town was born to wine. In the '90s there was a scattering of vineyards around Downey, and an Italian named Monteleone making wine there; but the big enterprise was the Downey Vintage Company, also known as the F. B. Weis Winery, after its founder. Weis died in 1894, but the winery continued to be operated by his widow, Margaret. In 1902 she is reported as planning a crush of some 2,000 tons—enough to yield 300,000 gallons of wine, mostly fortified. In the next year, however, after reportedly planning to add another 50 acres to her vineyards, she announced that she would make no more wine but would, in order to make more money, sell her grapes to others.[30] Santa Fe Springs, not far from Downey, also had four or five vineyards in the '90s; Artesia had even more, but there does not appear to have been any winemaking carried on in these two southern suburbs except at the Artesia Vineyard Company and the Santa Fe Winery.

The main action lay to the north and east of Los Angeles. Burbank (one of the new towns created by the boom of the '80s) had attracted a number of Italians: Matteo Brusso, Giovanni Gai, John Grangetto, and J. Randisi, all winemakers. Not far away, at West Glendale, Charles Pironi had his vineyard and winery. The scene was not wholly Italian. The biggest of the Burbank wineries began with the partnership of three Irishmen: John McClure, John Kenealy, and Richard Dillon. They were associated in business as dry goods merchants in Los Angeles

McClure's Sunnyside Winery in Burbank, built in 1905. Courtesy of the Huntington Library.

but were interested in the possibilities of winegrowing. In 1878 they took out, under the homestead law, 160 acres of raw land from the government at what was then called Roscoe and is now Sun Valley, over the Verdugo Hills north of Burbank. The vineyard that McClure planted prospered, a winery was built, and in 1886 the dry goods store was sold; the three Irishmen were now known as winemakers.[31] The vineyard was not irrigated, and although L. J. Rose had almost twenty years earlier shown that grapes would succeed without irrigation in Los Angeles County, McClure's example was regarded as something new. A Los Angeles paper described the "viticultural experiment" thus:

> These gentlemen [McClure et al.] have now a two hundred acre vineyard near Burbank, over towards the Verdugo range. Not one of these vines has ever been irrigated. They all show robust health, and have recorded a prolific yield, which fact shows that irrigation is shortly to become a thing of the past in the cultivation of the grape as respects most portions of Los Angeles county.[32]

In 1896, McClure, now acting independently, undertook a big new venture. He bought a thousand-acre property closer to Burbank and planted 350 acres of it to vines. In 1905 McClure built a winery there on a scale recalling the gaudy days of Shorb and Rose and Nadeau: the concrete buildings had a wine storage capacity of 700,000 gallons. This Sunnyside Winery, as McClure called it, operated down to Prohibition and was restored to activity after Repeal. McClure and the Italian wineries around Burbank and Glendale thus carried into the twentieth century the winegrowing tradition of the old Verdugo Ranch that went back to the late eighteenth century. It was the site of perhaps the earliest winemaking, apart from the Missions, in all of California.

Over the ridge of hills that separates the Burbank/Glendale region from the San Gabriel Valley to the east lay what may be called the classic ground of San Gabriel winemaking: Benjamin Wilson's Lake Vineyard, J. DeBarth Shorb's Mound Vineyard, and the vineyards of their neighbors—Kewen, Stoneman, Howard, Bacon, Mayberry, Titus, and many others. Now this region, too, was beginning to be crowded—not urbanized, to be sure, but definitely suburbanized.[33] Pasadena, founded in

1874, was growing mightily. Henry Douglas Bacon's Marengo Ranch, a property of almost 800 acres including a substantial vineyard and winery, was subdivided in 1884 (it is now part of South Pasadena);[34] General George Stoneman's Los Robles, Shorb's Oak Knoll, and other properties in the region of Pasadena were all developed for housing in the '80s. As a result, the vineyards and wineries of the San Gabriel Valley moved to the east, to San Gabriel, and, especially, to new places called Lamanda Park and Sierra Madre Villa.

Lamanda Park was laid out by L. J. Rose in the northwest corner of his Sunny Slope ranch in 1886 and named by adding the "L" of his first name to the name of his wife, Amanda.[35] There were already vineyards there, and now the area sprouted new vineyards and wineries. By 1888 there were seventeen vineyards listed in the Board of State Viticultural Commissioners' *Grape Growers and Wine Makers of California*, one of them belonging to the wealthy Abbott Kinney, now remembered as the founder of Venice, California. A bigger vineyard was developed on a part of the 1,100 acres of the Hastings Ranch, established by Charles Hastings in 1882. It has long since been subdivided but is remembered by Hastings Ranch Drive in northeastern Pasadena. Sierra Madre Villa was the work of William Cogswell, a successful portrait painter who came to California in 1873, bought 473 acres just above what would become Lamanda Park, built a hotel and sanatorium called Sierra Madre Villa, and planted 30 acres of vines. He sold his grapes to L. J. Rose. So did Mrs. Mary Cooper of Sierra Madre Villa, who had 13 acres of vineyard, and there were other small growers with that address who also regularly sold their grapes to Rose. From the point of view of grapes and wine, the two places called Lamanda Park and Sierra Madre Villa were indistinguishable, and the lists published by the State Board of Viticultural Commissioners sometimes give a name under the one place, sometimes under the other. So I will treat them together.[36]

The leading winery, biggest and most active in this region, was the Sierra Madre Vintage Company. It had complicated origins, beginning with Eliza Griffin Johnston, widow of the Confederate general Albert Sidney Johnston, who had been killed at Shiloh in April 1862. He had been military commander of the Department of the Pacific, stationed

Chinese workers picking grapes at Fair Oaks Vineyard. Courtesy of the Huntington Library.

in San Francisco, until the outbreak of the war, when he resigned and made his way to the Confederate States. Eliza Johnston accompanied her husband only as far as Los Angeles and remained in the region when he went on to the war. Her brother, Dr. John S. Griffin, was established in Los Angeles not only as a doctor but as an owner of large properties, including the San Pasqual ranch, now the site of Pasadena. In December 1862, Griffin sold a part of the San Pasqual to Benjamin D. Wilson, and on the same day Wilson sold 262 acres of his new purchase to the widow Johnston, no doubt by previous arrangement with Dr. Griffin.[37]

Mrs. Johnston named her property Fair Oaks, after her home in Virginia. In 1868 she sold it to Judge Benjamin Eaton, her brother-in-law, who planted a vineyard in the next year and was making substantial quantities of wine and brandy by the 1870s. His vines, according to Archduke Salvator, "have never been watered."[38] Under Eaton's ownership the Fair Oaks property came to be called Eaton's Vineyard, and its wine acquired a good reputation.[39] Eaton in turn sold Fair Oaks to J. F. Crank in 1877, by which time the vineyard, of Mission grapes, covered 60 acres. At first Crank sold the grapes to L. J. Rose, as did most of his grape-growing neighbors. In 1879 he is reported as making 28,000 gallons of wine and 9,000 of brandy at the Fair Oaks winery that Eaton had developed.[40] Later, he would go into the winemaking business with his brother-in-law, Albert Brigden, whose sister Crank had married.

Brigden, a native of upstate New York, came to the San Gabriel Valley in 1876, a year before Crank, and bought 135 acres of what had been part of the Fair Oaks property. There were already 40 acres of vines on the place when Brigden bought it; he set about at once on improving it, expanding the vineyard to 90 acres. The rest of the property was planted to citrus and other tree fruits. By 1879, if not before, he was making wine from the yield of his Highland Vineyard, as he named it. Both Brigden and Crank were experienced businessmen, and it must have occurred to them fairly quickly that combination would be a good idea. However that might be, they did not get around to joining forces until 1885, when they built a winery on Foothill Boulevard at Lamanda Park. They called it the Sierra Madre Vintage Company, formally incorporated in February 1886. The grapes came from Brigden's Highland Vineyard and Crank's Fair Oaks Vineyard, which had reached 140 acres by 1879.[41] Crank was the president of the company, Brigden the general manager and the man in charge of the winemaking.

The Sierra Madre Vintage Company's winery was built at the beginning with a capacity for crushing 1,000 tons of grapes—enough, approximately, for 150,000 gallons of wine from what were now among the standard varieties of Southern California: Zinfandel, Blaue Elba, and Muscat. The wine, according to a contemporary writer, found "a ready sale in home and eastern markets."[42] This, too, at a time of great difficulty in the wine trade—the late '80s and early '90s were a time of overproduction, falling prices, and widespread business failure.

Brigden died a terrible death in 1894. An addition to the winery was being built and new cooperage installed. Brigden was standing on the top of a tank then being steam cleaned when the pressure of the steam blew out the top of the tank and Brigden was thrown to the rafters and fell to the floor, fatally scalded by the escaping steam.[43]

Brigden was succeeded as manager by his assistant, a Milwaukee German named Herman Blatz. At some point after Brigden's death Crank sold out and Blatz became the owner of the Sierra Madre

Top: Interior of the Sierra Madre Vintage Co., Lamanda. Courtesy of the Huntington Library. Bottom: Workers in the vineyards of the Sierra Madre Vintage Co. Courtesy of the California Historical Society at the University of Southern California.

Vintage Company. The winery grew under Blatz; by 1902 production was up to 300,000 gallons. But by that time, too, expansion of the vineyards in the Pasadena region was no longer possible: real estate values were too high.[44] The company's vineyards, as did those of other Los Angeles County wineries, moved over the county line into San Bernardino County, to undeveloped land at Etiwanda. Here, in 1907, the Sierra Madre Vintage Company bought a thousand-acre property to grow the grapes that supplied it down to Prohibition. Blatz wrote at the time:

> Los Angeles and its satellites are growing so rapidly that the grape industry is being slowly forced down the San Gabriel Valley....The season's crop will be a heavy one, but will probably not exceed 5,000 tons. The old days when the green vineyards extended from the foothills almost to the sea are only memory now. The luscious clusters hang in Pasadena now, but in the social arbor....Grape growers are prosperous, but in the rush of things it seems this far-famed industry of Southern California is almost being shoved aside.[45]

A letter from Blatz to the *Pacific Wine and Spirit Review* in 1909 is interesting for the way in which it repeats, at that comparatively late date, the boasts and complaints that had been familiar since the beginning of the commercial development of California wines. He lists the gold medals that Sierra Madre wines had won at exhibitions at home and abroad (Paris, St. Louis, Portland, etc.), attributing these triumphs to the "purity" of the wines—a theme that California winemakers had been harping on for more than half a century, with implicit reference to the "impurity" of the imported stuff. Next comes the claim, echoing what many others had already said, that "we have worked hard and faithfully, all these years, to raise the standard of California wines," a claim tacitly acknowledging that improvement was greatly needed. This is then followed by the ritual complaint of neglect and falsification: "For years we have had to contend with a lack of appreciation on the part of customers who drink California wines under foreign labels while decrying the home product." Then a turn to the therapeutic benefits of their good wine: it was "a health-giving beverage...suitable particularly for family

Advertisement for the Etienne brothers' Golden Park Winery. In business since the 1890s, they felt the effects of the dwindling supply of grapes grown in Los Angeles County. Courtesy of the Huntington Library.

and medicinal purposes." Such claims could be made then, before the federal authorities forbade them, and few California winemakers failed to make them. Finally, an appeal is made to the connoisseur and the snob: "By strictly adhering to the policy of reserving most of the fine old vintages, our extensive cellars contain some of the rarest, oldest and most valuable wines in California."[46] Even for a successful enterprise such as the Sierra Madre Vintage Company the idea still prevailed that California wine was neglected, underappreciated, and misunderstood. No doubt Herr Blatz, or any of his contemporaries in the trade, could have given doubters an earful about what they had suffered.

The Sierra Madre Vintage Company was not the only active winery in the Lamanda Park–Sierra Madre Villa area, only the biggest. A brief account of some others will show the variety of origin that is typical in the history of American winegrowing. The Sphinx Winery was the work of William Allen, an Englishman who had spent many years as a cotton exporter in Egypt. He came to California in 1878 and bought 500 acres northeast of the present Allen Avenue (named for him) and New York

Drive. Here he built a fine house and brought over his large family from England. There were 50 acres of vines already on the property, as well as a small winery. Under Allen both of these were expanded, the vineyard ultimately covering 350 acres. Allen did not live long at his Sphinx ranch, dying in 1886, when the Sphinx Winery was reorganized as the Mountain Winery and continued to operate until Prohibition.

The Lamanda Park Winery, also known as the Golden Park Winery, founded in the 1890s, belonged to the Etienne brothers, John and Peter, who were Belgians. They had only a small vineyard and so depended upon purchased grapes for a fairly large volume of wine made in their winery at what is now the intersection of Allen Avenue and Villa Street. By 1907 they were hoping to make 100,000 gallons in that year's vintage but doubted that they could find enough fruit.[47] That must have been more and more the situation for those Los Angeles County wineries that had not moved into San Bernardino County for new vineyards to supply the grapes they needed. But the brothers stayed in business until Prohibition.

At Sierra Madre Villa (now just Sierra Madre), a small winery grew from an unlikely beginning. John Jacob Hart, a classically trained violin-

The adobe Monte Vina winery of John Jacob Hart as it is today in Memorial Park, Sierra Madre. From the author's collection.

ist, had suffered injuries to his hands from a hunting accident and was no longer able to perform. In 1884 he came to California to start a new life, bought property in Sierra Madre, planted grapes, and in 1885 built a small adobe winery. Hart continued to be active as a teacher of violin and as a composer as well as a winemaker; the winery, called Monte Vina, prospered under the management of his son. It did not, however, escape from the growing dry sentiment in the Protestant parts of Southern California. The winery had a small retail shop where locals could buy wine, and this was attacked by the local paper as a "grog shop" corrupting the husbands and sons of the women of Sierra Madre.[48] The winery closed in 1918, in anticipation of Prohibition, and the site is now Memorial Park in Sierra Madre, where the small winery building still stands.[49] Another Sierra Madre winery was that of the California Wine Company, with offices in Los Angeles. The president of the winery was Edward Germain, prominent also as a fruit dealer, seedsman, and wholesaler of wine purchased from other wineries in the south.

Under the pressure of urbanization in and around the city of Los Angeles, grape growing and wine making were steadily squeezed to the east of the county, all the way to the city of Pomona, on the border between Los Angeles and San Bernardino Counties. Pomona had been founded in 1874, but until the boom of the '80s it had not amounted to much. Since then it had done well from fruit growing, including grapes for wine. "Practically all the earlier settlers in the [Pomona] Valley planted vineyards, amounting altogether to hundreds of acres."[50] They had long-established precedent to give them the idea. Ignacio Palomares, who was granted Rancho San Jose, on which the town of Pomona would later grow, had a vineyard from an early date following the grant to him in 1837.

At Pomona, wines and vines had a distinctly French flavor.[51] The first Frenchman to arrive was the strangely named Grat (short for "Gratien"?) Mirande, who came from the Basses-Pyrénées via San Francisco and Los Angeles, where he raised large flocks of sheep. In 1879 he sold out of the sheep business and bought land in Pomona. In 1885, a boom year still for California vineyards, more than 800 acres were planted around Pomona, and in the next year another 500. To serve all this expansion, Mirande and John Westphal, one of the local vineyardists, built a winery in 1884. They made 25,000 gallons in that year. In the next year, Westphal made 55,000 gallons, Mirande having withdrawn from the partnership to build a winery of his own a few blocks farther north in town. This he operated successfully until 1901, when he retired and returned to France.[52] His production was small but of good reputation; a local article on Mirande in 1898 stated that he was then shipping his wine "to all parts of the country."[53]

Next in the line of Frenchmen was Jacques Tisnerat, who built a winery in Pomona in the late '80s or early '90s (precise date not known) and operated that until 1903, when he sold it.[54] Tisnerat was followed by Pierre Espiau, a winemaker by profession who came to Pomona in 1890 and planted a vineyard on West Holt Avenue.[55] In 1896 he built a winery and opened a restaurant. Vineyard and winery are long gone, but Espiau's restaurant still survives, although it has migrated from Pomona to Claremont and has become, in common with the region generally, Mexican rather than French.

The last Frenchman in this sequence is Jules Hugues, who was working for M. Tisnerat in 1900 and who bought the winery on Tisnerat's retirement in 1903. In the next year he put up "a fine stone winery" to

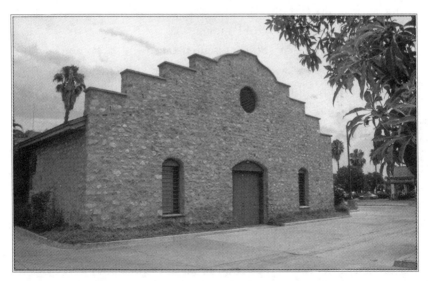

The winery of Jules Hugues on South Garey in Pomona. Built in 1904, it is now the breakfast room of a hotel. From the author's collection.

replace Tisnerat's and ran that until the city of Pomona went dry in 1912.[56] The winery building, a stout construction of twenty-two-inch-thick walls made of native stone and concrete, still stands on South Garey Avenue, where it has been incorporated into a new motel as the breakfast room.

As well as Frenchmen, there were Yankee vineyardists at Pomona. C. F. Loop and A. R. Meserve, both among the founders of the town, bought 2,200 acres of the Rancho San Jose in 1874. The property included Palomares's old vineyard of Mission vines, still intact, and this they set about expanding and improving with "choice varieties imported from abroad."[57] Meserve, born in Maine, the child of "ardent workers for the temperance movement," had been in California since 1852 and had evidently learned a more tolerant view of wine than prevailed in his home state.[58] Loop was an Anglican clergyman who did not share the prohibitionist convictions of his Baptist and Methodist confreres. He had been sent to California by the church as a "missionary at large" in the early 1860s, and by 1868 he was settled at San Gabriel, where he was surrounded by the vineyards of Wilson, Shorb, Rose, and others. Although he never ceased to be "the Reverend Loop," he was by this time apparently more horticultural than ecclesiastical. He soon planted a vineyard on his 180 San Gabriel acres. He was thus an experienced vineyardist before his move to Pomona.

It was Loop who, in 1889, presented the town of Pomona with a statue of the goddess Pomona, a copy of the ancient original in the Uffizi Gallery in Florence. This became the emblem of the town—grapes are the most prominent among the fruits the goddess holds in her basket—and may still be contemplated in the library there. J. DeBarth Shorb delivered a highly ornate speech at the unveiling of the statue but unfortunately omitted to say anything on the occasion about vine growing and wine making.

Another prominent investor in Pomona winegrowing was J. A. Packard, originally of Chicago, who planted what was described as a hundred-acre vineyard containing a surprising 150 varieties—"all of the French varieties of wine grapes that have proven of value in this country."[59]

Fred J. Smith, a young Englishman, came to California in 1881, when he made the acquaintance of C. A. Wetmore, the head of the State Board of Viticultural Commissioners and the founder of the Cresta Blanca Winery who was then living in Pleasanton. Wetmore filled young Smith with information about California wines and vines, of a kind positive enough to decide Smith to go into the business.[60] He went south, to Pomona, where, in 1881 he bought a hundred acres, bought cuttings from L. J. Rose, and planted a vineyard at what he named El Verde Ranch. He was thus one of the many who innocently joined in the planting binge of the early 1880s. His first crop brought the decent price of $18 a ton, but after that the annual price slid steadily downward, to a low of $6 a ton.

Since no one had any use for his grapes, Smith determined to learn how to make wine. He went to the Napa Valley, offered to work for Charles Krug without pay so he could learn the trade, and was set to work in the cellars. How long this may have lasted Smith does not say, but he returned to Pomona in time to join the enterprise of the Pomona Wine Company.

Fred J. Smith, a Yorkshireman who joined the grape-planting boom of the 1880s at Pomona, but, as did all his neighbors, turned to citrus growing at the end of the decade. Courtesy of Special Collections, Pomona Public Library.

This was an ill-timed venture. Formed in 1886 by a combination of local growers and investors, who, like Smith, badly needed a home for their grapes. The company took over the winery just built by Mirande and Westphal and, in 1887, enlarged it. Fred Smith was made secretary of the company; J. A. Packard was a major investor. The winery produced 120,000 gallons of wine in 1886, and 200,000 gallons in the next year.[61] By 1890 the Pomona Wine Company was the biggest industry in the town; it made a 50,000-gallon sale to New York in August 1889 and a 40,000-gallon sale of port, sherry, and claret in the next month to a Liverpool agency.[62] At vintage time one might see "as many as fifty wagons waiting in line to unload grapes."[63] But the company was making no money. The years of the decade beginning in 1885 were years of the locust for the California wine trade. Overplanting and the dumping of inferior wine had sunk prices to an unprofitable low. In 1892, only six years from its founding, the Pomona Wine Company wound up its affairs and went out of business.[64] It joined the many other winemaking firms to shut up shop and depress the market even further by disposing of their wines at distress prices. According to Smith, Packard "bought out everything at 15¢ on the dollar and then sold it all out to Mattei in Fresno."[65]

The building of the Pomona Wine Company as it looks today. When the winery closed down in 1892 the building was converted to the storage of lemons, symbolizing the triumph of citrus over the grape in Southern California. From the author's collection.

Not just the Pomona winery but Pomona winemaking in general did not survive the hard times of the late '80s and early '90s. Pomona, in common with nearly every other wine region in the county, took a double hit, the first of which was the seriously depressed market. The second was the damage done by Pierce's disease. Fred Smith, who became one of most prominent citizens of Pomona, turned from grapes to citrus, and so did everyone else in the Pomona Valley. The building of the Pomona Wine Company (which still stands at the corner of Park and Commercial Streets in downtown Pomona) was converted to a packing house for lemons.

THE COLONIZATION OF SAN BERNARDINO COUNTY

In the first decade of the twentieth century, there were substantial modern wineries at work in the city of Los Angeles and at various places in Los Angeles County. But further expansion of vineyards and winemaking facilities in the county was, as has been noted, increasingly expensive and difficult. And yet it was an expansive time, both for the wine business in general and for Southern California in particular. In 1900 California produced 23,433,383 gallons of wine; ten years later the figure was 45,486,868 gallons, almost doubling the quantity in a decade.[66] The usual explanation given for this startling jump is not that the settled white Protestant population of the country had learned at last to drink wine. Instead, it is explained by the flood of immigration in those years, a flood that suddenly added a big demand for wine where only a small one had been before. No doubt other things helped too: better-made wine, better transportation, more effective advertising. The near-monopoly power of the California Wine Association, beginning in 1894, contributed to stabilize and develop the trade. Whatever the reasons, these were good years for many California winemakers, although it was just at this time that Napa and Sonoma Counties were being devastated by phylloxera.

In Southern California, as in most of the rest of the state, the trend was upward. I do not have the figures for wine production by counties in these boom years, but the figures for vineyard acreage confirm the growth. The acreage of vines in Los Angeles County in 1904 was 6,825; by 1912 it had doubled to 12,075.[67] Evidently, there was still some room for expansion in the county. But the figure went no higher in the years following, in part because of high real estate values, and in part because of the growing threat of Prohibition. Meantime, Los Angeles was profiting, and not only from the growth of the national market for all wine. In 1906 the federal tax on brandy used for fortifying wines was reduced to 3 cents a gallon, and this set off a boom in the production of such wines in California, and especially in Southern California, which had long been identified, for better or for worse, as the ideal home of fortified wines. The production of sweet wines, as they were called in California, was 11,502,000 gallons in 1906; by 1910 it had reached 18,086,868.[68]

The problem of expansion in Southern California was solved by the simple expedient of planting vines in San Bernardino County, adjoining Los Angeles County on the east; the town of Pomona lies only a stone's throw from the border. The region of Cucamonga at the west end of San Bernardino County is a region of deep sandy soil at the base of the San Gabriel Mountains ("Cucamonga" means "sandy place" in Shoshonean). Wine had been made there since the beginning of settlement in the 1840s, but no sizeable business had developed. The main producer was the Cucamonga Vineyard Company, which descended from the vineyard planted by Tiburcio Tapia in 1840 and had been owned by Isaias Hellman since 1870. New interest was stirred in 1886 when George Haven and Daniel Milliken set out a 500-acre unirrigated vineyard south of the town of Rancho Cucamonga. The grapes thrived without irrigation, and that demonstration put Cucamonga in a new light. By the end of the century there were many scattered vineyards in the region, and more often than not they supplied wineries in Los Angeles, city and county both. Not much wine was made there: at the end of the century only two wineries operated in the district.

The big development of the Cucamonga vineyard region was a kind of colonial enterprise: the money, the direction of affairs, and the market were all in Los Angeles; the land and the labor were in Cucamonga. We have already seen that the Sierra Madre Vintage Company planted a thousand-acre vineyard at Etiwanda (now a part of modern Rancho Cucamonga) beginning in 1907. Secondo Guasti's big downtown Los Angeles winery depended largely on grapes from Cucamonga, since he was using quantities far in excess of the yields from the Los Angeles vineyards available to him. Giovanni Demateis, of the Italian-American Vineyard Co. on Alameda Street, had a Cucamonga property, and other Italian wineries in Los Angeles got at least some of their grapes there.

The next, inevitable step was to make wine where the grapes grew. This step was duly taken in 1900 by Secondo Guasti—he made it a giant step. Wanting to expand, and seeing the success of unirrigated grapes growing in Cucamonga, Guasti thought big. With fellow Italians in Los Angeles, some of them winemakers themselves, he formed the Italian Vineyard Company in 1900.[69] The company then bought 1,500 acres of raw land at Cucamonga, to be planted exclusively in grapes for sherry.[70] As Guasti said at the time, sherry grapes grew "to perfection" in Southern California and would earn for the region "the name of the best sherry producing section of America."[71] Guasti does not say what varieties he has in mind—perhaps Palomino was one. The method would be the standard California process of "baking" the base wine after fortification.

Guasti went on expanding. By 1903 his initial 1,500 acres of vineyard had doubled to 3,000; ultimately it would go to 5,000, making it "the biggest vineyard in the world," a claim that no one, so far as I know, has bothered to dispute.

The company was by no means confined to making sherry but had a complete line of fortified and table wines from "the very best varieties of wine grape known."[72] Grapes were brought in to the winery by a narrow gauge railway threading through the vineyard. The winery had refrigeration to combat the high heat of vintage time in that semi-arid region. There was a planing mill to provide lumber for tanks and barrels, and a cooper's shop to make them—200 barrels a day capacity.[73] A small company town called Guasti grew up on the site; besides the winemaking buildings, there were houses for the workers, a school, a fire station, a post office, and eventually a church. In 1903 Guasti folded his Los Angeles winery into the Italian Vineyard Company.

The firm of Secondo Guasti was swallowed by Guasti's Italian Vineyard Company, but the address in this ad from 1907 is still that of the Secondo Guasti Company in Los Angeles. The building shown, however, was the new winery in Rancho Cucamonga with a capacity of 5 million gallons, not replacing but greatly expanding the production of Guasti's downtown wineries. From *Pacific Wine and Spirit Review,* May 31, 1907.

Production in 1911 had grown to around 3 million gallons, from 20,000 tons of grapes. But all of this remained a colonial enterprise, financed and directed from Los Angeles, where wine continued to be made at Guasti's big property in the city.

The view that Cucamonga, and Guasti in particular, were simply extensions of the Los Angeles *vignoble* is evidenced by the establishment of an experimental vineyard at Guasti by the U.S. Department of Agriculture in 1905. Land for the purpose was made available by Secondo Guasti. The aim of the vineyard, which was laid out by George C. Husmann, son of the pioneering George Husmann of Missouri and Napa, was "to determine the kinds of grapes best adapted to the San Gabriel Valley."[74] Today, one might think it strange to test grapes in San Bernardino County for use in the San Gabriel Valley, but no one appears to have questioned the arrangement at the time. According to a later account, the experimental vineyard included for testing some five hundred varieties of grapes.[75]

Another Los Angeles winery that expanded by migrating to another county was the Stern Winery. It had deep roots in Los Angeles. The founder was the German Charles Stern, who had worked for Kohler and Frohling from their beginning and was the manager of their original New York agency in 1860. The association with Kohler and Frohling came to an end in 1869, but Stern remained in New York as a merchant of California wines. One of his important sources was L. J. Rose at Sunny Slope, and in 1878 Stern and Rose joined forces. The firm of Stern and Rose endured until the sale of Sunny Slope to an English syndicate in 1887. Stern, after a lapse of years, became a major Los Angeles wine producer on his own when the firm of Charles Stern and Sons was incorporated around 1890.[76] His winery at Macy and Mission in Los Angeles was said to have a capacity of 500,000 gallons. A year before Secondo Guasti was buying up land at Cucamonga in 1900, Stern and his associates were buying 2,500 acres at a whistle stop just south of Guasti's place but across the county line in Riverside County. The place—hardly a town—where the new vineyards grew was first called Stalder but was renamed Wineville when the Sterns

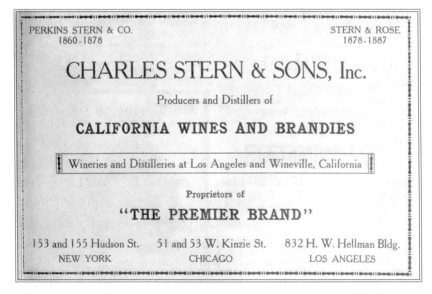

Advertisement for Stern's "Premier Brand" from the winery at Wineville, Riverside County. The date of 1860 in the upper left refers to the pioneer days of Kohler and Frohling in Los Angeles and of their New York agency, Perkins, Stern and Co. (see Chapter 3). From *Pacific Wine and Spirit Review,* June 30, 1911.

developed their establishment there.[77] In 1903 a big winery was constructed at the Riverside County vineyard, now expanded to 3,000 acres. Stern was killed that year in an accident; his sons (one of them named "Perkins," after Stern's old associate in the days of Kohler and Frohling) continued the business down to Prohibition, producing under the label "The Premier Brand."

Nothing remains of the Stern Winery—not even the name "Wineville." A sensational series of murders there in the 1920s gave the town a bad name and led the citizens to change it to "Mira Loma." A few structures at the big establishment of the Italian Vineyard Company at Guasti still survive in derelict condition and will no doubt soon disappear. Many of Secondo Guasti's thousands of acres are now occupied by the commercial developments that proliferate around a major airport.[78] A few token vines grow on the security fence that guards the idle remnants of the Italian Vineyard Company.

GOING DRY

While winemaking in Southern California was flourishing from the turn of the century, so too was the campaign to prohibit all alcoholic drink throughout the country. The "temperance" movement, so-called, has a long history in the United States, full of ups and downs, chops and changes, infighting and schism. But it also has a history, under some of its leaders, of undeviating determination to succeed in winning the struggle against Demon Rum. Such leaders were now in control of the movement, and had been since 1893, when the Anti-Saloon League had been formed in the college town of Oberlin, Ohio. The League was well organized and, through the Protestant churches, had friends and agents in every town in the country. It developed a great propaganda apparatus: a printing plant producing an unending stream of leaflets, pamphlets, magazines, and papers. It also had a corps of thousands of lecturers who fanned out over the country to spread the gospel of Prohibition—the promise of a sober, healthy, prosperous nation.

What really distinguished the League was its commitment to

single-issue pressure politics. It had but one goal—prohibition. It would support any politician who would vote as the League desired; it was the implacable enemy of any politician who failed to conform to the League's desire. No other issue mattered—foreign affairs, the economy, public welfare, conservation, education: the League cared nothing for such matters, since, in its view, they were all subordinate to the goal of a sober country. Once you had that, everything desirable would follow. In no very long time the political power of the League began to be felt by anyone who ran for office or who wanted to stay in office.

The League's strategy, apart from coercing politicians, was gradualism, drying up first a town, then a township, then a county, then a state. The success of this procedure was remarkable. Georgia went dry in 1907, Mississippi and North Carolina in 1908, Tennessee in 1909, West Virginia in 1912, Virginia in 1914—after which other states went down like a row of dominos. By 1916 there were twenty-six dry states. The next and final step would be national prohibition through constitutional amendment.

In California the situation facing the League was more complicated than in most other states, and, in fact, the state of California never voted Dry. The prosperous wine industry was one obstacle. The value of grapes and wine in the state's economy made a good defense against attacks on it. The Drys called this "skulking behind the grape."[79] The division between the increasingly Midwestern Protestant population of Southern California and the more polyglot, diverse population of the North was another complication. This made California not one but two states from the League's point of view. When the issue of statewide prohibition was put to the vote, as it was in 1914 and again in 1917, the measure was defeated by the northern vote. The city of Los Angeles itself did not vote for prohibition, but Los Angeles County then abounded in towns that had voted themselves dry. Sometimes the rule against alcohol was written into the property deeds of the town, as it was in Long Beach, Compton, and Ontario (in San Bernardino County). In Long Beach, for example, the deeds "provide that if liquor is dispensed on the property, in any manner whatsoever, the title shall immediately revert to the former owners."[80] More often dryness was established as a local

A response to the Dry effort to shut down the Los Angeles wineries in 1913. From *Pacific Wine and Spirit Review*, April 30, 1913.

option obtained by popular vote. By 1908 there were sixty incorporated dry towns, including towns where grape growing and winemaking were important: Glendale, Pomona, Sierra Madre, and Pasadena.[81]

Ironically, it was Pasadena that led the fight to obtain local option. Pasadena and its neighborhood was the historic center of winemaking in Los Angeles County: Benjamin Wilson at the Lake Vineyard, J. DeBarth Shorb at the San Gabriel Winery, General George Stoneman at Los Robles, J. C. Kewen at the Old Mill, Benjamin Eaton at Fair Oaks, L. J. Rose at Sunny Slope, Lucky Baldwin at Santa Anita, Albert Brigden at Lamanda Park—the list might go on at great length and would include wineries in Glendale, Burbank, San Gabriel, and El Monte. Pasadena's behavior exhibits the effects of the Protestant Migration. Although the original settlers in Pasadena found vines already planted on their new properties, some, at least, chose to ignore them, or at least not to talk about them. Or they pretended that they were table grapes, or raisin grapes (as some were).

I may note that there is no mention of vines or wine in almost all of the histories of Pasadena and its neighboring towns that I have looked at. Like the undesirables in Orwell's *1984* who become "unpersons" and are never heard of again, the wineries of Pasadena have become "unwineries." Charles Holder, in *All About Pasadena and Its Vicinity* (1889), speaks by way of exception of the "vast vineyards that cover miles of country here" and gives brief mention to the wineries of Shorb, Baldwin, and Rose. But far more typical is the Pecksniffian style of R. W. C. Farnsworth's *A Southern California Paradise* (1883). He declares that "the people of Pasadena are employed in fruit growing almost exclusively for a livelihood" but can hardly bring himself to admit that grapes are among those fruits. "We have several raisin vineyards" is all he can manage. There is no mention of wine. But the truth about dryness in Pasadena is well shown by the Pasadena City Directory for 1902/3. This carries a running ad at the foot of page after page for a Los Angeles liquor store promising free delivery of "bottle, gallon, or case put up in *plain* packages" (italics in original). That appeal to concealment is an emblem of how the local histories treated the Pasadena wine trade.[82]

Pasadena, which had been founded in 1874, passed an informal vote against the sale of liquor in the town in 1876, when it had not yet been incorporated. But when a saloon opened in 1884, the town was powerless to prevent it or to close it down. A public meeting was called; the saloon owner, a Mr. Campbell, was violently denounced while Campbell "sat in his carriage on the outskirts of the crowd and laughed at the helplessness of the orators."[83] The citizens then tried a boycott that failed. The next step was to incorporate and to require an expensive liquor license ($1,200 annually), but Campbell paid this and continued in profitable business.

An ordinance prohibiting the sale of liquor was then passed, despite the fact that local option had been, in 1874, declared unconstitutional in California.[84] The new ordinance—"the first prohibitory law...to go into effect in the State of California"[85]— was challenged in the courts, and in 1887 it was declared constitutional by the California Supreme Court.[86] Campbell was defeated. Dry sentiment was so strong in Pasadena that when President Benjamin Harrison visited in 1891 the town was scandalized by a banquet given in his honor at which wine was served. The president, to the relief of the townspeople, drank only Apollinaris water.[87]

Many other California towns followed Pasadena's lead—sixty by 1908, as we have seen. The terms of the proliferating antiliquor ordinances varied greatly, and so did the effectiveness of enforcement. It was easier to pass a law than to carry it into effect. And some of the laws were absurdly complicated and unenforceable.

The town of Pomona distinguished itself by the foolishness of its regulations. Things began mildly enough in 1889, when the town passed an ordinance modeled on the Pasadena law but allowing the purchase of wine in quantities of 2 gallons or more. This, it is said, was "inserted so as to exempt the Pomona winery, one of the largest in Southern California."[88] Things were toughened up in 1891, when a law was passed making it a misdemeanor punishable by fine or imprisonment even to enter a place where liquor was served. It was also a punishable misdemeanor to carry a bottle or container that might be used to hold liquor, and if a person knew where liquor was available and failed to inform the police, that failure was also punishable. Finally, the law prohibited anyone from having "any empty or filled bottles, jugs, casks, kegs, or barrels designed for liquors about his house or store."[89] The Puritans, Lord Macaulay wrote, hated bear-baiting not because it gave pain to the bear but because it gave pleasure to the spectators. That seems to have been the spirit behind the invention of many dry laws— an envious hatred of another's pleasure rather than concern for their welfare, and a determination to deny.

Pomona learned little from its earlier attempts at prohibiting alcohol; the following report comes under date of January 1914:

> The prohibitionists of Pomona are still in a quandary over the interpretation of their ordinance which provides that alcoholic liquors shall be used for scientific purposes only. One of the effects of the ordinance is the replenishment of the scientific chests of many families of Pomona. While clubs and similar organizations are not allowed to keep alcoholic liquors for scientific purposes, families are free to make demonstrations of the scientific value of alcohol by inviting guests to make bibulous analyses of the contents of brown, black and green bottles. The prohibitionists are now thinking of prohibiting science in Pomona.[90]

There must have been many such futilities enacted in the name of Prohibition. The city of Los Angeles itself had a long struggle to invent laws that would both make sense and actually work. Most of them were compromises and so were doomed to dissatisfy both sides, as, for example, an ordinance passed in 1917 for closing the saloons but allowing the continued sale of wine and beer.[91]

In most places in Los Angeles County where wineries existed they were not much affected by local anti-saloon ordinances and continued to make and to sell wine. That immunity did not continue. The Anti-Saloon League mounted a number of offensives with the aim of closing the wineries, for it was the first article of Dry faith that if you removed the supply, people would no longer be thirsty, a belief that the nearly fourteen years of national Prohibition proved sensationally wrong. The County Board of Supervisors, which had authority over licensing, was pressured into considering an ordinance to put approval or denial of a winery license to a popular vote. In the election of 1912 a form of this measure was passed. In April 1913, all of the wineries in Los Angeles County had their applications for renewal of license to operate refused; the Board of Supervisors was under the thumb of the League, which "threatened to recall them if they did not abide by the will of the people."[92] The wineries were unable to do any business at all for a time, but the measure apparently did not survive challenge, for the wineries in Los Angeles continued to operate.

The response of the liquor trade to the attacks of the Anti-Saloon League were belated, uncertain, and divided. The wine people said the proper targets of Prohibition should be beer and spirits, for wine was the drink of temperance. The beer and spirits people were outraged by such a betrayal of common interest. The *Pacific Wine and Spirit Review*, the leading trade journal on the West Coast, treated the activities of the League with mockery at first; many pages carried items exhibiting the foolishness of its measures. After a time the tone changes: things are getting serious, even though the actions of the League still appear farcical. At last, the note is desperation: What can one do with such people? But at no time does the *Pacific Wine and Spirit Review* publish a coherent defense of its industry or recognize a specific organization as leading the fight. For a long time the wine men deluded themselves with the notion that wine, somehow, would not be among those things prohibited, and so they need not mount a defense.

Among the wine people who did undertake a defense against Prohibition, Andrea Sbarboro, founder of the Italian Swiss Colony winery in Asti, Sonoma County, was easily the most active. A native Italian, he found it incredible that people concerned with temperance should be opposed to wine, and he labored hard to persuade the infidels. But even Sbarboro was slow off the mark. His California Grape Protective League was not founded until 1908, a decade after the Anti-Saloon League had taken up its work in California. Sbarboro worked hard; he traveled the state and the country addressing any audience that would listen. He went to Washington for congressional hearings; he published tracts and pamphlets and gave them out wholesale. One of his aides was a publicist who had worked for him at the Italian Swiss

Colony, Horatio Stoll. Stoll devised print ads and highway signs warning of the devastation that Prohibition would produce in California, and he sent cameramen out to the vineyards and wineries to make films for a movie showing the good solid people who made wine and the productive, beneficial work they did. This was probably not the first propaganda movie, but it must have been one of the earliest.[93]

All was in vain. The national mood was in favor of Prohibition, for which it had a wide choice of reasons. Prohibition was prosperity: it would reduce crime, it would enhance productivity, it would preserve the country's youth from destruction, it would boost the health of the nation. One of the most potent appeals was to the supremacy of white, rural, Protestant America. The saloon, an urban institution patronized by Catholic immigrants, was a dangerous cultural and political threat—a combination of the City, the Foreigner, and the Catholic, as

One of Andrea Sbarboro's pamphlets defending wine against the Anti-Saloon League. His appeal to wine as the drink of "true temperance" fell on deaf and uncomprehending ears. Courtesy of the California Historical Society.

well as the Inebriate. Hence the leading body in the fight was not called the Anti-Alcohol League or the Anti-Liquor League, as one might reasonably expect, but the Anti-Saloon League, the saloon in its most offensive terms being an urban institution. There were other arguments available if these were not enough.

By 1916, preparations for a national Prohibition were complete.[94] A Congress dominated by members approved by the Anti-Saloon League had been elected that year. In the next year, Congress voted to submit to the states for ratification a constitutional amendment creating national Prohibition. The required two-thirds majority of the states ratified the amendment by January 1919. The Volstead Act, spelling out the terms under which the amendment would be enforced, was passed in 1919, and at midnight on January 16/17, 1920, national Prohibition went into effect. It would endure, against repeated legal assault and under growing popular disregard, for almost fourteen years.

8

THE DRY YEARS

In order to make any sense out of what happened to the wine business in general and in Los Angeles County in particular, one needs to know what the legal provisions were. The language of the Eighteenth Amendment to the Constitution, the Prohibition amendment, is simple enough, as legal statements go:

> The manufacture, sale, or transportation of intoxicating liquors within, the importation thereof into, or the exportation thereof from the United States and all territory subject to the jurisdiction thereof for beverage purposes is hereby prohibited.

The Volstead Act, spelling out the terms under which this general Prohibition would be enforced, defined "intoxicating" as anything containing one half of one percent alcohol, a measure that had been traditionally used for tax purposes. That clearly prohibited anything recognized as alcoholic drink—every sort of wine, beer, and spirit without exception. It is said that sauerkraut has more alcohol than the law would allow. Yet, despite this severe limitation on allowable alcohol, home winemaking was permitted under Prohibition. How that exception came about and what effect it had are among the many curiosities of the Prohibition era.

It came about in this way: Paul Garrett, the producer of Virginia Dare wine, an energetic and resourceful winemaker with properties in North Carolina, New York, and California, called on Wayne Wheeler, the chief counsel of the Anti-Saloon League, and the Reverend E. C. Dinwiddie, legislative superintendent of the League, at their Washington office in 1919. The two were then engaged in writing the Volstead Act, nominally the work of Andrew Volstead, Republican congressman from Minnesota and chairman of the House Judiciary Committee, but essentially the work of the League and especially of Wheeler, the legal brains of the Prohibition movement. Garrett, who had heard Dinwiddie at congressional hearings say that the League had no wish to injure any agricultural interest, wanted to ask what they meant to do for the grape growers of the country. After some discussion, Wheeler wrote out what became Section 29, Title II of the Volstead Act. It read:

> The penalties provided in this chapter against the manufacture of liquor without a permit shall not apply to a person manufacturing non-intoxicating cider and fruit juice exclusively for use in his home, but such cider and fruit juices shall not be sold or delivered except to persons having permits to manufacture vinegar.[1]

Paul Garrett, the master salesman behind Virginia Dare wine. He helped enable home winemaking during Prohibition and so provided a brief prosperity to the nation's grape growers. From Clarence Gohdes, *Scuppernong: North Carolina's Grape and Its Wines* (1982).

A response to one of the periodic threats to investigate grape sales in order to prevent bootlegging. From the *San Francisco Bulletin,* reprinted in the *California Grape Grower,* May 1, 1929.

"It's None of Your Business, Sir," She Said - By Rodger

WHERE ARE YOU GOING MY PRETTY MAID?

CALIFORNIA GRAPES

From San Francisco Bulletin

When this section was introduced into the bill as it was being debated in the Senate, there were questions about its puzzling language: Why call "fruit juices" "non-intoxicating"? And why should anything "non-intoxicating" have to be exempted from the Prohibition law? How did you "manufacture" these things? And so on. Garrett, too, was troubled by the language, but Wheeler assured him that it would do the job.[2] And so it did; the authorities, for the most part, acted as though this section permitted home winemaking. The key term appears to be "non-intoxicating." Although the "intoxicating" level of alcohol was defined as less than one half of one percent elsewhere in the Volstead Act, here it was deemed to be without definition. The courts would have to prove that any suspect beverage was in fact intoxicating, and that would entail an impossible waste of time, especially since the defendant would probably be tried before a jury of his friendly neighbors. The permission as Wheeler wrote it was certainly unclear, but it was a permission that produced spectacular results.

Home winemakers, especially in the big cities with large immigrant populations—greater New York, Philadelphia, Chicago, San Francisco—made staggering quantities of wine. Since home winemaking was domestic and unpoliced, there was no way to know exactly just how much wine was made that way, or what was done with it once it had been made. One guess put it at 111 million gallons annually from 1922 to 1929.[3] In 1919, the last year before Prohibition, the commercial production of wine in the United States was 55 million gallons. The grapes required for the immense production of homemade wine mostly came from California, and were mostly shipped out by rail. In 1920, the first year of Prohibition, 26,000 cars of fresh grapes left California; by 1927, the peak year, the count was 72,000 cars. The prices paid for these grapes were the highest that growers had ever received—up to $185 a ton for a brief moment in 1924.[4] In short, the first years of Prohibition were years of an unprecedented boom for grape growers, not just in California but everywhere that grapes fit for winemaking were grown— New York, Ohio, Missouri, and a few other states. At the beginning of Prohibition, there were about 300,000 acres of bearing grape vines in California; in 1927, after seven years of dryness, there were 577,000. And as the acreage of grapes had almost doubled under the Volstead Act, so too did the size of the crop: from 1.25 million tons in 1920 to 2.5 million in 1927. And, at least according to one estimate, twice as much wine was made at home as had been made commercially on the eve of Prohibition. As one wit put it, America might have become a wine drinking country if only Prohibition had lasted long enough. The good times did not last; first, overproduction let the air out of inflated prices for grapes, and then the Depression shrank the market. But the Dry people—at least those honest enough to admit what had happened— must have wondered where they had gone wrong.

The boom in planting was only faintly heard in Los Angeles County; most of the expansion took place in California's Central Valley, where new vineyards were limited only by the availability of water. There was, however, a mild growth in Los Angeles County, from 4,600 acres in 1920 to a high point of 5,996 in 1929.[5] Even in a place like Pomona, where the orange had long since driven out the grape, there were 350 acres of vineyards in 1925, no doubt generated by the boom in the fresh grape market.[6]

The growers prospered—some of them, at least, and for a time—but for the winemakers under the Volstead Act it was a different story. At the beginning of Prohibition, there were just under 700 bonded wineries in California; twelve years later, the number had fallen to 177. But how, one may ask, did any wineries survive at all? Part of the answer lies in the fact that the Eighteenth Amendment prohibited alcoholic liquors only "for beverage purposes." If you were not going to drink it, wine could be made and sold for certain specific purposes. Wine could be prescribed for medical reasons, and wine could be used as a sacrament. These were the best-known exceptions, and many myths have grown up about their abuse—how doctors prescribed it for no ailment whatever, and how phony religions were invented by self-ordained priests. The fact is that the few wineries in that business had to be licensed and were closely supervised, so abuses were easily discovered. Doctors' prescriptions were on record, as were the requests for sacramental wine. Neither the sacramental nor the medical trade in wine ever amounted to much. The quantity of wine for sacramental use never exceeded 3 million gallons in a year, and was usually much less than that. Other "non-beverage" uses were for flavoring food—Campbell's Soup used a lot of sherry—and for curing cigar tobacco. Wine could be distilled for the brandy used in fortifying other wines, or it could be converted to vinegar and sold. All of these permitted uses were allowed only to licensed wineries, and the demand for them did not grow.

Some wineries, especially those that owned vineyards, made grape concentrate for those home winemakers who did not use fresh grapes. Concentrate, diluted with water to its original strength, could be fermented at any time of the year, and was offered in a variety of kinds. Fruit Industries, a combination of California wineries created toward the end of Prohibition, offered port, muscatel, tokay, sauterne, Riesling, claret, burgundy, and Virginia Dare concentrates. If desired, Fruit Industries would deliver the concentrate, manage the fermentation, and bottle the resulting wine. Another way to use grapes was in wine tonics, wine candy, wine jellies, and anything else of the kind. These, too, had very limited markets and could not keep many wineries in business.

And yet, at one time or another in California during the Prohibition years, 694 wineries were licensed to operate by the Bureau of Prohibition (later the Bureau of Industrial Alcohol).[7] Since the vineyards were not only intact but expanding, and since not all of the crop could be profitably sold fresh, a substantial part of the crop remained on the vines each year. In order not to let the fruit go to waste, the Prohibition authority licensed commercial wineries to make wine—but not to sell it for drink, since that was what was explicitly prohibited. According to the official records, 139 million gallons of wine were legally made during the Prohibition years, and nearly 43 million of these gallons were sold for permitted uses.[8] That left 96 million gallons slowly turning to vinegar in the vats and tanks of commercial wineries across the country. The situation made no sense, but the history of national Prohibition is rich in such nonsense.

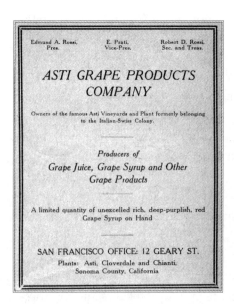

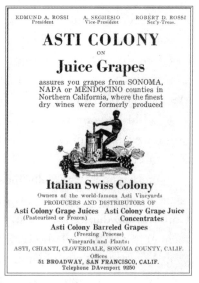

Two ads for Northern California's Asti Colony. The first, from 1920, does not include the word "wine"; the second, from 1929, nine years into Prohibition, is clearly about wine. In the later ad, the grapes are still "juice" grapes (the standard euphemism), but it is noted that they formerly produced "the finest dry wines," and the purpose of the man at the press is unmistakable. From *California Grape Grower*, May 1, 1920, and July 1929.

STORIES FROM LOS ANGELES

Most of the wineries in California, as has been said, simply went out of business; they may have sought permits at the beginning of Prohibition, but for most of them a brief experience of operating under the new conditions was enough. They soon shut down. Of the 694 bonded wineries in California holding permits to make wine in 1922, only 177, as has been said, still held permits by 1933.[9] And of that number, only a small fraction came from Southern California. The statistics usually give only the figures for all of California, but for a few years the numbers for Southern California are specified in the reports. They tell a clear-enough story: in 1927 there were 28 bonded winery permits in the South; in 1929 there were 25; in 1930, only 19.[10]

Those that elected to keep going had to apply for permits (there were thirteen different permits for winery operations; not everyone applied for all of them), and then to submit to regular inspections.[11] The reports of inspection are among the records of the federal Bureau of Alcohol, Tobacco, and Firearms, now in Special Collections at the Shields Library at the University of California, Davis. They give an intimate account of what it was like in those days. The case histories that follow are all taken from this source.

Vito Franco, operating Bonded Winery 32[12] at 542 Alpine Street in Los Angeles, applied for a license to produce "non-beverage" wine in 1920. Since he held a bonded winery number, he evidently had been making wine for several years before 1920, but his place was very small—a cement-floored cellar under his house and a dirt-floored cellar under another frame building at the same address. The neighborhood, the inspector noted, was one of "good repute"—it was in what was then Little Italy and is today Chinatown. Franco had a lease on a vineyard and needed a permit to make wine from the grapes that he could not sell in the fresh market. In 1921, 1,800 gallons of wine were reported on the premises; in 1922, 1,200. But Franco died that year, and his wife, Rosina, had to jump through all the bureaucratic hoops to get a license in her name. Mrs. Franco then fell ill, so that a daughter had to take over. The widow recovered, but by 1924 there were 5,250 gallons of wine on hand and nothing to be done with it except let it turn into vinegar, which it would readily do on its own. In July 1925, the wine was "destroyed" and the winery permit returned to the authorities. The story belongs to the short and simple annals of the poor. "Destroying" wine was a carefully prescribed procedure, lest any of the wine to be dealt with should end up being drunk. Usually it was run down the drain, in the presence of an inspector.

Rosina Franco's neighbor at 424 Alpine Street, Giovanni Guglielmo, had a similar story to tell. He had been making wine since 1916 and possessed a permit for Bonded Winery 18. His place was small—a frame building at the rear of his house lot. He applied for a license from the Prohibition Bureau to make wine in 1921, and he continued to make wine in 1922, but, it was discovered, he had no permit for that year. When he applied for another license in 1923 his application was refused and he was told that he could sell the older wine but that the newer wine must be destroyed. By the end of 1923 he had sold none of the 7,000 gallons he had on hand, and in the next year he gave up his bond and retired from winemaking. The record does not say what became of the wine, but presumably it was dumped under the watchful eye of an inspector. What Guglielmo thought of all this may be imagined.

Lorenzo Clemente, of 828 N. Broadway, an Italian-born naturalized citizen, had a wholesale fruit business. He sometimes bought grapes in large quantities, occasionally the produce of an entire vineyard. If he could not sell all of his grapes as fresh fruit, he could salvage the unsold lot by converting it into wine. Clemente held a permit to manufacture for this purpose, but for some reason it was revoked in 1923, leaving Clemente licensed only to sell, not to make, wine. A license to sell, however, as so many small-scale winemakers discovered, was a practically worthless piece of paper. Home winemakers could provide their own supply; ambitious home winemakers, of whom there must have been countless numbers, could make a lot more than the permitted 200 gallons and sell it quietly to their neighbors and friends. The small, licensed, officially inspected producer, hoping to sell his wine for "non-beverage" purposes, had a hopeless prospect. Who would buy it under all the burdensome procedures required and for so few legally permitted uses? So it was with Clemente. His wine—he called it "claret"—spoiled and was destroyed in 1925.

The Lotito brothers, Cristofaro and Giuseppe, of BW 50 at 615 Cleveland Street, Los Angeles, took out a permit in 1920 for their small winery—a brick-walled cellar twenty-five by thirty feet beneath a frame building, where they currently had 750 gallons of wine. By 1923 they had 4,700 gallons but had apparently sold nothing. The inspector noted that the brothers had "no legitimate market" and recommended that they not be permitted to make any more wine. Then inspection showed that the wine on hand had been watered, no doubt to replace the volume of wine that had been sneaked out. The Lotitos were in trouble; an action was considered but was not brought. Giuseppe—"Joe"—swore that the wines were made from "water grapes," and this absurd explanation seems to have been accepted, perhaps because the Feds did not want to bother with such small fry.[13] But the watered wine was destroyed and the winery closed in 1925.

Hirsch Genss, BW 41 at 1263 East Twentieth Street, Los Angeles, the Rabbi of Congregation Adath Israel, had a small winery in his basement from which he had provided wine for other rabbis. He was issued a permit to make sacramental wine in 1920, but when he applied also for a permit to purchase wine for resale to other rabbis the request was denied: "Let them get wine from a winery," the inspector wrote. Genss quit business in November 1921.

A complicated succession at a bigger establishment is an interesting illustration of persistence. A Mr. Julius, first name not known, had been in business since 1912 at 330 N. Anderson Road making retsina wine for the Chicago market. (Anderson Road was later changed to Mission Road; it runs northeast from Cesar Chavez Avenue toward the County Medical Center in a region of railroad tracks.) When Prohibition came in 1920 he sold the place to Harry and Louis Burnstein, of the California Sacramental Wine Co., BW 408. Their permit was for a modest 5,000 gallons at first, but by 1925 this had risen to 29,000 gallons. In that year the authorities demanded that Harry Burnstein account for an unexplained loss of wine. In an affidavit Burnstein testified that, because the winery had previously been making retsina wine, the new wine in the storage vessels had been given a strong resinous flavor. To reduce this, they had been obliged to transfer their wine many times in order to aerate it, and in the process some wine was lost. Presumably this explanation was accepted, but in 1927 the California Sacramental Wine Co. was in receivership.

The next owner was Louis Guerrieri, who bought the Burnstein winery in 1927, renamed it the California Mission Vintage Co., BW 166, and greatly expanded it—to 385,000 gallons capacity by 1935, by which time Prohibition had been repealed. Louis was the son of Giuseppe Guerrieri, who had been winemaker for Secondo Guasti at the Italian Vineyard Company and had then gone into business for himself and was now the proprietor of the Santa Fe Winery. Louis sold the California Mission Vintage Co. in 1935 and then joined his father at the Santa Fe Winery.

The buyer of the Mission Road winery, now in its third change of ownership in fifteen years, was Antonio Moramarco, who had behind him a troubled history as a winemaker during the Prohibition years. His original winery, BW 65 at 750 Yale Street, was issued a permit for 20,000 gallons in 1920.[14] It appears to have been an adjunct of Moramarco Brothers, Produce and Fruit Dealers of Van Nuys. It was supplied by 77 acres of vines in Cucamonga. Trouble started in 1923, when the winery was found to contain more wine than allowed by its permit. Action was threatened but only threatened. In 1925 Moramarco was again found to have more wine than had been reported. A hearing was held to decide whether to revoke his permit for improper record keeping and was decided in Moramarco's favor. Then, in 1929, Moramarco was arrested for bootlegging, but again he was cleared of the charges. Still, the inspector recommended that the winery be closed: "There seems to be no reason for this winery being in business, or making more claret wine."

But Moramarco persisted. The winery was now strictly a salvage operation. "The proprietor stated," according to the inspector's report in February 1930, "that as owner of vineyards, he ships most of his grapes and converts into wine only a small part of his grapes that will not come up to shipping standard. He intends to continue making wine." But the Prohibition men now gave him a permit only to sell wine, not to make it. Moramarco protested, unsuccessfully, because, the administrator told him, there was already too much claret in California: "There are millions of gallons of this class of wine in this state for which there is no market, and which is deteriorating to such an extent that it will soon be valueless for any purpose." Moramarco tried again in the next year to regain a manufacturing permit, but by this time he appears to have lost heart, and the story of BW 65 is downhill to the end. In 1931 the winery is "in an old unsanitary and insecure building…wine on hand of doubtful quality." Yet only four years earlier, in 1927, the inspector found the "cooperage in winery in splendid condition" and the wine appeared to be "well taken care of." Not now. The winery was derelict, and the official file on it was at last closed in 1945, following Moramarco's death in 1944. No wine had been made at the place since 1935, when there must have been a brief episode of winemaking following Repeal at the end of 1933.

One further case history from Prohibition shows how a winery, having hung on to precarious life for years, could be reinvigorated by the belief that Repeal was coming. The San Gabriel Vineyard Co., BW 46, housed in a sizeable brick building along the Southern Pacific tracks in east San Gabriel, began life as the Italian-American Vineyard Co. of Giovanni Demateis, founded in 1888 on Alameda Street. In 1920, at the beginning of Prohibition, Demateis bought the San Gabriel Vineyard Co., which had been founded by a German from Frankfurt named Jacob Rudel. In 1883 Rudel had bought raw land at San Gabriel, cleared and planted it, built a winery, and continued to expand; by 1902 he had 120 acres of vineyard, and a partner named Henry Goetz.[15] Rudel retired some years before Prohibition; Goetz carried on until the sale to Demateis, who moved out of his Alameda Street place but kept its name: the San Gabriel Winery was now the Italian-American Vineyard Co., and it operated under that name until the very end of the Prohibition years.

Demateis was making wine at the relocated Italian-American Vineyard Co. from the moment he bought it in 1920, but I have no information about his operations then. In 1925 an inspector's report notes that Demateis is of "good reputation, had been in business for forty years, and sells mostly in the east"—hardly anything locally. Giovanni Demateis died in 1929, when Prohibition still seemed as firmly fixed in the land as it ever had been. He was succeeded at the winery by his sons, Robert and Charles. In August 1932, just after the Democratic Convention in Chicago had nominated Franklin D. Roosevelt for president and put a Repeal plank into the party platform, the brothers sprang into action. They applied to the Prohibition Bureau for permission to produce 500,000 gallons of wine and 100,000 of brandy from the coming vintage! These were impossible numbers except on the assumption that Repeal was on its way. It was indeed, but not for more than a year yet.

The Demateis brothers were not the only winemakers who had sniffed a change in the weather. The *California Grape Grower* reported in 1932 that "a number of owners of unused wineries…plan this year to crush their surplus grapes and make wine."[16] But the brothers were making a bold bet; they would be stuck with a lot of unsalable wine if Repeal were delayed or somehow evaded. It appears, in fact, that they had started making wine in very large quantities much earlier, for the Bureau's inspector reported these quantities at the winery in January 1932: 154,000 gallons of wine and 4,000 of brandy on hand in January 1931, to which 35,000 gallons of wine and 15,000 gallons of brandy were added during 1931, for a total of 208,000 gallons. The wines were identified as claret, Riesling, port, sherry, muscat, and Angelica.

Probably the biggest winemaking enterprise in all of California during the ostensibly dry years was Secondo Guasti's Italian Vineyard Company in San Bernardino County. Given its 5,000 acres of vineyard, it had to think big. Its permit from the Prohibition Bureau in 1920 was for 2.5 million gallons of wine. When the inspector called in 1925 he found the plant in full operation. At that moment it was turning out a new product: grape syrup. The manager stated that the company had shipped out between four and five hundred carloads of grapes in that season, and that it depended largely on the market for grapes whether any considerable amount of wine would be made. Five years later—still under the rule of Prohibition—the inventory of wine on hand showed the following amounts, divided into dry and sweet (that is, fortified) wines:

Dry Wines		Sweet Wines	
Claret	47,900	Angelica	54,670
Burgundy	22,620	Marsala	8,500
Grignolino	36,200	Tokay	6,110
Red wine	283,470	Port	472,230
Riesling	41,560	Muscat	60,150
Sauterne	8,500	Malaga	9,560
White wine	4,830	Sherry	878,665
Dry wine lees	9,050	Sweet wine lees	7,700
	454,150 gallons		1,497,585 gallons

Evidently the market had told them to make wine; most of it had probably been made since the decline of the fresh grape market after 1926. The list also shows that Guasti was counting on his eastern Italian market for dry red wines whenever Repeal should come: the proportion of red to white among the dry wines in the inventory is nearly seven to one. This must have been at the time the largest quantity of wine at one place in the whole of California; and was any one else then making a Grignolino?[17]

REPEAL, UP TO A POINT

By the end of the 1920s people had grown weary of Prohibition, now widely regarded as a failure. None of its promises had been fulfilled. The stock market crash of 1929 and the Great Depression that followed destroyed any economic claims it might make, and its moral claims had long been discredited. It threatened to make a nation of lawbreakers rather than a nation of clear-eyed, sober, productive citizens. The Dry

Herbert Hoover had defeated the Wet Al Smith in 1928, a year of prosperity, but by 1932 the scene had changed. The Democrats favored Repeal, and Roosevelt's landslide victory made the end of Prohibition certain. A Repeal amendment, the Twenty-First, was submitted to the states in early 1933 and by the end of the year it had been ratified. This was the first ever repeal of a constitutional amendment in American history.

The Repeal amendment was not passed in the way that the Prohibition amendment, the Eighteenth, had been. Prohibition was brought about by the votes of the state legislatures, and it was widely held that political cowardice was a powerful force affecting the politicians' votes on the question—the Anti-Saloon League, carrying a big stick, stood behind many of them. The Repeal amendment would be voted on by specially elected conventions; when enough conventions in favor of Repeal had been elected, the passage of Repeal was made certain, well before the actual ratification of the amendment, which took place on December 5, 1933.

The wine industry had begun to show stirrings of activity almost as soon as Roosevelt had been nominated in 1932; how the Demateis brothers responded to that signal has already been described. In 1933, the Prohibition Bureau (now officially called the Bureau of Industrial Alcohol), knowing that its end was near, began granting with a liberal hand licenses to make wine. Many winemakers whose wineries had lain dormant for the near-fourteen years of Prohibition now moved back into action, preparing for the day when wine would once again be a legal drink. Even more newcomers now sought and received licenses. In Los Angeles at least 32 new winemaking enterprises were licensed in 1933, in advance of the moment of Repeal at the end of the year. In the state at large the number of licensed wineries at the beginning of 1933 was 177; by the end of the year it was 380 and climbing, and in that year California produced some 20 million gallons of wine, even though Prohibition was still the law of the land. There was an eager rush to be ready when the new day dawned.

They had some frustrations in the meantime. Congress in 1933 was at last prepared to do what it had steadily refused to do in the preceding thirteen years—that is, to raise the limit on the alcoholic content of legal alcoholic drink from the one half of one percent set down in the Volstead Act. An act was passed allowing the sale of beer at 3.2 percent, and this went into operation in April 1933, to the accompaniment of celebrations that were said to have exceeded in enthusiasm even those that greeted the final extinction of Prohibition seven months later. The winemakers hoped they might get a relaxation of the rules such as the brewers had been given, and so they asked to make "light wines" of around 10 percent. Nothing doing. The proposal was seen as asking too much, or, as President Roosevelt wrote, "I am convinced that 10% is unconstitutional."[18] They could have the same concession as the brewers and make a 3.2 percent wine, although such a compound could not in seriousness be called wine. Nevertheless, a few winemakers, more or less shamefacedly, proceeded to make 3.2 percent "wine" under various names. When Repeal came at last this stuff disappeared from the market. At least one winemaker in Los Angeles actually made the ersatz for sale.[19]

Repeal, like Prohibition, brought about a very mixed and contradictory condition. The amendment had two parts. The first was quite clear: a statement that the Eighteenth Amendment was thereby repealed. The second part turned out to be deeply problematic. It read: "The transportation or importation into any State, Territory or possession of the United States for delivery or use therein of intoxicating liquors, in violation of the laws thereof, is hereby prohibited." In other words, states' rights were now supreme in the matter of liquor. And since the end of 1933 the fifty states have exercised their freedom by contriving a huge tangle of differing schemes of regulation and taxation applied to the traffic in spirits, wine, and beer, a tangle so dense that only a highly practiced lawyer can dare venture into it.

At the same time that the states were laying on their new regulatory schemes, a new federal authority with powers over the wine trade was created. This is now, after several name changes, called the Alcohol and Tobacco Tax and Trade Bureau, "TTB" for short, an agency belonging to the Department of the Treasury. Its main purpose is to guard the revenue, but in connection with that function it has acquired much authority in such matters as the legal definition of wines, the standards and

ANNOUNCING

THE

CLARETTE COMPANY'S

3.2% WINE BEVERAGE

"SPARKLING CLARETTE"

Made from Sonoma County's choicest dry Claret wine.
Packed 24 - 12 oz. bottles in the winery of

SCATENA BROS. WINE CO.

Healdsburg, California

for

THE CLARETTE COMPANY

Offices: HEALDSBURG and SANTA ROSA, CALIFORNIA

Prices Quoted to Distributors on Request

Ad for a "wine beverage" that, at 3.2 percent alcohol, was legal in 1933. From *California Grape Grower,* June 1933.

methods of winemaking, and the regulation of labeling and advertising. Wineries find it hard to comply with all the regulations since they are so complex. Labeling requirements are particularly troublesome: they are a contradictory mix of indulgent permissions (for instance, the use of "burgundy," etc., as wine names) and strict prohibitions, especially as regards anything remotely resembling a medical claim. Whether a Treasury agency should preside over such things is highly doubtful, but there it is. All of the agency's rules are written out in a document called "Wine. Code of Federal Regulations. Title 27. Part 24," which, in its current edition, runs to thirty-nine pages of close print.

The effects of the long years of Prohibition were not easily shaken off. The authorities were nervously anxious about guarding against a "return to the saloon," for the saloon, one remembers, had been the main object of attack in the run up to Prohibition, an attack led by the Anti-Saloon

League. President Roosevelt declared, "The policy of the government will be to see to it that the social and political evils of the pre-prohibition era shall not be revived nor permitted again to exist."[20] All sorts of regulations were enacted in state after state to ensure that the old "social and political evils" did not return, mainly by seeking to make liquor as unattractive as possible. Liquor stores were not allowed window displays; if women were allowed in drinking places, they could be served only when sitting down; liquor advertising was severely restricted; prices could not be given. In some places you couldn't get a drink at a bar, and in others no drinks were served in hotels, restaurants, or clubs. In Kentucky, a drink could not be more than two ounces; in Maine, restaurants could not sell spirits; in Michigan, taverns could sell only beer. The proliferation of such nuisance regulations went on endlessly.

California, mindful of its important wine industry, has kept things relatively simple in comparison to what other states have done. In California, wine may be sold by license-holders throughout the state; wine may be shipped direct from producer to consumer within the state; wine may be sold in grocery stores; wine is not taxed in a prohibitive way; and so on through a list of permissions regularly denied in other states.

The chaos of legislation following Repeal is the most troublesome and enduring of Prohibition's legacies. Another bad effect, although one that has by now been largely overcome, was the degradation of California's vineyards. Prohibition had seen the great expansion of vineyards in order to supply the demands of home winemakers, but the only consideration in that business was quantity, not quality. If the grower had any superior varieties, they were likely to be replaced by vines bearing large quantities of coarse grapes—the Alicante Bouschet was the great favorite. There was not much demand for white varieties among home winemakers, and what there was could be readily supplied by the Thompson Seedless grape, grown to be used as a fresh fruit, or for raisins, and, as an afterthought, for white wine as well. By the time Repeal was achieved, the Thompson Seedless, according to Charles Sullivan, was "by far California's most extensively planted grape variety," covering, as it did, some 200,000 acres.[21] Other white wine varieties had essentially disappeared, and it was long before any superior kinds were planted to any extent. In

1940, six years after Repeal, it was estimated ("on the high side") that there were only 50 to 100 acres of Chardonnay in the state.[22]

Other effects of Prohibition that had to be faced immediately were many: the ongoing tradition of winemaking had been broken, no adequate supply of practiced winemakers existed, and no coming generation had been trained. No research in viticulture or enology had been carried out in this country, and there had been no reason to pay any attention to what other countries might be doing. The material requirements of winemaking were either missing or decayed. Buildings were derelict; machinery rusted; vats and barrels dried out and falling apart.

Prohibition had also created a general suspicion of anyone engaged in the trade of alcoholic drink. It would be long before the idea of a winemaker could be separated from bootlegger, and that suspicion was not confined to the general public; it determined the official idea shared by the bureaucrats and legislators who had authority over the business.[23] In earlier years, the American government had eagerly helped to promote winegrowing in this country. Now just the reverse was true. And, worst of all, the American public knew nothing about wine apart from a few debased ideas acquired during Prohibition. Fortified wines, called by such names as port, sherry, and muscatel, were the main thing. For the next generation, the California wine trade obligingly supplied port, sherry, and muscatel and did little to change the situation, in which it simply followed the line of least resistance. Add to all these obstacles the fact that the nation, at the end of 1933, was sunk in the deepest economic depression in its history, and you have business conditions about as inauspicious as you could imagine.

9

DEPRESSION, WAR, AND AFTER

After Repeal, many ventured into the wine business, and, predictably, many failed.[1] Perhaps the worst reason to start a winery in those hard times was to make money. This truth was quickly discovered by the hopeful men who founded California Winery Inc., BW 3610, at 1711 N. Spring Street, Los Angeles, in 1934. They made 97,000 gallons of wine that year, went into receivership in March 1935, and quit business in May. Thomas Cowen, who held the license, was an unemployed salesman who, as an inspector put it, was "desirous of starting a winery as he feels that there is money to be made in the business." His winemaker, M. A. Berardini, is described as a rancher, laborer, and doer of odd jobs. Poor Cowen had borrowed $7,500 from a friend to get started, and instead of making money in the wine business lost whatever he had. Under Prohibition the California Winery's unsold wine would have been run down the drain—"destroyed"—but not now. It was bought by the big Mt. Tivy winery of Reedley, in the Central Valley, and no doubt disappeared into one of its blends. The fate of Cowen and the California Winery may stand for any number of like ventures into the renewed wine business by men who had no idea what they were getting into, apart from thinking that there was "money to be made in the business."

Another misguided effort at making money was the Franco-American Import Co., BW 3604, of 9628 Kalmia Street in Watts. The brothers Landier—hence the "Franco-American" identity—operated a bus service but thought they saw a way to profit from making carbonated sparkling wine. They called it "Marquis de la Fayette champagne" and made 10,000 gallons of it as early as 1933, one of the many vintages made in anticipation of Repeal. But that was their only vintage: in 1936, the wine was "disposed of" (how that was done is not said), and the Landiers discontinued the Franco-American Import Co. One hopes that they still had the bus business to fall back on.

Many other new ventures had only a brief life. Anthony's Winery, BW 3737, at 4328 Produce Plaza, was owned by Anthony Dinardo and managed by G. Dinardo. They had a small operation of 10,000 gallons storage capacity and made dry wines only. They began in January 1934, but lasted only a couple of years, after which Anthony's disappears from the record. The Gold Coast Wine Co., BW 3783, at 6428 Selma Avenue, started out in 1934 and disappeared in 1937. Fuscaldo Wines, BW 244, of 1574 E. Slauson Avenue, under president Dr. A. Sabato, was more ambitious. It made "wines of high alcoholic content, natural fermentation"—whatever they might be—on a substantial scale. In 1936 Fuscaldo planned to crush 3,500 tons of grapes to make 50,000 gallons of dry wine, 250,000 of "sweet" (fortified), and 20,000 of brandy. In the next year Fuscaldo was out of business. In its brief life it had the distinction of naming Franchot Tone, the movie actor, as its vice president. Whether Tone was serious about winemaking or simply wanted an investment I do not know. There does not appear to have been much connection then between Hollywood and Los Angeles wine, perhaps evidence of the low social prestige of the trade in those days.

Other ephemeral enterprises may be named from a long list. Kessler Brothers, of 823 S. Alameda Street, lasted only a couple of years, as did Mike King, of 2413 S. Walker Street in San Pedro; the Monte Cristo Vintage Co. of 1621 Atlantic Street, Los Angeles; the Orlando Winery, of 608B Alpine Street, Los Angeles; and Freda G. Poggi, of 24516 S. Vermont Avenue, Harbor City. Many others had a tenure of three or four years before expiring. There was a fearful mortality between 1935 and 1939. In 1935 there were ninety-seven wineries listed in Los Angeles County; in 1939, only thirty-five.[2] Two-thirds had gone under in the space of four years.

In these tough times some small enterprises did, after all, manage to survive, although none of them for a very long time. One of the longest lasting was Joe Vernaci, BW 3644, of 6012 Vineland Avenue, North Hollywood (in the San Fernando Valley). Joe had 14 acres of vines, including 8 acres of Zinfandel. He made his wine from the Zinfandel, some 3,000 or 4,000 thousand gallons a year, and sold the crop from the other varieties in his vineyard. The wine was sold at retail from Vernaci's store at the winery. I doubt that sales did much more than meet his expenses, but making a lot of money must not have been what he had in mind. Vernaci's sons Billy and Victor worked with him until after the war. When two other sons, Henry and Frank, came back from the war, they became partners with Joe in place of their brothers. The Vernacis continued to make wine until 1956, when, I suppose, the booming real estate market in the San Fernando Valley persuaded them to sell out.

An even longer tenure among the small producers was held by Matteo Brusso, BW 3789, on Thornton Avenue in Burbank, where he had 15 acres of vineyard. He operated through Prohibition down to 1967, at first making all types of wine but ultimately concentrating on dry table wine sold only at retail. His winery, of 6,000 gallons capacity, was, by today's standards, so small as to be nearly invisible.

It will have been noted that most of the names so far mentioned in the renewed winemaking of Los Angeles are Italian. That was overwhelmingly the case: Cuccia, Fanelli, Napolitano, Grangetto, Randisi, Guglielmo, Polito, Spirito, Ficarella—the list of names ending in vowels might go on at great length. As has already been shown, the names during the Spanish and Mexican eras of Los Angeles history were of course Spanish, and even before the American takeover the French had appeared, led by Vignes and the Sainsevains. After the conquest, a mixture prevailed: Yankee, German, Irish, French. Italian names appeared in rising volume from late in the nineteenth century down to Prohibition. Now, following Repeal, the Italians were everywhere, while the other communities seem to have lost interest. It is this post-Repeal development that has established the popular idea in America that winemaking has always been a proprietary province of the Italians. That is not so, but the mistake is easily understood. I have never

Wines of Old San Gabriel are sweet wines of tradition. Into them is woven the romance of California's vintage beginnings. Founded in 1888 by George Demateis, the organization has never ceased to be active. Grown in our own vineyards, the vintages of 1926 are still available for your distribution, rich in the bouquet and flavor which only a truly good wine can have. *From the wineries of Old San Gabriel shall come only the best.*

SAN GABRIEL VINEYARD COMPANY
San Gabriel   •   California

Wines of OLD SAN GABRIEL

Top: The San Gabriel Vineyard Co. (formerly the Italian-American Vineyard Co. of Los Angeles) made substantial quantities of wine under Prohibition. Some apparently stayed in condition long enough to be offered for sale upon Repeal. Here the wine of 1926 is "still available" eight years later. From *Wine Review*, April 1934. Bottom: Orange wine came on the market in 1936 but had only a brief vogue. From *Wine Review*, August 1937.

seen a persuasive explanation of the overwhelmingly Italian character of California winemaking immediately following Repeal. One suggestion is that the Italians then had an "in-between" social status: they were above untrained manual labor but not yet seen as eligible for professional standing. They could, however, have respectable, independent status as winemakers. Maybe so.[3]

There was some uncertainty about, and some variety in, the sorts of wine offered immediately after Repeal. It is interesting to note that some Prohibition wine was advertised—that is, wine that had been made during the Prohibition years but that could not have been sold then. Perhaps most of that wine was of doubtful character, being "pricked," or on its way to vinegar. But some was put out for sale. The San Gabriel Vineyard Co., early in 1934, offered "Old San Gabriel" wine from the vintage of 1926, "grown in our own vineyards."[4] Then there were novelty wines: carbonated "champagne" was one. Around 1936 there was a flurry of interest in orange wine, an alcoholic beverage fermented from oranges and then fortified with spirits distilled from the resulting "wine." This was made by several wineries—the Hendrickson Winery, the Wine-o'-Gold Winery ("naturally fermented citrus champagne"), and the big Pacific Wine Co., which was advertising orange wine down to the late 1930s, after which it is heard of no more.[5] I suppose that the attraction for the winemakers was a glut of oranges to be had cheaply, the sort of abundance in the midst of want that so often occurred in the Depression years.

Two wineries were devoted to making retsina. The George Alexakis Retsina Wine Co. operated from 1935 to 1946 at 659 S. Anderson Street. Nicholas Verry, at 526 West Garfield Avenue in Glendale, had a much bigger and enduring operation. Beginning in 1933, Verry built up his specialized winery to a capacity of 135,000 gallons of storage before moving, in 1943, to Parlier, in the Central Valley, where he, and his family after him, continued to operate into the 1990s, one of the few wineries in California producing only a single wine.[6] What the winery in Van Nuys with the unlikely name of "Old English" was making is hard to guess.

Among the more exotic of the new wineries was the oddly named Infanta Pomona, with downtown premises at 450 Broadway. The "Pomona" in the name alludes not to the city but to the Roman goddess of fruits, for the Infanta Pomona company had been founded in 1932 to make fruit products, including preserves, nectars, and cordials. The head of the enterprise was Constantine Lukis, formerly a government chemist and now an eager experimenter with wine. He had, according to an inspector's report, "crushed his grapes and fermented his wine in sealed hermetically 5-gallon bottles." Another inspector, after observing Lukis's methods, wrote excitedly: "I believe if experiments are successful they will revolutionize wine industry to the advantage of United States and California over foreign countries." Lukis was said to be building a winery at 1630 S. Essex Street in order to produce his revolutionary wines, but the promise was unfulfilled. He returned his license in April 1936, and no more is heard of the enterprise.

Another venture into the unorthodox was made by the Vesuvio Vintage Company, proprietor Mary Diliberto, at 1770 N. Main (premises earlier occupied by Peter Manuele, BW 196, one of the ephemeral wineries brought forth at Repeal). After trials with Zinfandel and Muscat wines, she turned to making honey wine and vermouth before going out of business.

A number of Los Angeles wineries in the '30s made wine only irregularly, business was so slow. One of these, the De Bartolo Winery, BW 1417 in Culver City, continued a winemaking business begun by Gioacchino De Bartolo in 1900. He had tried to continue under Prohibition, but, like so many others, made wine only to see it spoil as it lay in storage. Whether he lived to see Repeal I do not know. His daughter Mary revived the business in 1934, assisted by her daughters Mary and Frances and her son Frank. At first they were full of hopeful energy, installing "a pasteurizer, filter, new crusher and stemmer, and a continuous press, all part of a general expansion program."[7] The De Bartolos made a substantial quantity of wine, both dry and fortified, in 1935, 1936, and 1937. But after that they made no more wine, although they stayed in business until 1942, by which time their inventory of wine had dwindled nearly to a vanishing point. The war perhaps gave them a reason to quit.

Some wineries, although fully licensed, made no wine at all. Angelo Lispi, the owner of the Imperial Winery, BW 3575 of 1700 Gage Avenue, was one of the few who had, in the final months of Prohibition, made the so-called wine of 3.2 percent alcohol that was then permitted. When Repeal was achieved he of course dropped that line and began making real wine, mostly fortified. He had about 5,000 gallons on hand in 1936, but, as an inspector reported then, Lispi had "no intention to crush grapes and produce wine in the future." He had winemaking equipment, but he also had a bottling line, and there was not room enough at his winery to carry on winemaking and bottling together. Since he could buy wine cheaply and bottle it at a profit, he chose to be a bottler, although still officially the owner of a bonded winery. He made no wine after 1936 and got out of the business in 1942.

A variant of this scheme was provided by the Lombardi Winery, BW 3610 of 1711 N. Spring Street (an address formerly belonging to the unfortunate California Winery, as detailed above). Michael Lombardi, the president, held a bonded winery license; he had a winemaker, Frank Bartolone; and he had 160,000 gallons storage capacity. But he made no wine. Instead, he sold wine from the north-coast counties and from the Central Valley. He was, in fact, a wine wholesaler, as Angelo Lispi was a wine bottler. Lombardi continued in business on this basis until his operation was bought out by the New Jersey firm of Renault and Sons during the war. Renault was a producer of wine as well as a distributor of wines from other sources. It obviously wanted the Lombardi Winery for its inventory at a time when there was a scramble for supplies of wine under wartime conditions.

To end this sketch of the many wineries in and around Los Angeles that came and went after Repeal, there is the winery called, interestingly, Le Solitaire, BW 3904 at 15633 S. Western Avenue in Gardena. Originally, in 1935, it was called Emile Leydet's Winery, after the proprietor. The name was changed—who knows why?—in 1936. Leydet made only a modest quantity of wine: the inventory was 2,868 gallons of dry wine at the end of 1940, and 6,473 gallons of fortified wine. He did not bottle his wine but sold it directly from the barrel. On one occasion he was cautioned by the authorities that he must not move wine from the bonded storage room to his retail sales room by unpermitted methods; he had simplified the work by running a hose through the wall between storage room and shop to keep his retail barrel full. The guardians of the revenue were not amused. Leydet shut down the place in 1944, the building was demolished the following year, and now no material trace of Le Solitaire remains, no doubt the fate of most solitaires.

LARGE-SCALE WINEMAKING

Secondo Guasti's Italian Vineyard Company in Guasti, just over the Los Angeles County line, was, as we have seen, one of the biggest operations in the state under Prohibition. Guasti died in 1927, but the business continued to grow after Repeal. In the city of Los Angeles itself there were three big wineries, all of them founded before Prohibition and now put back to work. One of these was the California Mission Vintage Co., which, as has been noted, was sold by Louis Guerrieri to Antonio Moramarco in 1935, when it was already a sizeable operation, having a 385,000-gallon storage capacity. Despite the hard times in the 1930s, the California Mission Vintage Co. somehow managed to grow in those years: by 1940 it had reached a storage capacity of a million gallons. The winery had a brand for retail sales—"Old Mission" it was called— but the main business was in selling wine in bulk to such big producers as the Petri Winery in Escalon. In February 1942, the property at 330 N. Mission Road was condemned for a federal housing project, and Moramarco was compelled to move his wine—180,000 gallons of it at the time—across the street to 331 N. Mission Road, where the city had given him some property in compensation. The road had been closed by the construction on the housing project, so it was possible to run a hose across the street—a bonded hose, since it conveyed wine not yet tax-paid from a bonded premise—and the buildings, too, were moved one at a time across the road. The move was successful and business continued even under wartime conditions.

When Louis Guerrieri sold the California Mission Vintage Co. to Antonio Moramarco it was not in order to leave the wine business but

Wine from the biggest of the post-Repeal wineries in Los Angeles, which made wine into the 1950s. *From Wines and Vines Directory*, 1949.

to join his father at the Santa Fe Vintage Co., BW 55 at 1700 N. Spring Street. The elder Guerrieri had been superintendent and winemaker at Secondo Guasti's big Italian Vineyard Co. winery before Prohibition. In 1919 he bought the Santa Fe Winery at Santa Fe Springs, some ten miles south of downtown Los Angeles. Presumably he got it at distress prices, since Prohibition was about to descend. Guerrieri must then have been taking very long views. The winery did not operate during Prohibition, and no one could know how long Prohibition might last, so Guerrieri was holding an unprofitable investment in hopes for a change. Perhaps he bought only the name "Santa Fe," for when Repeal came the reactivated Santa Fe Winery, now called the Santa Fe Vintage Co., was relocated in central Los Angeles. Whether anything was salvaged from Santa Fe Springs I do not know.

The new business began in 1935, father and son running it together, and making it run indeed. The Santa Fe Vintage Co. quickly became the giant among Los Angeles wineries. The storage capacity at the outset was 260,000 gallons; this was raised to 550,000 gallons in 1938, and ten years later it was 1.25 million gallons. At the end of the winery's independent existence, in 1955, it had reached 2.5 million gallons, dwarfing anything else in the city.[8]

Production rose along with storage capacity. The Guerrieris owned 200 acres of vineyard at Mira Loma (the former Wineville, in Riverside County), but that could supply only a part of the winery's needs, which ran to thousands of tons. In 1938, for an early example, the Santa Fe Vintage Co. crushed more than 3,000 tons of grapes to make 75,000 gallons of dry wine, 275,000 gallons of fortified wine, and 10,000 gallons of brandy.

Unlike the California Mission Vintage Co., which depended on bulk sales, the Santa Fe Vintage Co. concentrated on selling bottled wines under its own labels. It also made Southern California its prime territory. This plan was so successful that in 1953 the Santa Fe Vintage Co. bought the Morello Winery at Kerman, near Fresno, in order to supply its growing needs. The Kerman winery added 2 million gallons of storage capacity and probably a greatly increased source of grapes as well. But other wineries were in expansive mode at this time, and the big Santa Fe Vintage Co. was swallowed up in 1955 by the even bigger Di Giorgio Wine Co., the property of the Di Giorgio Fruit Company in Kern County. When the Santa Fe Vintage Co. was added to its possessions, the Di Giorgio Wine Co.'s capacity stood at 9.5 million gallons. The new ownership ended the Santa Fe Vintage Co.'s life as a producing winery, and by 1958 it had been converted into a bonded wine cellar, in effect a warehouse for the storage and distribution of wine, not for its manufacture.

The third of the big downtown wineries was the Pacific Wine Co., BW 1318 at 218 North Avenue 19. Its history went back to around 1889, when the founder, Giovanni Piuma, planted a vineyard at El Monte and then, in 1902, built a winery on North Avenue 19 that he named the El

Monte. He lived in apartments above the winery with his family, and so the sons who succeeded him after Repeal may be said to have grown up in a winery. Piuma, who was born near Genoa in 1864, came to Los Angeles in 1884 and became, in time, a man of high consideration in the Italian community—"a brilliant industrialist and merchant," in one description.[9] He served as Italian consul in Los Angeles from 1911 to 1921. His winery was closed by Prohibition and reopened in 1933 as the Piuma Winery, a named soon changed to the Pacific Wine Co.

Giovanni Piuma was still identified as head of the company then, but I do not think he was very active in it. An item in the *Wine Review* in November 1937 reports that Piuma was returning from Italy that month: "Mr. Piuma has been in Italy for more than a year, and has made 28 trips across the Atlantic."[10] That would not seem to leave much time for work back in Los Angeles, where Piuma's two sons, Frank and Joseph, were running the business, with Frank as president.

The winemaker there had the fine Italian name of Attilio Boffa, and the business was in expansionist mode. New storage tanks, new refrigeration equipment, and a new still were added in 1934, and new cooperage added in 1935 raised the storage capacity to 400,000 gallons, and then to 450,000 gallons in 1937, and to 650,000 gallons in 1940. The company put up new buildings in 1937 to accommodate its increased capacity and announced that it would now make all of the wine that it sold instead of buying from others as it had been doing.[11]

Fortified wines dominated the winemaking at Pacific Wines, but dry wines were also made in substantial quantity: in 1935, the plan was for 150,000 gallons of fortified wine, 100,000 dry; in 1936, 175,000 fortified, 150,000 dry; and in 1938, 100,000 of each.[12] These wines went to market under the bad old system of borrowed names, as did almost all of the wine then produced in California—the exceptions were very few. Much California wine went to market as Haut Sauterne, or Chianti, or Moselle, or even as St. Julien, Margaux, or Pontet Canet. The Pacific Wine Co. offered to the public a "Chateau Yquem," which won a prize at the Los Angeles County Fair in 1936. In the next year they were told by the authorities that they could no longer use that name, so the wine went to market simply as "Chateau."[13]

A 1937 ad for the Burbank Winery, which also had a distillery at Selma, in the Central Valley. The line about "Cognac and Grape Brandy" is evidence of the careless freedom in naming allowed during this era. From *Wine Review,* August 1937.

The Pacific Wine Co. continued a steady production though the 1940s of large quantities of wine: a high of 498,000 gallons in 1942, a low of 236,000 in 1947. But it did not long survive the postwar years and by 1953 was out of business.[14]

The biggest winery outside the city was the Burbank Winery. This went back to 1896, when Irishman John McClure planted a 300-acre vineyard north of Burbank of Mataro, Grenache, Zinfandel, and Burger grapes. In 1905 he built a substantial winery of 700,000 gallons capacity to process his grapes, calling it the Sunnyside Winery. It is said that in McClure's time the winemaking was in charge of a Chinese winemaker.[15] Sunnyside did not operate during Prohibition but reopened in 1933 as the Burbank Winery (BW 194), still the property of the McClure family. The company had 400 acres of vineyard, although most of those acres were now in the Cucamonga district rather than around Burbank, and by 1935 the winery had a capacity of 850,000 gallons. Two years later this had leaped to 1.8 million gallons, mostly of fortified wines. One of the brands was "Sunnyside," after the original name of the winery. Another was "San Marino," although whether there was much demand for the wine in that exclusive community may be doubted.

In 1943, when supplies of wine were being eagerly sought by bottlers and wholesalers from all over the country, the Burbank Winery was bought from the McClure family by the Eastern Wine Company, the biggest New York City wine bottler, selling wine under the Chateau Martin label in eastern markets. What Eastern wanted was the Burbank inventory, at the time of the sale reported as 188,603 gallons of dry wine and 857,000 gallons of fortified wine. Having possessed themselves of these more than a million gallons, the Eastern people then leased (and ultimately sold) the winery back to John C. Randisi, who had been the general manager of the Burbank Winery under the McClures.

Randisi operated the winery under the same BW number as before (194), together with the token 10 acres of Burbank vineyard that remained from John McClure's original 300, but the winery was now called, after its owner, the Randisi Winery. In 1948, when the city of Burbank incorporated what had been rural territory, "Mr. Randisi, a very shrewd and competent businessman, sold the 10 acres for lots and the winery for a warehouse."[16]

The San Gabriel Vinyard Co.—renamed from the Italian-American Vineyard Co. that once belonged to the Demateis family—has already been described as an instance of the early revival of winemaking during the terminal agonies of Prohibition. Its "Old San Gabriel" wines, fortified only, were mostly sold in the East.

The combined storage capacity of the five wineries described here—California Mission Vintage Co., Santa Fe Vintage Co., Pacific Wine Co., Burbank Winery, and San Gabriel Vineyard Co.—was 5.2 million gallons, only a fraction of California's capacity, but hardly a negligible quantity. Wine from Los Angeles was still an important element in the market. Most of the wine was fortified, and all of it of standard quality only, but that was the case almost everywhere in California. A crucial difference between the southern and northern sections of the trade was that the north had a few big wineries, such as the Italian Swiss Colony, making decent table wine, plus a few smaller wineries devoted to making table wines of high quality—among them Inglenook, Beaulieu, Larkmead, and Louis Martini—but the south did not, and could not have, given the irresistible transformation of Los Angeles, city and county.

The Italian element stubbornly refused to give up on dry table wines. There had been a large acreage of Zinfandel in the south before Prohibition, and much of this remained, since Zinfandel was one of the popular varieties for home winemaking. Other red wine varieties in the southern vineyard included smaller quantities of Mataro, Barbera, Grenache, Grignolino, Alicante Bouschet, and, of course, the apparently ineradicable Mission. Some small wineries—all Italian—made dry wine exclusively: Anthony's, Delellis, Sorrento, Sunland (the Giobinazzo family), Vernacci, and Ardizzone. And most of the bigger wineries made substantial quantities of dry wine: Pacific Wine Co. (Piuma family), the Santa Fe Vintage Co. (Guerrieri family), the San Gabriel Vineyard Co. (Demateis family).

Since the Los Angeles winemakers had conceded the superiority in dry table wines to the north coast at least as early as the 1870s, one wonders whether the production of an attractive dry wine was ever a possibility in Los Angeles. I think the answer is certainly yes, although it seems to have happened only by way of exception. There are a host of "ifs" to consider. If Pierce's disease had not devastated the vineyards and so destroyed confidence in the future of viticulture; if the coming of the railroad from the east had not ended the isolation of Los Angeles and released a flood of immigrants into what had been a quiet agricultural region; if severely depressed economic conditions had not coincided with the attack of Pierce's disease and with a mass immigration to further impede and disrupt the winemaking business; if Prohibition had not cut off all orderly development so that better varieties and better methods might have been introduced into winemaking practice; if all of these things had not happened, then the fate of wine in general and of dry wine in particular in Los Angeles might have been different.

With the modern understanding of varietal character and of viticultural practice, with modern equipment, and with scientific understanding of winemaking procedures, there is no doubt that Los Angeles could produce excellent dry wines. The county abounded in favorable sites, largely built over now; the climate, as was clearly recognized in the nineteenth century, is highly favorable to grape growing. One can imagine the San Gabriel Valley and its foothills as one vast vineyard, the source of a variety of sought-after dry wines. But the bright prospects were cut off and the region ran out of time. When winegrowing was restored in 1934, all the conditions were hostile: unimproved vineyards, unchecked urbanization, uninstructed winemakers, undercapitalized wineries, unresponsive markets—one could go on. Los Angeles winemaking, although it was carried on in substantial volume in the years immediately following Repeal, was living on borrowed time.

After Repeal, Los Angeles did not recover whatever leadership among California's winemakers that it had had before Prohibition. The wines from Los Angeles do not appear in the judgings at the state fair, nor are there Los Angeles winemakers among the judges.[17] The trade journals pay little attention to Los Angeles, and no spokesman there gives them anything to report. There was a lot of wine made there, but city and county had no public identity as wine country. In 1941 the WPA Federal

Photograph published with the caption "Wine Experts Taste and Classify California Vintages," in Los Angeles in the 1930s: from *The WPA Guide to the City of Angels*, originally published in 1941. The scene used to illustrate wine in Los Angeles is actually of the Inglenook Winery in St. Helena, Napa Valley; the gentleman standing with a glass of wine is Carl Bundschu, manager of the winery in the 1930s. Nothing in the picture has anything to do with Los Angeles—but who knew or cared? Courtesy of the Wine Institute.

Writers' Project published its guide to Los Angeles, describing the city as it was in the 1930s.[18] The wine industry figures in this as one of the minor tourist attractions, listed along with the tuna industry and walnut packing. Fair enough; Hollywood and oranges certainly took up more of the public mind than wine, which was still, at that time, anything but a glamorous subject. The guide prints a photograph of "wine storage vats" and a carefully composed but unidentified photo captioned "Wine Experts Taste and Classify California Vintages." They of course did no such thing in Los Angeles, where vintage-dating was unknown and where, as the Wine Advisory Board was then assuring the public about California, every year was a vintage year.

The photo of "wine experts" shows four gentlemen sniffing at grotesquely oversized German *Römer*s in a room such as one might find in a *Weinstube*; the picture is uncredited, but it does not originate from Los Angeles—it comes from Napa.[19] It does, however, illustrate the very limited notions about wine that would satisfy the American public at the time—wine vats, and experts sniffing at comic glasses satisfy quite uninstructed expectations. Apart from the photographs, the only other attention given to winemaking in the WPA guide, which is otherwise a thorough and very well informed piece of work, is an outline of winemaking procedure, particularly as it was carried on at the Italian Vineyard Company at Guasti, in San Bernardino County! *Not one word* is said about the active winemaking in Los Angeles, so little had the many wineries still operating in and around Los Angeles imposed themselves. That was not a good sign for the future.

WAR AND POSTWAR

Roosevelt's New Deal struggled in vain to drag America out of the Great Depression. Then the war galvanized all the West Coast cities, Los Angeles prominent among them. As a great port and a great center of manufacturing, the city grew explosively. The aircraft industry, including Douglas, Lockheed, Consolidated, Hughes, and Northrop, reached monster size, employing 220,000 people in Los Angeles by 1943. The navy took over the Port of Los Angeles, where more than a thousand ships were built during the war. At the same time that these industrial feats were being performed, the long-declining agriculture of Los Angeles County was brought back to energetic life. In 1942, a peak year, 318,000 acres were farmed in the county.[20] Comparable developments were scattered all over California.

The wine industry in the state was affected, of course, but not in a crippling way, and some of the changes brought about by the war had quite positive effects. The labor pool was reduced, and materials were in short supply, but that was true for any enterprise not making war materials. The biggest change immediately affecting the wine business was through an order from the government that the entire crop of Thompson Seedless, Sultana, and Muscat grapes be made into raisins, effectively diverting them from the wineries. Since these varieties had made up 44 percent of the entire grape crush in 1941, mostly going into fortified wines, their loss meant a precipitous drop in wine production in 1942; California produced only 54 million gallons in that year. But some people saw this development as a hopeful sign. If the California wineries learned to do without raisin and table grapes but turned to true wine varieties instead, the result would be a dramatic improvement in wine quality. This was probably not a popular view, although it was certainly the right one.

At the same time that production was falling, demand was sharply rising: an all-time high of 92 million gallons were sold in 1942. Inventories of wine quickly dwindled under these conditions, but good harvests in 1943 and 1944 meant that production recovered: 80 million gallons in 1943, and 90 million gallons in 1944. To produce this wine, now that the supply of raisin grapes was cut off, the California wineries desperately sought every available grape, with the result that grape prices zoomed.

In hopes to keep down inflation, Congress had created the Office of Price Administration (OPA) early in 1942, and this agency had set the ceiling on the price of wine at the level of the highest price prevailing in March 1942. Since the highest prices had been paid for bottled wine rather than anonymous bulk wine, here was a powerful argument for bottling wines. Another argument was that the tank cars used to ship bulk wine to the East were now in short supply, many of them having been converted to carrying war materiel. Bottled wine, or case goods, as they were called, could find ready transport in boxcars being returned empty from the West Coast. The winemakers, naturally, scrambled to get bottling equipment and enter what had, until then, been a very minor part of the business. That was another of the good effects of the war from the point of view of the wine trade. Once started on bottling its own wines, no winery wanted to go back to the old system, which had put them at the mercy of regional bottlers and had done nothing to help them to develop an identity or to encourage the planting of better varieties or to improve the methods of winemaking. This change, according to a retrospective in *Wines and Vines*, was "the major development in the industry during the war."[21] Incidentally, it was at this time that the quart bottle was replaced by the smaller fifth-of-a-gallon bottle as the standard wine bottle size. I do not know that this had anything to do with the war. Consumers resented it, but the wine industry seems to have made no protest.

A change that created more excitement than the prosaic struggle with supplies and prices was the sudden entry of the country's biggest distillers into the California wine business. Historically, the distillers had had no interest in the winemakers. That suddenly changed when the government directed that all whiskey production would cease on November 1, 1942, and the distilling capacity of the whiskey firms be devoted to producing industrial alcohol. That was a profitable activity for the distillers, but they worried that without anything to sell to their retail trade their lines of distribution would dry up. Since wine was still being made, owning a winery now seemed a good idea. The Big Four distillers—Schenley, National Distillers, Seagram's, and Hiram Walker—now, with Schenley in the lead, began buying big wineries at a fast pace. Schenley bought Cresta Blanca, Elk Grove, Roma, Louis Martini's Kingsburg winery, and the Greystone Winery, all in 1942. National Distillers bought the Italian Swiss Colony; Seagram's the Mt. Tivy winery and Paul Masson; and Hiram Walker the Valliant and R. Martini wineries. By early 1943 the distillers were the biggest players in the California wine game. Some of the major wine bottlers, fearing that the distillers might shut them out from their sources, began buying wineries too, although never on the distillers' scale.

The winemakers were of course keenly suspicious of the distillers but need not have worried. After the war the distillers got out of the wine business rather quickly, and during the war they, too, produced some good effects. They had money, and used it to promote wine as no one in California had yet done, by print, outdoor, and radio advertising. Americans, even in those many regions essentially unacquainted with wine, now had wine thrust upon them. Presumably this had some effect, although the wine in question was mostly the usual sweet, fortified standard wine that had dominated the market since Repeal. If anyone had thoughts of changing that situation, the war years were not the time to try it.

The wineries in Los Angeles County operated under the conditions just described, and as was true elsewhere in the state, some did not survive. By my count thirteen wineries in Los Angeles and Los Angeles County went out of business between 1941 and 1946. That was certainly the biggest disturbance of the trade. How many such losses were the immediate effect of the war, who can say? I know of only one for certain. The Briano Winery (BW 13), south of El Monte, was an almost comically typical small Italian winemaking enterprise. Paolo Briano, the father, had been making wine from his 30 acres of Zinfandel since 1898, although he had had to stop during Prohibition and earn his living from a small farm. He died shortly after renewing his license in 1933; he was, as one of his character references put it in Paolo's application for that license, a "high-class Italian."

His wife, Maria, then took over, with her son, Paul Jr., who left his job as a pharmacist to be manager and winemaker. They produced red wine and a little white, both dry and fortified, in a winery of 35,000 gallons storage capacity. In a good year they might get 12,000 gallons from their vineyard; in a bad one, only half that. They may have sold a little wine in bulk, but the main reliance was the retail store adjoining the winery. Then, like the people at the Imperial Winery in Los Angeles, they found that it was cheaper to buy wine and resell it than to make it themselves. So in the years from 1938 through 1942 no wine was made. Early in January 1943 the winery was closed. In returning her winemaker's license to the Bureau of Alcohol, Tobacco, and Firearms (BATF), Maria Briano explained: "My son, Paul Briano, Jr., will be called to the Army in February and it will be impossible for me to continue operations without him."[22] That story must have been repeated at least a few times among the small wineries of Los Angeles.

There were also some purchases of wineries. Burbank, as we have seen, went to the Eastern Wine Company, the California Mission Vintage Co. to Chicago distillers, and the Lombardi Winery to Renault. But none of these new owners stayed very long. When wartime conditions were lifted, what was left of the Los Angeles winemaking establishment went back to what it had been doing before, with very little observable change. There was, however, a swirling, exciting set of changes going on all around them—changes whose effects could not be avoided.

California before the war had been an underpopulated state; in 1940 there were only 6,907,000 people living on its 158,693 square miles, meaning fewer than 45 people per square mile of territory. During the war, countless newcomers—soldiers, sailors, war workers and their families—got their first glimpse of California. A great many of them, tens of thousands from all over the country, either stayed or returned to the state as soon as they could. The resulting population boom was not just a boom, it was an explosion, especially in and around Los Angeles. In 1950 the population of the state had zoomed to 10,586,223; by 1960 the number was 15,717,000, more than twice as many people as had been in the state only twenty years before. More than half of this growth had occurred in Southern California.

To accommodate the new thousands, vast acreages of agricultural land were paved over or built upon—for the growth was not so much urban as it was suburban. Los Angeles, already regarded as the most centrifugal of cities, where everything moves away from the center, became ever more sprawling. The city of Los Angeles had a population of 1,504,277 in 1940; in 1960 it was 2,481,595, not yet doubled. But the county grew from 2,785,643 in 1940 to 6,038,771 in 1960, more than doubling.

Such growth was, of course, fatal to agriculture. The most conspicuous loss was the orange groves, for vineyards had already been in retreat for many years. Now the landscape was dominated by housing tracts, shopping malls, warehouses, commercial buildings of all kinds. Freeways cleared new paths for further development, which swallowed up more and more land. By the 1960s one could drive from central Los Angeles to the eastern border of the county at Pomona, forty miles away, and not see an acre of plowed ground along the way. The polluted air, trapped between the mountains that ring the Los Angeles Basin and heated by the California sun, became a choking smog, threatening to plants and humans alike.

The smog has now been more or less controlled; development continues, but not quite so destructively; public transport, once almost annihilated by the freeways, is making a comeback. But the oranges and

The current seal of Los Angeles.

the grapes are gone. Their memory is embodied in the oranges and grapes that form minor ornaments on the official seal of the city of Los Angeles. In the popular imagination, oranges were the signature fruit of Southern California. But the orange was in fact a substitute crop, distinctly secondary to the grape until the misfortunes of the 1880s destroyed confidence in viticulture. As the original seal of the city made plain, Los Angeles was a place to grow grapes and make wine.

The current seal is very different but historically correct. The quarterings of the seal are flanked on the left by an olive branch and on the right by some oranges; at the top, signifying its primacy, is a small bunch of grapes. And that is the way it was in Los Angeles.

CODA

Winegrowing of some sort and on some scale will probably never die in Los Angeles, given the climate and the topography. Backyard growers, hobbyists and curious amateurs, and wealthy wine lovers will always want to give it a try, and so a good many do today. The scale, however, remains small. Los Angeles County had 212 acres of bearing vines and 12 acres of nonbearing—that is, newly planted—vines in 2015, not a significant contribution to the total of almost 500,000 acres of wine grapes grown in California in that year.[23] But the people concerned continue to keep the interest alive. They are currently concentrated in the Santa Monica Mountains that parallel the Malibu coast, the city's nearest relatively undeveloped land.

There has, in fact, been so much activity in and around Malibu as to provoke hostile reaction. A ban on new vineyards and on the expansion of existing vineyards in a large area of the coastal mountains was established by a new coastal plan approved in 2014. In a region to the north of the coastal zone new vineyards are limited to 2 acres, a compromise arrived at with the many people who wanted a complete ban.[24] But there is continued pressure to allow new plantings. Other urban vineyards are planned or planted from time to time in Los Angeles and always generate conflict.

By far the largest vineyard in the county—65 acres—is on the Saddlerock Ranch of the Semler family in the Malibu region. They operate as Malibu Family Wines. At the other extreme there are backyard vineyards of a half acre or less. In the isolated region of Agua Dulce, on the road to Palmdale, the Reyes Vineyard of 16 acres was planted in 2004 and bonded in 2009 by Robert Reyes, a native of the Dominican Republic. The two unquestioned stars of contemporary Los Angeles winemaking were, until recently, George Rosenthal of the Rosenthal Winery, cultivating 30 acres in Malibu, and Tom Jones of the Moraga Vineyards on 16 acres, not in the relative wilds of Malibu but in the fully-developed and exclusive residential neighborhood of Bel Air. Jones first planted vines on his property in 1978; Rosenthal in 1987. In

2005 Jones licensed a winemaking facility at Moraga and so became the first integrated producer in the region.[25] Most of the others depend on so-called custom crushing to make their wines; there are convenient facilities in nearby Ventura County or, farther away, in Santa Barbara County. The very small growers cannot justify the capital expense of a fully-equipped winery; those who can afford one don't really need one.

Both the Jones and the Rosenthal estates were put up for sale in 2013, by which time their owners were well past the age of retirement. Moraga went to newspaper mogul Rupert Murdoch for nearly $30 million; Jones died a few months later. Rosenthal's estate, a much bigger property, is still on the market at the time of this writing for $59.5 million. If, in new hands, these properties should drop out of the wine game, the region will lose a lot of glamour—but the game will go on.

APPENDIX 1

The Native Vine of California

There are two related species of grape vine in the state: *Vitis califor-nica*, growing along streams in Central and Northern California, and *Vitis girdiana*, the desert grape, growing in Southern California. No dis-tinction of species appears to be made in the various early references to the "native vine" or the "native grape" that I have seen. But T. V. Munson (*Foundations of American Grape Culture*, 1909) is quite emphatic about it: the two species, he writes, are "widely separated."[1] *V. californica* belongs to the northern half of the state, where it produces fruit that is "very sugary and pleasantly flavored" but is of a "skinny, seedy nature."[2] U. P. Hedrick, in the monumental *Grapes of New York* (1908), agrees with Munson about the habitat of *V. californica*: it belongs to the northern half of the state. Its fruit he describes as "pleasant" but "too small to be of cultural value."[3]

V. girdiana, named by Munson for a Mr. Gird of Fallbrook, California, from whom Munson had his first specimens of the grape, is described as producing fruit that, when compared to the fruit of *V. californica*, is found to be "deficient in sugar, tartaric acid and tannin," although when very ripe "it is agreeably sweet."[4] Both *californica* and *girdiana* are found hybridized with *vinifera*; the fruit from such an accidental hybrid can, according to Munson, produce "quite a good grape," a fact that may help to explain some of the statements included in this note.[5]

Munson and Hedrick agree in holding that both *V. californica* and *V. girdiana* are without resistance to phylloxera. Hedrick says that *californica*, native to a region without phylloxera until it was introduced by American settlement, has less resistance than any other American species.[6]

As for the winemaking value of the native vine, there is some disagreement. A. J. Winkler, in his authoritative *General Viticulture* (1962), says simply that the "wild vine" the Spanish colonists found in Southern California "was itself of no value," although it was valuable as indicating the possibility of grape growing there.[7] In their *Winemaking in California* (1983), Ruth Teiser and Catherine Harroun write, "From time to time…the padres tried to make palatable wine from the fruit of these temptingly prolific vines, but always they found their effort unrewarding."[8] The authors don't say the wine was undrinkable, but evidently the Franciscans gave up on the native vine. I know of no record of wine made at any of the missions from native grapes. E. W. Hilgard, the distinguished dean of the College of Agriculture at the University of California, writing in the 1878 yearbook of the Department of Agriculture, calls the fruit of *V. californica* "somewhat acid and unpalatable."[9]

Yet there is evidence that something could be done with California's native grapes. Alexander Forbes, in his *California: A History of Upper and Lower California* (1839), wrote that brandy was being produced from native grapes in 1835.[10] Forbes had not yet been in California at the time he published his book, but as a British merchant in Mexico he had access to current information about Alta California, and his account of things there is accepted as generally reliable. In 1840, Captain John Sutter, in his fort at New Helvetia (now Sacramento), had plans "for the manufacture of brandy from the wild grapes which grew in great abundance in the region of New Helvetia,"[11] and he apparently did produce it in commercial quantity.[12] The attractions of the grape as they appeared to the surveyors of the *Pacific Railroad Report* in the Tejon Valley of California are thus described:

> The borders of the creek were overgrown in many places
> by thick masses of grape vines, loaded with long and heavy
> clusters of fruit. This grape is deserving of attention, as it
> is probable that it will be found an exceedingly valuable

variety for the manufacture of wine. The berry is small and round, and much resembles the ordinary Frost grape of New England, but it is larger, more juicy, and rich in flavor, and also has a high color, yielding a juice of rich claret color.[13]

Hubert Howe Bancroft has little to say about the native grape apart from one noncommittal note: "There are some traditions of wild grapes found in the country near San Antonio, and improved by cultivation."[14] "Cultivation" by itself does nothing to improve a grape variety, but the statement may at least indicate that some people, somewhere, made an effort to use the native grape.

There are some surprisingly enthusiastic statements about the wine of the native vine. Matthew Keller, in his account of California wine for the U.S. Patent Office report for 1858, distinguishes three different species of wild vine, two of which are useless. (There must have been much confusion in the classification of the native grape.) The third, according to "old Californians," makes an "excellent" wine, "resembling in flavor, color, and aroma, the clarets of Bordeaux. It is replete with coloring matter, and I have no doubt that, if properly tested, it will prove an invaluable acquisition to the State."[15] It is not clear from Keller's remarks that he had in fact drunk any of this wine, but he was at least prepared to believe in its possibility.

More positive, although still not quite direct evidence, is a statement in "Culture of the Grape Vine in California," a report in 1861 of the Special Committee on the subject in the state legislature:

> We have been informed...that there is now growing a wild grape in the County of Los Angeles, near the San Gabriel River, of surpassing excellence for wine purposes, and that it is gathered extensively by the wine-makers in the neighborhood to give flavor and value to the wine from the common Mission grape, the only species found in their vineyards. At the annual exhibition of the California State Agricultural Society in 1858 there was exhibited a wine, made near Marysville, from the native California grape, growing on the banks of the Feather River, which its exhibitor called the California Frost Grape. It was pronounced by the Committee

> on Wines to be very fine. We must not…neglect the search
> and domestication of such of the wild grapes of California,
> as a beneficent Providence has given us.[16]

It is quite likely that winemakers in the Los Angeles region did add wine from *V. californica* to their Mission wines, since the one has excellent color while the other has inadequate and unstable color.

Even more surprising, and evidently based on direct experience, is the following statement in a letter of 1873 from J. DeBarth Shorb, then managing the Lake Vineyard in the San Gabriel Valley, to Benjamin D. Wilson, Shorb's father-in-law and partner:

> Have made a pipe of wild grape wine which promises to
> be very fine—to my astonishment I found the must to con-
> tain 21 per cent sugar though not dead ripe—my opinion is
> that we have in this neglected grape of the country, the very
> best variety under cultivation and care for making the long-
> sought-for fine claret.[17]

Nothing more is heard about this wine. But in 1882 a "rich and tannic" wine from *V. californica* was exhibited and praised at a meeting of the St. Helena Vinicultural Club.[18] And in 1883 a Mr. Mattier of Harbin Springs in Lake County is reported as making a wine from *V. californica*; it was said to have 11.5 degrees of alcohol and a deep red color and to have been approved by the experts at the university.[19] Presumably Dean Hilgard was among those "experts" at Berkeley. Mattier had evidently been experimenting with *V. californica* for some time. In the *First Annual Report* of the Board of State Viticultural Commissioners (1881), Charles Wetmore, the chief executive officer of the Board, reported on his studies of the native grape in California and named Mattier, who was then making wine from the native vine at his "little Hermitage near Harbin's Springs," as a source of useful information.[20] Mattier was planting *V. californica* from seeds, hoping to find useful qualities in the seedlings. Wetmore himself recommended such experimental planting of seeds for the same purpose; he was also convinced that the native vine was resistant to phylloxera (it isn't), and that when used as a rootstock, it powerfully invigorated the grafted scion (it does).[21]

Wetmore also reports on the results of the chemical analysis of wines made from *V. californica* and from *V. arizonica* (native to the high regions of Arizona) made by the eminent enologist Frederico Pohndorff. Pohndorff was cautiously optimistic about the possibilities of *arizonica* and fairly enthusiastic about *californica*: the latter, he wrote, "can and ought to be used for wine purposes," especially for its deep color, its adequate alcohol, and its resistance to phylloxera.[22]

I am not aware that any wine is currently made from the native grapes, although there are still plenty of wild vines in California. Charles Sullivan's modern experience is interesting:

> I once made wine from [*V. californica* grapes] that grow along Guadalupe Creek in Los Gatos. For a day or two after fermentation the wine was fruity and drinkable. A week later it had a foul flavor, even though it was chemically sound. What must its distillate have tasted like? It is not surprising that this early fire-water was used mostly to pay Indian workers.[23]

In his *Companion to California Wine* (1998), Sullivan dismisses *V. californica* in a single sentence: "Its fruit is useless for making wine." But would someone like to give it another try?

APPENDIX 2

Street and Place Names in Los Angeles, City, and County,
Commemorating the Wine Industry

In central Los Angeles today there are four Grape Streets, one Grape
Place, a Vineyard Avenue, a Vineyard Drive, and two Vinevale Ave-
nues. Some of these may be developers' names, but some at least may
remember an earlier condition of things. More particular names appear
in the following lists, which do not pretend to be complete.

CITY OF LOS ANGELES

Aliso Street: After the great sycamore tree marking the site of Jean
Louis Vignes's El Aliso winery (1831).

Avila Street: After Januario Avila, who had a vineyard before 1831.

Bauchet Street: After Louis Bauchet, the first French vineyardist and
winemaker (1828) in Los Angeles, at the site of his property.

Beaudry Avenue: After Prudent Beaudry, who came to Los Angeles in
1851 and developed a vineyard and winery on Boyle Heights.

Boyle Avenue, Boyle Heights: After Andrew Boyle, winemaker from
1862 at the Paredon Blanco (White Cliff) winery.

Childs Way: On the campus of the University of Southern California,
of which Ozro Childs, nurseryman and winemaker, was one of
the founders. He came to Los Angeles in 1850. A Childs Avenue
(Newmark, *Sixty Years in Southern California*, 69) no longer exists.

Dalton Avenue: No longer extant; named for George Dalton, who
grew grapes and made wine on his property east of Central on

Washington. Dalton Avenue in Azusa is named for his brother Henry.

Hoover Street: After Dr. Leonce Hoover (originally Huber), a Swiss immigrant who came to Los Angeles in 1849 and produced wine commercially from his vineyard south of town.

Keller Street: After Matthew Keller, a prominent winegrower since the early 1850s, whose original property is now the site of Union Station. Keller Street, on what was once the vineyard, is now a stub running between the river and the Piper Technical Center.

Kohler Street: Marking the site of Kohler and Frohling's Pioneer Winery (1854). Charles Kohler was the first to distribute his California wines all over the country.

Mateo Street: After Matthew (Don Mateo) Keller (see also Keller Street), and marking the site of the property he called the Rising Sun Vineyard.

Mesnager Street: After Georges Le Mésnager, who built L'Hermitage winery and distillery on North Main Street in 1874. He also owned a large vineyard at La Crescenta. The winery property had formerly been that of Louis Wilhardt (see Wilhardt Street).

Moran's Lane: No longer extant; described by Newmark (*Sixty Years in Southern California*, 662n) as "east of Main Street." John Moran's winery and vineyard were on San Pedro Street near Ninth.

Naud Street: After French merchant Emile Naud, who lived in Los Angeles from 1856 and dealt in various commodities, including wine. He also owned a 20-acre vineyard. Naud Street runs between both Mesnager and Wilhardt Streets, and so connects three of the early winemaking names of the city.

Ogier Street: No longer extant; named for Isaac Ogier, a lawyer and a judge, who came to Los Angeles in 1851 and owned a vineyard between San Pedro and Main Streets and Fourth and Fifth Streets, a region dense with vineyards.

Requena Street: No longer extant; named for Manuel Requena, a highly regarded winemaker. Requena Street bounded his vineyard on the south along the east side of Los Angeles Street.

Sainsevain Street: Now called Commercial Street; named Jean-Louis

Sainsevain, who, with his brother Pierre, continued the winery founded by his uncle, Jean Louis Vignes (see Vignes Street). The street runs across what would have been the northern end of the Vignes vineyard.

Vignes Street: After Jean Louis Vignes, developer of the first big commercial winery in Los Angeles (1831). The street, cut off at the south end by Highway 101, runs to the north from what were the Vignes vineyard and winery.

Vine Street: Called Olvera Street since 1877. A number of wineries clustered on or around it. Some writers identify it as Wine Street, but "Calle de las Vignas" appears to be the correct name.

Weyse Street: Paralleling Naud Street across from the Los Angeles State Historic Park. Julius Weyse was a partner of Emile Naud and had a vineyard planted in 1856 on Eighth Street near San Pedro Street that he called "Fernheim." Weyse was a politcal exile from Germany.

Wilhardt Street: Louis Wilhardt had a vineyard and made wine as early as 1848 at his place on Main Street north of the plaza.

Wolfskill Road: No longer extant; named for William Wolfskill, whose great vineyard lay between Fourth and Seventh Streets and from Alameda to San Pedro Streets. Wolfskill was contemporary with Jean Louis Vignes and, like Vignes, made wines on a large commercial scale.

Workman Street: William Workman, nephew of pioneer winegrower William Workman at Rancho La Puente and son-in-law of pioneer winegrower Andrew Boyle, greatly developed his father-in-law's vineyard and winery on Boyle Heights before the vineyard was annihilated by Pierce's disease in 1888.

LOS ANGELES COUNTY

Allen Avenue (Pasadena): Named for the Englishman William Allen, owner of the Sphinx ranch and winery. Allen Avenue bordered the west side of the 350-acre vineyard.

Brigden Road (Pasadena): After Albert Brigden, owner of the Highland Vineyard and partner with J. F. Crank in the Sierra Madre Vintage Co. of Lamanda Park.

Dalton Avenue (Azusa): Named for Henry Dalton, owner of Rancho Azusa (1844), where winegrowing was a major economic activity. His brother was George Dalton, of Dalton Avenue in Los Angeles.

Del Vina Street (Pasadena): In the Lamanda Park/Sierra Madre Villa vineyard region.

Eaton Drive (Pasadena): After Benjamin Eaton, of the big Fair Oaks Vineyard. Eaton Canyon and Eaton Wash also bear his name.

El Molina Avenue (San Marino): E. J. Kewen (see Kewen Drive below), a Los Angeles lawyer, was given the Old Mill property by his father-in-law, Dr. T. J. White, in 1859. Kewen made wine there from 50 acres of vines, adjacent to B. D. Wilson's Lake Vineyard.

Fair Oaks (Pasadena): Originally the property of Eliza Griffin Johnston, widow of Confederate general Albert Sidney Johnston. Judge Benjamin Eaton bought the property in 1868, developed a vineyard and winery in 1870, and sold it to J. F. Crank in 1877. The vineyard then supplied grapes to the Sierra Madre Vintage Co.

Hastings Ranch Drive (Pasadena): After Charles Hastings, who bought 1,100 acres in the foothills of the San Gabriel Mountains in 1882 and planted a vineyard, which was destroyed not long after by Pierce's disease.

Kewen Drive (Pasadena): Named for E. J. Kewen (see El Molina Avenue above), as is Kewen Place in San Marino. He lived at the Old Mill.

Lake Avenue (Pasadena): Originally Lake Vineyard Avenue. The street was laid out by Benjamin D. Wilson leading to his home property, the Lake Vineyard. The lake in question has been filled in and is now Lacy Park.

Mataro Avenue (Pasadena): After the Spanish name of the wine grape variety known as Mourvèdre in French, which was widely grown in Southern California. The street lies near where the Sierra Madre Vintage Co. stood in the Lamanda Park district of Pasadena.

Muscatel Avenue (Rosemead): The town Rosemead was laid out on the property where the winemaker L. V. Rose stabled his thoroughbred horses and is named for him: Muscatel probably alludes to grapes in Rose's big vineyard.

Nadeau Street (Florence): After Rémi Nadeau, whose winery and great 2,700-acre vineyard was destroyed by Pierce's disease at the end of the 1880s.

Oak Knoll Avenue (Pasadena): Named after a large property, including a vineyard, that was adjacent to the Lake Vineyard and inherited by J. DeBarth Shorb from Benjamin Wilson and later sold to speculators during the boom of the 1880s.

Packard Drive (Pomona): After J. A. Packard of Chicago, who planted 80 acres of vines near Pomona in the 1880s. He was an investor in the Pomona Wine Company, at one time the biggest industry in town.

Pelancoli Avenue (Glendale): After Lorenzo Pelancoli, who moved from Los Angeles, where he had inherited an Olvera Street winery, to his vineyard property in what was then Tropico and is now part of Glendale.

Scott Road (Burbank): Named for Jonathan Scott, a Los Angeles lawyer who planted a vineyard in 1862 on the 4,603 acres of the San Rafael ranch he had bought in 1857.

Shorb Street (Alhambra): After J. DeBarth Shorb, who laid out the town of Alhambra in 1871. To name the streets he used not only his name but those of his eleven children: Benito, Ramona, Campbell, Marguerita, etc. Another main street he called "San Marino," after the house he had built before there was a town of San Marino. Beginning in 1881 Shorb developed the San Gabriel Winery, "the world's largest winery," and a large vineyard on property he called Ramona. After his death in 1896 Shorb's property was bought by Henry E. Huntington; Ramona was absorbed into the city of Alhambra.

Stoneman Avenue (Alhambra): Named for Civil War general George Stoneman, who after the war bought his Los Robles estate in 1871 and by 1879 had a vineyard of 200 acres and a winery producing 40,000 gallons a year. Stoneman was elected governor of California in 1883. Stoneman Avenue was no doubt named by Shorb in 1871, although he and Stoneman later quarreled.

Sunny Slope Avenue (Pasadena): Named for L. J. Rose's great winemaking estate, established in 1861.

Vinedo Avenue (Pasadena): In the old winemaking district of Lamanda Park; "vinedo" means "vineyard." See also the entries for Del Vina Street, Mataro Avenue, and Vineyard Street in the same neighborhood.

Vineyard Street (Pasadena): In the Lamanda Park winemaking district. According to Hiram Reid (*History of Pasadena*, 362), Vineyard Street was named for Martha's Vineyard in Massachusetts. Reid was so fanatical a prohibitionist that he could not bear to admit the obvious source of the name.

Wilson Avenue (Pasadena): Named by Benjamin D. Wilson for himself in 1876, on the Lake Vineyard Tract he was then developing.

NOTES

CHAPTER 1

1. Missionary bodies in Mexico had vainly sought permission to found missions in Alta California since early in the seventeenth century, but it was only when a political threat, or what the Spanish imagined to be a threat, developed toward that region that the Spanish government decided to support such a move. See Bolton, "The Mission in the Spanish-American Colonies," 49.

2. The belief rests on a note written by Comandante Mariano Vallejo in 1874. It stated that his father, a soldier who had arrived in California in 1774, told him that Serra brought the vines to San Diego in 1769. Since the elder Vallejo was not present at the founding, and since Comandante Vallejo was writing more than a century after the date, the note cannot stand against the strong contrary evidence. The note is in *Documentos para la Historia de California*, Bancroft Library, University of California, 36:288.

3. Brady, "Alta California's First Vintage," 10–15.

4. Bowman, "The Vineyards in Provincial California," 10.

5. Letter in the archives of Mission Santa Barbara, cited in Bowman, "The Vineyards in Provincial California," 10n6.

6. Humboldt, *Political Essay on the Kingdom of New Spain*, 2:234.

7. See Appendix 1: The Native Vine of California.

8. "From time to time...the padres tried to make palatable wine from the fruit of these temptingly prolific vines, but always they found their effort unrewarding." See Teiser and Harroun, *Winemaking in California*, 1. The authors give no authority for the statement.

9. Neuerberg, "The Beginnings of the Wine Industry in California," 10–12.

10. Brady, "Alta California's First Vintage," 12. Presumably the snow in question was on the mountains rather than on the coastal plain where the Capistrano mission lies, although Charles Sullivan (personal communication) calls attention to the fact that climatological study shows coastal California to have been measurably cooler and wetter in the eighteenth century than it is now.

11. The story is complicated. From an examination of shipping records, Roy Brady ("Alta California's First Vintage," 14) concluded that vines must have arrived at San Juan Capistrano in May 1778; the mission, however, was moved to a new site in the summer of 1778, meaning vines planted at the original site would not have been transplanted during the

269

summer but would have been transplanted while dormant the following winter, to be replanted in the spring of 1779, the beginning of their continued growth. Whether this was in fact what happened, no one can now say.

12. J. N. Bowman, a careful student of the documents, concludes that the first vineyard in Alta California was planted at Mission San Diego in 1781 (Bowman, "The Vineyards of Provincial California," April 1943, 10). But he apparently missed the reference to vines in Mugártegui's letter of 1779. Since we are guessing, there is room to guess that at least a token amount of wine was made in 1781: Mission grapes planted in 1779 would have been in their third leaf that year and are likely to have produced a small crop. It is more than likely that Mugártegui made trial of his grapes then rather than leave them on the vine.

13. It is often said that early California winemakers—Jean Louis Vignes, for instance—recognizing the defects of the Mission variety, brought in superior varieties, but such statements are never, so far as I know, accompanied by any evidence or even by any particularization. Nothing is said about what, or where, or how, or when, or how many—details one would like to know by way of evidence. Still, it is reasonable to suppose that some new varieties were brought in and experimented with, even though the dominance of the Mission grape was never in question. It is stated, with some plausibility, that Muscat vines were growing in mission vineyards. See M'Kee, "The Grape and Wine Culture of California," 338–39.

14. Tapia, Fernando, J. A.Cabezas, F. Cabello, T. Lacombe, J. M. Martinez-Zaparer, P. Hinrichsen, and M. T. Cervera, "Determining the Spanish Origin of Representative Ancient American Grapevine Varieties." *American Journal of Enology and Viticulture*, 58 (2007) 242–51.

15. Brady, "Alta California's First Vintage," 15.

16. Hendricks, "Viticulture in El Paso del Norte during the Colonial Period," 181–200.

17. For an account of these and other afflictions of the grape, see Winkler et al., *General Viticulture*.

18. Ten years was the statutory term for each mission, after which it would be turned over to the secular clergy. A few of the California missions endured for more than sixty years.

19. See, for example, Servín, "The Secularization of the California Missions," 133–49.

20. See Street, *Beasts of the Field*, 27.

21. G. H. Phillips (*Vineyards and Vaqueros*, 329) notes that the Mission Indians "have been identified as 'slaves,' 'wards,' 'vassals,' 'peons,' 'serfs,' or 'inmates'" without being exactly any of these things; he suggests the neutral term "workers," which is certainly correct as far as it goes.

22. Duhaut-Cilly, *A Voyage to California*, 167.

23. Phillips, *Vineyards and Vaqueros*, 126.

24. Bolton, "The Mission in the Spanish-American Colonies," 57.

25. They are as follows, in approximate sequence from south to north, with their dates of founding: San Diego (1769); San Luis Rey (north of San Diego, 1798); San Juan Capistrano (in what is now Orange County, 1776); San Gabriel (eight miles east and north of Los Angeles, 1771); San Fernando (twenty miles north of Los Angeles, 1797); San Buenaventura (on the coast at Ventura, between Los Angeles and Santa Barbara, 1782); Santa Barbara (1786); Santa Inés (in Santa Barbara County, 1794); La Purísima Concepción (near Lompoc, 1787); San Luis Obispo (1772); San Miguel (north of San Luis Obispo, 1797); San Antonio (at the head of the Salinas Valley, 1771); Soledad (in Monterey County, 1791); San Carlos (Carmel, 1770); San Juan Bautista (1797); Santa Cruz (1791); San José (1797); Santa Clara (1777); and San Francisco (1776).

26. Brady, "Alta California's First Vintage," 12. Since 1784 is only two years after the conjectured first vintage of 1782, it seems unlikely that the production of wine could have been considerable or general in 1784, but winemaking had by then at least been shown to be practical.

27. Bowman, "The Vineyards of Provincial California," April 1943, 22.

28. A mission unable to grow its own grapes might get them from some other source and

make its own wine: William Heath Davis wrote that he frequently drank wine made at Mission Dolores from grapes grown at Mission Santa Clara and Mission San José (Davis, *Seventy-Five Years in California*, 5).

29. The Mission is a productive grape; I have seen a yield of 15 tons an acre claimed for it. But a cautious estimate would be 2 tons to the acre under the conditions of early California. Using the conventional measure of 150 gallons of wine from 1 ton of grapes, an acre of Missions would produce 300 gallons. How much of that yield would not yet have turned to vinegar after a few months is another question.

30. Dana, *Two Years Before the Mast*, 1:120.

31. Duhaut-Cilly, *A Voyage to California*, 114. The term translated as "white port" is in the original *"porto depouillé,"* roughly "port that has cleared," indicating, perhaps, a red wine that has lost color, rather than a white port. "Paxarete," however, indicates a white wine, although the comparison is to taste not color.

32. Palóu, *Life of Fray Junípero Serra*, 179.

33. The early descriptions of California's vineyards typically give an estimated count of vines rather than a statement of acreage. There was no strict rule for the number of vines per acre, but it appears that the common measure was 1,000 vines to the acre, more or less. J. N. Bowman ("The Vineyards of Provincial California," July 1943, 22) estimated a density of from 854 to 876 vines per acre spaced at seven feet between rows and seven feet between vines in a row. According to John S. Hittell (*The Resources of California*, 198), 1,000 vines to the acre was customary in Los Angeles, while 680 to the acre was common in Sonoma and Napa. The usual spacing between vines and between rows in Los Angeles was six feet by six feet.

34. If there were 1,000 vines to the acre producing, say, a very modest 2 tons to the acre, then the San Gabriel vineyards produced at least 106 tons of grapes. At an estimated 150 gallons to the ton, the yield is 15,900 gallons of wine. Many grapes were no doubt eaten fresh, and much of the wine was no doubt distilled as brandy, but that would still leave a very generous supply of wine on hand.

35. San Fernando, with 32,000 vines in 1835, came second; these two missions in what is now Los Angeles County gave the region a commanding lead in wine production in California.

36. The authority is Colonel J. J. Warner, as reported in John Albert Wilson's *History of Los Angeles County* (p. 27). Warner gives the following menu for "the usual dinner at San Gabriel Mission during the years of its prosperity":

Bill of Fare

First Course.

Caldo.

Plain broth, in which meat and vegetables had been boiled.

Second Course.

La Olla.

Meat boiled with vegetables and served separately.

Third Course.

Al Bondigas.

Forced meat balls—in gravy.

Fourth Course.

Guisados.

Stews—generally two.

Fifth Course.

Azado.

Roast—beef, mutton, game, fowls.

Sixth Course.

Fruit and sweetmeats.

Seventh Course.

Tea, coffee, cigarritos.

Pork was eaten sparingly at every meal. Wine was served *ad libitum.* On Fridays, fish followed the caldo, and the meats were dispensed with.

37. Dale, ed., *The Ashley-Smith Explorations*, 195. At least some of the Americans misbehaved about the wine; as Harrison Rogers records, "Our blacksmith, James Read, came very abruptly into the priest's dining room while at dinner, and asked for aguardiente. The priest ordered a plate of victuals to be handed him. He eat a few mouthfuls, and set the plate on the table, and then took a decanter of wine, and drank without invitation, and came very near breaking the glass when he set it down. The Padre, seeing he was in a state of inebriety, refrained from saying anything." (Engelhardt, *Mission San Gabriel*, 151.) Sánchez was notably long suffering, since these Americans camped on him for two months.

38. Duhaut-Cilly, *A Voyage to California*, 148.

39. Of the twenty mission priests named in the list drawn up by Serra in 1777, nineteen were born in Spain. See Serra, *Alta California's First Census and Directory*.

40. Phillips, *Vineyards and Vaqueros*, 68, citing Robert H. Jackson, *Indian Population Decline* (Albuquerque: University of New Mexico Press, 1995), 54; and Antonio Coronel, *Tales of Mexican California* (Santa Barbara: Bellerophon Books, 1994), 104n2.

41. The willow fence was still in common use in the 1850s and '60s in Los Angeles. The approach to Los Angeles from the east in 1858 was along a "road, street, lane, alley, or avenue, so unlike anything else seen, that we know not what to call it. It is sixty or eighty feet broad, very serpentine in its course, and entirely closed in on both sides by live willow-fence; the heads of the trees spreading fifteen or twenty feet wide, and so completely interwoven (the bodies being originally only a few inches apart) that there is one continuous row of deep green foliage, twenty or thirty feet high, and drooping over on either hand." In the town itself each of several wineries was "entirely surrounded by the dense willow fence" and "so shut up that it appears like a world by itself." (California State Agricultural Society, *Transactions 1858*, 282, 287.)

42. Blake, *Report of a Geological Reconnaissance in California*, 77–78.

43. In the pre-phylloxera era (i.e., before the last quarter of the nineteenth century) the rule had been scattered planting. One notable exception was John Wolfskill, who in the 1840s in Los Angeles rejected the Indian method of hoe cultivation and planted vines in straight rows to enable cultivation by plow. Maynard Amerine, enumerating the modern advances in winegrowing, named straight-row planting as one of them. See Amerine, "The Golden Age of Wine," (London: Institute of Masters of Wine, 1969), quoted in Thomas Pinney, *Makers of American Wine* (Berkeley: University of California Press, 2012), 192.

44. Dakin, *A Scotch Paisano in Old Los Angeles*, 270.

45. Phillips, *Vineyards and Vaqueros*, 69.

46. Hugo Reid, quoted in Phillips, *Vineyards and Vaqueros*, 152.

47. Some missions had outlying properties (ranchos or "estancias") to increase the production of crops and livestock. San Gabriel had a dozen or more, extending all the way east to San Bernardino. If there were vineyards on these, then transport *would* have been a problem, unless the grapes were made into wine at the estancia itself. This appears to have been done at one or more of the estancias belonging to the Santa Barbara mission. See Street, *Beasts of the Field*, 35.

48. The first method is as described by Carlos Hejar, quoted in Bowman, "The Vineyards of Provincial California," June 1943, 20; the second is from Newmark, *Sixty Years in Southern California*, 202–3; and the third is from Bancroft, *California Pastoral*, 371–72. Another account, from 1849, about the winemaking at Pokamongo [Cucamonga?] Ranch, is similar: the Indians are naked, and the pole by which they support themselves is fixed horizontally across the cowhide. See Caughey, "The Jacob Y. Stover Narrative," 177. The long, long period of fermentation could be accounted for by the fact that the missions were dependent upon whatever strain of wild yeast was used. As described by Jean J. Jacobson ("Upsides of Wild Fermentations," 35), "Wild primary and secondary fermentations can take months to complete, and each year is different."

49. See the illustration opposite page 214 in Webb, *Indian Life at the Old Missions*. Webb makes the common mistake of confusing crushing the grape with pressing the grape, and calls the structures illustrated "presses." They are evidently receptacles for treading grapes by foot: shallow cisterns or troughs known as *lagares*.

50. Sullivan, "Wine in California: The Early Years," *Wayward Tendrils Quarterly*, July 2010, 27.

51. Webb, *Indian Life at the Old Missions*, 220.

52. Hugo Reid, writing of the San Gabriel Mission under Zalvidea (1806–26), notes that while most of the skilled trades were carried out there by Indians, they were never coopers; only "foreigners" were. See Dakin, *A Scotch Paisano in Old California*, 271. Alfred Robinson, however, in listing the "various occupations" of the Indians at San Luis Rey in 1829, includes "coopers." Robinson is writing some years after the event, and in constructing a long list of "occupations" may not have paid strict attention to accuracy. But it is also possible that by 1829 the art of the cooper had been taught at the missions. See Alfred Robinson, *Life in California*, 24.

53. Webb, *Indian Life at the Old Missions*, 223.

54. Hilgard, "The Agriculture and Soils of California," 504.

55. Sullivan, "Wine in California," 28.

56. Webb, *Indian Life at the Old Missions*, 222.

57. Three, at least, of the Mission grape vines planted in early California grew to giant size: one at Montecito, another at Carpenteria, and a third at the San Gabriel mission. The Montecito vine, displayed at the Centennial Exhibition at Philadelphia in 1876, was nearly ten feet in circumference at the base; in 1857 it was reported to have produced 5,000 bunches that year. (A street in Montecito, Parra Grande Lane, has been named for it.) Oddly, no such gigantism has been reported in modern times, a fact perplexing to scientists. When A. J. Winkler, the dean of California viticulturists, retired from the University of California at Davis in 1962, his colleagues planted as a memorial to his work a Mission vine in the university's experimental vineyards. The hope was that it might grow to giant size, and so it did, before succumbing to disease. A successor vine has been planted.

58. It must, however, have been quite early in mission history. According to J. N. Bowman ("The Vineyards of Provincial California," 11), several stills were at work by 1799. As described by an

observer in California as late as 1834, these brandy stills were very simple devices. They were "copper containers in the form of jars covered with a kind of lid. They put in two tubes and then heated the liquid to induce evaporation and condensation." See Carlos Hejar, in Bowman, "The Vineyards of Provincial California," 20.

59. Sullivan, "Wine in California," 28.

60. To my knowledge, the only attempt at a classification of the wines made at the missions is by Father Narciso Durán, then president of the missions, in a letter of 1833. It is more confusing than enlightening. "There are two kinds of red wine," he writes. "One is dry, but very good for the table; the other is sweet, resembling the juice pressed from blackberries and so rather unpleasant. There are also two kinds of white wine. One of them is from pure grapes without fermenting, I mean from pure grape juice without fermenting it with the skins of the pressed grapes. This produces the white wine. The other of the same juice is fermented with a quantity of grape brandy. These two make a most delicious drink for the dessert. The wine from the pure grape juice is for the altar; the other for any use whatever." Durán is quoted in Webb, *Indian Life at the Old Missions*, 222–23. I can make little sense of this description. The white "fermented" with brandy is presumably an early version of Angelica. The sweet red wine was no doubt fortified.

61. Boston merchants were the leaders in the business; the hides went to make shoes for the Yankees, the tallow went into candles and soap.

62. Sullivan, "Wine in California: The Early Years," *Wayward Tendrils Quarterly*, July 2010, 31. On October 25, 1815, Father Zalvidea at Mission San Gabriel wrote to Captain De La Guerra at the presidio of Santa Barbara advising him that wine was available: "If you wish, you may send a barrel that it may be filled for you, and also a keg for the Muscatel. Send the casks and let me know to whom I should deliver them." See Engelhardt, *Mission San Gabriel*, 94. The reference to "Muscatel" would appear to confirm that Muscat grapes as well as Mission grapes were known at the missions. See also note 13 above.

63. Bancroft, *History of California*, 2:494. In 1831, Michael White, an English resident of Los Angeles, took wine and brandy as part of his cargo on the schooner *Guadalupe*, sailing for trade with Mexico; the brandy he identified as "mission *aguardiente.*" See White, *California All the Way Back to 1828*, 32.

64. Duhaut-Cilly, *A Voyage to California*, 169.

65. Alfred Robinson, *Life in California*, 32–33.

66. In some early statements a "barrel" is said to hold 18 gallons. See F. P. F. Temple, letter, December 27, 1845, in Rowland, *John Rowland and William Workman*, 86. If that is what Robinson means, then the San Gabriel vineyard could easily have produced an annual 600 barrels of wine and 200 of brandy, with a good deal left over. That would be 10,800 gallons of wine; the brandy, allowing a modest 3 gallons of wine to produce 1 of brandy, would require another 10,800 gallons, for a total of 21,600 gallons. But there is no way of knowing what measure Robinson has in mind. Father Zephyrin Engelhardt, after quoting this statement about the wine of San Gabriel, says, "Some one at the Mission must have been practicing on Robinson's credulity." See Engelhardt, *San Gabriel Mission*, 157n.

67. Bowman, "The Vineyards of Provincial California, " July 1933, 23.

68. Engelhardt, *San Gabriel Mission*, 133.

69. Cole and Welcome, eds., *Don Pío Pico's Historical Narrative*, 150.

70. Street, *Beasts of the Field*, 84–85.

71. A token quantity of land was restored to the church on its appeal to the American authorities in the 1850s.

72. "The Decay of the Mission," from Hugo Reid, *Letters on the Los Angeles County Indians*, quoted in Dakin, *A Scotch Paisano in Old Los Angeles*, 280.

73. From the diary of William Hartnell, June 1839, quoted in Phillips, *Vineyards and Vaqueros*, 170–1.

74. California State Agricultural Society, *Transactions 1858*, 293.

75. J. Q. A. Warren, *American Stock Journal*, March 1861, reprinted in Gates, *California Ranchos and Farms*, 93.

76. Teiser and Harroun, *Winemaking in Califor07na*, 65.

77. Bryant, *What I Saw in California*, 391.

78. *Los Angeles Star*, June 24, 1854.

79. *The Southern Vineyard*, August 7, 1858 (an early Los Angeles newspaper).

80. John Albert Wilson, *History of Los Angeles County*, 105.

CHAPTER 2

1. As were all of the pueblos of Spanish America. According to J. M. Guinn, writing in 1895 ("The Plan of Old Los Angeles," 40), "The Spanish poblador...went where he was sent. He built his pueblo after a plan designated by royal reglamento and decreed by the laws of the Indies. His planting and his sowing, the size of his fields and the shape of his house lot, were fixed by royal decree." Whether a strict enforcement of the rules in remote Los Angeles was carried out may be doubted.

2. The name of the Italian church, Porciúncula, meaning "little portion [of land]," refers to where the Franciscan order originated.

3. Bolton, *Fray Juan Crespi*, 148.

4. Gumprecht, *The Los Angeles River*, 141; and California State Agricultural Society, *Transactions 1858*, 294.

5. California State Agricultural Society, *Transactions 1858*, 284.

6. W. W. Robinson, *Los Angeles from the Days of the Pueblo*, 25.

7. Willard, *Herald's History of Los Angeles City*, quoted in *El Pueblo*, 12.

8. Gumprecht, *The Los Angeles River*, 311n10.

9. Gumprecht, *The Los Angeles River*, 311n10, from Guinn, *History of California*.

10. The names of the original settlers are: Antonio Villavicencio, with wife and daughter; Josef de Velasco y Lara, with wife and three children; Antonio Mesa and wife; José Vanegas, with wife and son; Pablo Rodriguez, with wife and daughter; Manual Camero and wife; Josef Navarro, with wife and three children; Josef Moreno and wife; Josef [or Basilio?] Rosas, with wife and six children, including Alexander Rosas and wife; and Luis Quintero, with wife and five children. All of the wives were named "Maria." Mesa, Lara, and Quintero, with their families, were expelled from the pueblo in March 1782. Although an alcalde, or mayor, was elected in 1788, it is said that Corporal José Vicente Feliz, who had accompanied the settlers to Los Angeles, remained to manage the town. See Security Trust and Savings Bank, *El Pueblo*, 15.

11. Gumprecht, *The Los Angeles River*, 46.

12. Later statements about the age of vineyards in Los Angeles are notoriously unreliable. A typical instance is the statement by Major Ben Truman (*Semi-Tropical California*, 59) that Dr. T. J. White's property "is the site of the first vineyard that was planted in the city of Los Angeles" and that the vines still growing there from the original planting were then ninety years old. When a committee of the California State Agricultural Society visited White's establishment in

1858, however, they found that two-thirds of his 16,000 vines were then eight years old and the other third, fifteen years old, so that White's oldest vines went back only to 1843, meaning that when Truman saw them they were not ninety but twenty-seven years old. But the same committee, reporting on a Dr. Hoover's vineyard next door to White's, notes that some of Hoover's vines were then "over eighty years old." See California State Agricultural Society, *Transactions 1858*, 283, 285. That would put the original planting not later than 1778, three years before the town was founded. No serious effort to determine when and where vines were first planted in Los Angeles seems to have been made.

13. Geiger, "The Building of Mission San Gabriel," 37. The first reference to winemaking at San Gabriel is from 1796 (see Bowman, "The Vineyards of Provincial California," April 1943, 24), but there must have been considerable winemaking before 1796, although there is no documentation of the subject.

14. Cleland, *The Cattle on a Thousand Hills*, 17, 285n44.

15. Cleland, *The Cattle on a Thousand Hills*, 13; and W. W. Robinson, *Southern California Local History*, 47.

16. Cleland, *The Cattle on a Thousand Hills*, 16.

17. Shaler, *Journal of a Voyage between China and the North Western Coast of America*, 64.

18. Wolcott, ed., *Pioneer Notes from the Diaries of Judge Benjamin Hayes*, 98. Still, if Mission San Gabriel had vineyards by 1783, Los Angeles may well have had vineyards very shortly afterward.

19. Sullivan, "Wine in California: The Early Years," *Wayward Tendrils Quarterly* 20 (October 2010): 19.

20. J. A. Wilson, *History of Los Angeles County*, 65. I do not know that arrope would retard fermentation, but it would increase the alcohol content of the resulting wine.

21. Guinn, "The Plan of Old Los Angeles," 43.

22. J. A. Wilson, *History of Los Angeles County*, 64. The list is from information provided by J. J. Warner, who came to Los Angeles in 1831. The complete list is as follows:

> Northeast of Aliso Street: Tiburcio Carillo, 4 acres; Ybarra, 5 acres; Tapia, 2 acres; Louis Bouchette, 4 acres; Henriques Sepulveda, 4 acres; Yanuario Abila, 6 acres; Apablasa, 2 acres; Juan Ramirez, 5 acres.

> East side of Alameda Street: Ballesteros, 4 acres; Luis Vignes, 5 acres; Maximo Alanis, 5 acres.

> East side of San Pedro Street: N. M. Pryor, 2 acres; Antonio Mario Lugo, 8 acres; Cota, 4 acres; Rice and Temple, 4 acres; Vicente Sanchez, 8 acres; Benedicto Palomares, 4 acres; Antonio Sanchez, 2 acres; Jose Maria Abila, 8 acres; M. Requena, 2 acres.

> West of San Pedro and South of Main Street: Romero, 5 acres; Vejar, 2 acres; Moreno, 6 acres; Valdez, 4 acres; Urquivez, 5 acres; Alvarado, 2 acres.

> Together this is 112 acres, or, say, 100,000 vines, making a grand total not to exceed 200,000 bearing vines then in the county.

23. Ibid.

24. *California Farmer* 4, 127.

25. California State Agricultural Society, *Transactions 1858*, 286.

26. Ibid.

27. Iris Wilson, *William Wolfskill*, 158; and J. A. Wilson, *History of Los Angeles County*, 65. The other winemaker was William Wolfskill, who contributed a barrel of port. Buchanan is said to have accepted the gift "with quiet cordiality," adding that he "claimed to be a good judge of wine." This was not the first gift of California wine to a president. A cask of 1846 white wine from Jean Louis Vignes, decorated with a silver plate engraved with the words "California Wine," was sent to Franklin Pierce for his inauguration in 1853. See Bowman, "The Vineyards of Provincial California," 22. And the Sainsevain brothers managed to send a case of their sparkling wine to Buchanan in January 1857, ahead of the Requena and Wolfskill wine, which did not leave Los Angeles until September of that year. See Teiser and Harroun, *Winemaking in California*, 21.

28. Perkins, Stern and Co., "Catalogue of California Wines"; and J. A. Wilson, *History of Los Angeles County*, 64.

29. Workman, *The City that Grew*, 35.

30. Harlow, *California Conquered*, 33.

31. Or he had been captured at Monterey or at Refugio; there are several differing stories.

32. W. W. Robinson, *Los Angeles from the Days of the Pueblo*, 43.

33. Scott, "Why Joseph Chapman Adopted California and Why California Adopted Him," 244.

34. Alfred Robinson, *Life in California*, 101.

35. Charles Chapman had 2,500 vines from which he sold seven and a half tons in 1860. See Perkins, Stern and Co., "Catalogue of California Wines."

36. Perkins, Stern and Co., "Catalogue of California Wines"; and Iris Wilson, *William Wolfskill*, 81.

37. Newmark, *Sixty Years in Southern California*, 293.

38. Leonard Pitt and Dale Pitt (*Los Angeles A to Z*, s.v. "Temple, John") note that Temple "conducted a brisk trade in *serapes*, *rebozos*, and wine."

39. Macy Street no longer exists, having been annihilated by the construction of Cesar Chavez Avenue. Bauchet Street is now a stub off Alameda just north of the Terminal Annex post office.

40. Peninou and Greenleaf, *Directory of California Wine Growers and Wine Makers in 1860*.

41. Street, *Beasts of the Field*, 136.

42. Street, *Beasts of the Field*, 137.

43. Duhaut-Cilly, *Voyage to California*, 145, 148.

44. Alfred Robinson, *Life in California*, 220.

45. He was said to have been born in Bordeaux according to the obituary published in the *Los Angeles Star* on January 18, 1862. His parents lived in the commune of Béguey, near Cadillac. See Jore, "Jean Louis Vignes of Bordeaux," 291–92.

46. Jore, "Jean Louis Vignes of Bordeaux," 294.

47. Ibid.

48. Wilson, *History of Los Angeles County*, 35. Such was the local legend in 1880, when Wilson was writing his history.

49. Vignes's entry into this neighborhood may have marked the beginning of what became known as "Frenchtown," south of Aliso Street. By 1850, one in every five Angelinos claimed French ancestry. See Gumprecht, *The Los Angeles River*, 49.

50. See note 22 above.

51. Another explanation is given in an outdoor display of photographs of early Los Angeles that is mounted in the Patsaouras Transit Plaza adjoining the headquarters of the Metropolitan Transit Authority in downtown L.A. The accompanying text says that Vignes simply took the land from the Indians. No authority is given for the statement. Since all of California was taken from the Indians, it seems an invidious distinction to single out Vignes as a thief of land.

52. Guinn, "The Plan of Old Los Angeles," 43.

53. Gumprecht, *The Los Angeles River*, 306n34. "Aliso" means alder, not sycamore. J. Gregg Layne (*Annals of Los Angeles*, 89) explains that the Spanish called the American sycamore "aliso" since the California sycamore "looks more like an alder tree of Spain than it does like the European sycamore."

54. Matthew Keller wrote in 1858, "Most of our vineyard labor is done by the Indians, some of whom are the best pruners we have—an art they learned from the Mission Fathers." See United States, *Report of the Commissioner of Patents 1858*, 347.

55. According to the census of Los Angeles in 1836 there were then two coopers at work in the town, so a supply of barrels was available. Neither was of Mexican origin. They may have been Vignes himself and fellow cooper and winegrower Louis Bauchet.

56. J. Ross Browne in the *Los Angeles Star*, December 13, 1874, quoted in Sherwood, *Days of Vintage, Years of Vision*, 354.

57. Phelps, *Alta California, 1840–1842*, 70–71.

58. Davis, *Seventy-Five Years in California*, 120. If Davis is right about wines "ten years old" in January 1843, then Vignes must have made wine as early as 1833; but Davis is not upon oath, and there are other reasons to think that some of his account is exaggerated.

59. J. A. Wilson, *History of Los Angeles County*, 35.

60. Iris Wilson, *William Wolfskill*, 149.

61. "A quarter mile" is a slight exaggeration. A contemporary description measures the arbor as 9 feet wide, 10 feet high, and 250 yards long. See California State Agricultural Society, *Transactions 1858*, 285.

62. Davis, *Seventy-Five Years in California*, 120–21. Davis's statement has been many times repeated, sometimes with added ornament. Idwal Jones (*Vines in the Sun*, 212) writes, "Every plant had been sent from Bordeaux, the Sauvignon Blanc and Cabernet, wrapped in moss or stuck in potatoes, coming by trade ships round the Horn." Iris Wilson (*William Wolfskill*, 148) says of the imported varieties, "Several of these…began to produce in large enough quantities to be used in wine making in the early thirties." Leo Friis (*John Fröhling*, 11) writes that Vignes "imported numerous varieties of grapes from Europe which enabled him and other vintners to produce many kinds of wine." None of these writers has anything resembling evidence, and what Jones has written is clearly a pastiche of items drawn from various sources having nothing to do with Vignes.

63. McKee, "Historic Winegrowers of Southern California, 1850–1890." The often-repeated claim that Vignes was the first to import superior varieties has generated some elaborate variations, as, for example, Richard Steven Street's statement (*Beasts of the Field*, 95) that "Vignes paid the passage of experienced Frenchmen who labored for years grafting the imported vines onto native rootstock while they paid off their debts." Why these imaginary Frenchmen should have wasted their time grafting imported vines onto native rootstocks is not said; vinifera vines can of course be planted directly, and in pre-phylloxera California no such grafting was done.

64. J. DeBarth Shorb, at his big San Gabriel winery, struggled to make an acceptable "claret" out of Mission grapes as late as 1884. By this time, the abundant Zinfandel in the northern vineyards had long since been producing a dry red wine that Southern California's Mission grapes could not compete against. As Shorb's manager, F. W. Wood, suggested, buying wine

from the north would make more sense than trying to make something equivalent out of Mission grapes. See F. W. Wood to J. DeBarth Shorb, June 9, 1884, J. DeBarth Shorb Papers, Huntington Library). Zinfandel was widely planted in Southern California by the 1880s, but although a great improvement over the Mission for red wine, it did not have the quality of Zinfandel from the north.

65. Sullivan, "Wine in California: The Early Years," *Wayward Tendrils Quarterly* 20 (October 2010): 28–31.

66. The fact that Vignes was joined in California by a nephew suggests he was not wholly alienated from his family in France. Yet his wife remained in France until her death in 1843.

67. W. W. Robinson, *Ranchos Become Cities*, 109.

68. Larkin, *The Larkin Papers*, 1:10, 13, 14.

69. Janssens, *The Life and Adventures in California of Don Augustin Janssens*, 105. Bandini, a native of Peru, lived in California from around 1822. He became a prominent citizen in both San Diego and Los Angeles. Bandini as a young man is described thus by Richard Henry Dana (*Two Years Before the Mast*, chapter 27): "He had a slight and elegant figure, moved gracefully, danced and waltzed beautifully, spoke the best of Castilian, with a pleasant and refined voice and accent, and had, throughout, the bearing of a man of high birth and figure"—and was at that time penniless.

70. Larkin, *The Larkin Papers*, 1:116.

71. Wood, *Wandering Sketches of People and Things in South America*, 219.

72. Alfred Robinson, *Life in California*, 207.

73. McKinley to Larkin, *The Larkin Papers*, 4:134, 180–81. James Santiago McKinley (d. 1875), a Scotsman said to have come to San Francisco on a whaler, had a long career in California. In 1845 he became part owner of both the San Juan Capistrano and San Luis Obispo mission properties. For a time he owned the schooner *Ayacucho*, the fast-sailing ship engaged in the Pacific coastal trade and often mentioned in Dana's *Two Years Before the Mast*. See Bancroft, *History of California*, 4:725.

74. Dakin, *A Scotch Paisano in Old Los Angeles*, 105.

75. Larkin, cited in Cleland, *The Cattle on a Thousand Hills*, 33 and note.

76. Davis, *Seventy-Five Years in California*, 120.

77. Phelps, *Alta California*, 70–71.

78. Guinn, "The Plan of Old Los Angeles," 46. "Vinatero" means "wine merchant." Harris Newmark (*Sixty Years in Southern California*, 231) says that Calle de los Chapules was named in the late 1850s by Mrs. O. W. Childs simply "because of some grasshoppers in the vicinity." That seems the more likely story.

79. J. A. Wilson, *History of Los Angeles County*, 65. The mildew was the powdery variety, the downy variety being unknown in California.

80. Phelps, *Alta California*, 320.

81. Bancroft, *History of California*, 2:111.

82. Ibid., 425n.

83. Duhaut-Cilly, *Voyage to California*, 159.

84. George Simpson, *Narrative of a Journey Round the World*, quoted in Cleland, *The Cattle on a Thousand Hills*, 75.

85. On the system of Indian labor in Los Angeles, see McWilliams, *Southern California Country*, 45, quoting Horace Bell; and Cleland, *The Cattle on a Thousand Hills*, 58–59, which adds the

interesting detail that the brandy destined for the Indians was often adulterated, even poisoned (although one wonders why). On the prominence of Indian labor in Los Angeles, see Street, *Beasts of the Field*, 78–79, 95–97. The law by which the auction system was created is also described by Street (*Beasts of the Field*, 121); he interprets it as a measure intended to deal with a labor shortage, particularly in the vineyards.

86. Street, *Beasts of the Field*, 681n18.

87. Bancroft, *History of California*, 2:574n.

88. Dana, *Two Years Before the Mast*, 1:82.

89. Pinney, *History of Wine in America*, 486–87n.

90. Neuerberg, "The Beginnings of the Wine Industry in California," 10.

91. Iris Wilson, *William Wolfskill*, 87.

92. William Wolfskill to John Wolfskill, August 10, 1847, MS WO 411, Huntington Library.

93. Iris Wilson, *William Wolfskill*, 160. The *Southern Vineyard* periodical (December 10,1858) called Wolfskill's the largest vineyard in Los Angeles County, with 55,000 bearing vines.

94. Bryant, *What I Saw in California*, 412. Bryant also says that Wolfskill had 4,000 or 5,000 vines; those numbers are either his mistake or, more likely, a typographical error, as 40 acres of vines planted according to Los Angeles practice would contain 40,000 vines.

95. Bryant, *What I Saw in California*, 405.

96. Buffum, *Six Months in the Gold Mines*, 145.

97. William Wolfskill to John Wolfskill, May 30, 1842, MS WO 398, Huntington Library.

98. California State Agricultural Society, *Transactions 1858*, 287.

99. Ibid.

100. Iris Wilson, *William Wolfskill*, 214–15.

101. See the list in Beck and Haase, *Historical Atlas of California*, no. 37.

102. Cleland, *The Cattle on a Thousand Hills*, 53.

103. Alfred Robinson, *Life in California*, 203. Leandri had arrived in Los Angeles in 1823, perhaps the first Italian to live there.

104. Jackson, *A British Ranchero in Old California*, 74.

105. When General Stephen Kearny's army, after defeating General José María Flores, approached Los Angeles in the afternoon of January 9, 1847, the fact that the town was "known to contain great quantities of wine and aguardiente" led Kearny to hold his men outside the town until the next morning, when the men could be better controlled. See Emory, *Notes of a Military Reconnaissance,*187.

106. Emory, *Notes of a Military Reconnaissance*, 122; Griffin, "A Doctor Comes to California," 353; Revere, *A Tour of Duty in California*, 282; and Pinney, *History of Wine in America*, 249–50.

107. Lt. Henry Watson, quoted in John Mark Faragher, *Eternity Street*, 168.

108. Bryant, *What I Saw in California*, 405–6.

CHAPTER 3

1. When General Persifor Smith arrived to take command in California in February 1849, he found that "the wages of a good carpenter were more than the pay of the major general commanding the army (himself)." See Harlow, *California Conquered*, 300.

2. Ord was not the only army officer so employed. Lieutenant William Tecumseh Sherman, later General Sherman of Civil War fame, laid out the city of Pittsburgh in 1849, and a

Colonel William M. Smith laid out the Northern California city of Martinez that same year. See WPA, Federal Writers Project, *California in the 1930s,*, 584–85.

3. The map itself carries the date of August 29, 1849, but it was not presented until early September. Hutton, while at work on the survey, also made drawings of Los Angeles that are among the earliest images we have of the place. See Hutton, *Glances at California.*

4. The original of the map has been lost (see Hayes, *Historical Atlas of California,* 149); the Huntington Library has a copy, and a reduced reproduction of it was published in *Historical Society of Southern California Quarterly* 17 (December 1935) as a fold-out insert between pages 142 and 143. Hutton (*Glances at California,* 21) wrote that the map was to include, among other things, "all the cultivated ground between the hills and the river, within two miles of the church." He also reported on September 1, 1849, that the map "is finished and is a very pretty one." See ibid., 31.

5. Ord has identified different uses of the land by a simple set of visual signs: short vertical lines for plowed ground; close-set dots for gardens; short, branching lines for corn; and short slanted lines for vines.

6. Sullivan, "Wine in California: The Early Years," Part II, *Wayward Tendrils Quarterly* 21 (July 2011): 32.

7. Newmark, *Sixty Years in Southern California,* 3rd ed., 134.

8. Bryant, *What I Saw in California,* 405; Buffum, *Six Months in the Gold Mines,* 144; Newmark, *Sixty Years in Southern California,* 25, 134; Thomas J. White, quoted in "Los Angeles Vineyards," *California Farmer* 4 (October 5, 1855):107; and Townsend, *The California Diary of General E. D. Townsend,* 104. Los Angeles was still a city of vineyards twenty years later, in 1875, when William Seward, President Lincoln's secretary of state, visited and pronounced its vineyards more beautiful than those of Burgundy. See Mrs. A. S. C. Forbes, "When Los Angeles Was the 'City of Vineyards,'" 339.

9. A federal census in 1850 put the state population at 92,597; a state census in 1852 gave 260,000. Neither figure is reliable. See Cleland, *The Cattle on a Thousand Hills,* 319.

10. By 1854, so one man claimed, "the Americans have got nearly all the vineyards from the Spaniards." See James Clarke to his brother, December 6, 1854, in Davies, "An Emigrant of the Fifties," 113). No doubt Clarke exaggerated.

11. Louis Wilhardt is remembered by Wilhardt Street, near the Los Angeles State Historic Park just north of Chinatown. Wilhardt Street is connected by Naud Street to Mesnager Street; all three names are those of early winemakers in this neighborhood, the other two being Edward Naud, and Georges Mésnager.

12. Newmark, *Sixty Years in Southern California,* 185.

13. Newmark, *Sixty Years in Southern California,* 185; and J. Q. A. Warren in *American Stock Journal,* April 1861, reprinted in Gates, *California Ranchos and Farms,* 105. There was general agreement that California wines were sent to market too soon. As Matthew Keller wrote ("The Grapes and Wine of Los Angeles," *U.S. Patent Office Annual Report 1858,* 346), "We cannot afford to wait until they have age. We expose them for sale, regardless of reputation, a few months after they are made, and are satisfied that they find purchasers. But we are convinced that if California wines had the same age as many of foreign production…ours would far surpass them." J. Q. A. Warren, writing in 1860 (Gates, *California Ranchos and Farms,* 102), says that the "excellent quality" of the wines of B. D. Wilson was "owing to the care taken in manufacture, and sufficient time allowed to age—none allowed to be sold under three years." The statement seems doubtful. Giving dry wines from the Mission grape some age would, under proper conditions, improve them, but achieving those "proper conditions" was a problem.

14. *Los Angeles Star,* August 8, 1863. "Paredón Blanco" translates to "White Cliff"; Boyle's

vineyard stood at the foot of the bluff on which Boyle Heights developed, across the river to the east of Los Angeles. The 30-acre vineyard was planted by José Rubio in 1835 and bought by Boyle in 1858 for the "astonishing" price of $3,000 an acre, or so it is said. See Peninou and Greenleaf, *A Directory of California Wine Growers and Wine Makers in 1860*, 14.

15. *Los Angeles Star*, August 5, 1868. This is the only reference I have seen to P. Downey & Co.

16. The omnium-gatherum character of storekeeping in early Los Angeles is well illustrated by the list on Beaudry's letterhead in 1865. His store dealt in "Groceries and Liquors, / Dry Goods, Clothing, Boots and Shoes, / Paints, Oils and Varnish, / Cane and Wooden Chairs, Crockery, Wall Paper, Window Glass, Cordage, / San Francisco Flour Depot." See Benjamin Wilson Papers, box 32, Huntington Library.

17. *New York Times*, February 20, 1887. Beaudry, a former mayor of Los Angeles, owned the San Rafael winery.

18. Newmark, *Sixty Years in Southern California*, 199. The Committee of the State Agricultural Society reported (*Transactions 1858*, 285) that some of Hoover's 7,000 vines were "over eighty years old," yet they were "more heavily laden with fruit than any that are younger." Los Angeles was only seventy-seven years old in 1858.

19. California State Agricultural Society, *Transactions 1858*, 285.

20. Ibid., 286.

21. *Southern Vineyard*, November 13, 1858.

22. California State Agricultural Society, *Transactions 1858*, 286.

23. "California as a Vineland," 603.

24. Sullivan, "Wine in California: The Early Years," *Wayward Tendrils Quarterly* 21 (October 2011): 21–22; and Pinney, *History of Wine in America*, 253–54.

25. California State Agricultural Society, *Transactions 1858*, 286.

26. An unidentified clipping dated September 11, 1863 (Bancroft Scraps, California Agriculture, vol. 18, part 4, Bancroft Library) reports that a firm called Mercado and Morris, identified as "successors to the Sainsevain Brothers," were producing 100,000 gallons of wine annually at Los Angeles. They may have succeeded immediately following the closing of the sparkling wine operation and before the sale of the property in 1867, but I have no information about that. The firm of Mercado and Seully had been agents for Sainsevain wines in San Francisco.

27. Newmark, *Sixty Years in Southern California*, 291.

28. Ayers, *Gold and Sunshine*, 292.

29. Frederick Keller, speech to the Native Sons of California, n.d., Matthew Keller Papers, box 4, file 2, Huntington Library.

30. Keller published this statement in an unidentified newspaper: "M. L. Pasteur has just published from the imperial printing office in France his 'studies on wines, its maladies, the causes, which provoke them, and new processes to conserve and age it,' a copy of which he has been kind enough to forward to me." From a cutting dated March 19, 1867, in Bancroft Scraps, California Agriculture, vol. 18, part 4, Bancroft Library. One wonders where this copy is now.

31. Sullivan, "Wine in California: The Early Years," *Wayward Tendrils Quarterly* (October 2011):

32. A typescript copy of Keller's obituary from the *Los Angeles Express* of April 11, 1881 (Matthew Keller Papers, box 4, file 19, Huntington Library), says that Keller planted 500 acres of vines at his Malaga Ranch, as the Malibu property was called. There may have been some vines there, but none planted by Keller; the statement about 500 acres is fantastic.

32. *Los Angeles Times*, clipping dated only "November" [1939?], Matthew Keller Papers, box 5, Huntington Library; and J. Gregg Layne, *Annals*, 53. In 1858 Keller wrote that his vineyard was

then fifty-five years old—that is, planted in 1803. There could only have been an anecdotal history of the place, subject to the usual confusions and exaggerations, so that one should probably make a large deduction from those fifty-five years. See Keller in U.S. Patent Office, *Report of the Commissioner of Patents 1858*, 345.

33. California State Agricultural Society, *Transactions 1858*, 288; the vines are said to be "of all ages from 1 to 54 years."

34. Sullivan, *Like Modern Edens*, 17, 20.

35. U.S. Patent Office, *Report of the Commissioner of Patents 1858*, 346–47. Since the grape vine does not breed true from seeds but produces many unpredictable variations, one might hope to get an improved variety by that means. But it would be wholly accidental, and no one could know how long the process might take.

36. L. J. Rose, "Appendix" to Garey, *Orange Culture in California*, 222.

37. Keller, letter in unidentified cutting, Matthew Keller Papers, box 5, file 24, Huntington Library.

38. Keller, letter dated February 22, 1871, published in the *Alta California*, February 27, 1871.

39. *Report of the Eighth Industrial Exhibition of the Mechanics' Institute of the City of San Francisco...1871* (San Francisco, 1872), 131. The Mission grape, as has been said, was commonly referred to as the "native" grape, and later importations of European varieties were known as "foreign" grapes. The Mission is of course wholly foreign itself.

40. February 9, 1871, Matthew Keller Papers, box 5, file 24, Huntington Library.

41. Keller to J. Lancaster Brent, March 7, 1868, J. Lancaster Brent Collection, Huntington Library. Quoted in Apostol, "Don Mateo Keller," 105.

42. Neither name appears in the encyclopedic *Wine Grapes* by Robinson, Harding, and Vouillamoz (2012). "Grizzly Frontignan" is no doubt one of the many varieties of Muscat. According to Charles Sullivan (personal communication), Grizzly (or Gray) Frontignan was not a wine grape but a table grape, one of many table varieties imported into California from New England nurseries in the 1850s and tried in winemaking.

43. Spalding, *Los Angeles Newspaperman*, 61.

44. *Transactions*, California Vine Growers' and Wine and Brandy Manufacturers' Association, 1872, in *Transactions 1872*, by the California State Agricultural Society, 474–75.

45. Keller obviously enjoyed writing; he was an inveterate writer of letters to periodicals such as San Francisco's *Alta California* in the 1860s and '70s.

46. *U.S. Patent Office Annual Report 1858*, 344.

47. The smaller figure probably comes from the county assessor's returns. It appears not only in *Transactions 1858* of the California State Agricultural Society but also in the *California State Register and Year Book of Facts* (p. 243) and in the statistical summary published in *Report of the California State Board of Agriculture, 1911* (p. 184). The creative character of early California statistics is well shown by those for Los Angeles vineyards in 1858. In addition to the conflicting numbers given by Keller and the State Board, the *Southern Vineyard* (April 8, 1858), a Los Angeles semiweekly, gives 500 acres in the city, with 350 more about to be planted, and 600 acres in the county, for a total of 1,450. Bancroft's *History of California* (4:47n) says Los Angeles had "nearly 2,000,000 vines," or 2,000 acres.

48. Los Angeles County had 11,333 people according to the census of 1860.

49. Leggett, *Early History of Wine Production in California*, 51; Leggett's figures come from the 1859 *California State Register and Year Book of Facts*.

50. If a Los Angeles vineyard produced at least 1,000 gallons to the acre, and there were 2,385

acres of bearing vineyards, then the vintage of 1858 would have been 2,385,000 gallons. Keller himself puts it at 325,000 gallons, but adds that "not more than half" of the Los Angeles grape crop is made into wine. "The natives dry and lose much of the fruit, for want of proper fences; a considerable portion is shipped in various directions, and the Indian consumption is extensive" (*U.S. Patent Office Annual Report 1858*, 345). Keller's estimate of 6.5 to 13 tons per acre is probably only a little exaggerated. J. DeBarth Shorb, writing in 1875, boasted of Lake Vineyard's Mission vines, "now sixty years old," that were producing "from 25,000 to 30,000 pounds per acre" (Hawley, ed., *The Present Condition, Growth, Progress, and Advantages of Los Angeles City and County*, 113). In my estimates of wine production in Los Angeles I have not ventured to use such extravagant figures, although there can be no doubt that they were often reached.

51. The California State Agricultural Society's *Transactions 1859* (p. 343) gives even more sensational figures for this growth. According to this source there were 324,234 vines in the state in 1855 and 6,668,717 in 1859, an increase of 6,344,483 in four years. That number of vines translates to something around 6,000 acres, a perfectly possible figure, although not, perhaps, a likely one.

52. *California State Register and Year Book of Facts* (1857), 206.

53. *Two Years before the Mast and Twenty-Four Years After*, 392. In Dana's journal, from which *Twenty-Four Years After* is derived, the entry for his visit to Los Angeles on August 22, 1859, reads: "Los Angeles prosperous, growing. All engaged in grape growing. Vineyards everywhere." (See *The Journals of Richard Harding Dana, Jr.*, edited by Robert F. Lucid, Cambridge, MA, 1968, 3:848.) In 1859, 500,000 gallons was the figure for wine production in Los Angeles according to both the *California State Register* and M'Kee's "The Grape and Wine Culture of California"; Keller gives 325,000, a more likely quantity.

54. Hilgard, "The Agriculture and Soils of California," 506.

55. *U.S. Patent Office Annual Report 1858*, 347–48.

56. Matthew Keller Papers, box 5, file 24, Huntington Library.

57. Keller to unidentified recipient, April 13, 1877. My guess is that the letter is to Isaias Hellman of the Farmers' and Merchants' Bank, who held the mortgage on Keller's Los Angeles Vineyard. A draft of the letter is in the Matthew Keller Papers, box 2, file 25, Huntington Library.

58. Matthew Keller Papers, box 4, file 21, Huntington Library.

59. Mahony to Keller, May 13, 1878, Matthew Keller Papers, box 3, file 5, Huntington Library. Quassia (*Quassia amara*), bitterwood, is still used to flavor soft drinks and as an element in bitters.

60. Sullivan, "Wine in California: The Early Years," *Wayward Tendrils Quarterly* 21 (October 2011): 31.

61. J. DeBarth Shorb to Charles Leoser, June 21, 1877, J. DeBarth Shorb Papers, Huntington Library. Leoser was the editor of *Bonfort's Wine and Spirit Circular* in New York.

62. Keller obituary, *Los Angeles Express*, April 11, 1881. Keller's papers show that he was making large sales of wine to Benjamin Dreyfus in San Francisco in 1879 (Matthew Keller Papers, box 2, file 10, Huntington Library).

63. Keller Papers, box 2, file 32, Huntington Library.

64. Apostol, "Don Mateo Keller," 112. On a letter of September 26, 1884, the company letterhead reads "Successors to Don Mateo Keller, Established 1852." See J. DeBarth Shorb Papers, box 70, Huntington Library.

65. Peninou, *History of the Los Angeles Viticultural District*, 17.

66. Bellini's *La Sonnambula* was performed in San Francisco as early as 1851.

67. *Alta California*, November 8, 1857.

68. In the name of the firm, "Frohling" was always spelled without the umlaut; I follow that practice. Kohler Street in Los Angeles, named for Charles Kohler, crosses Seventh Street just west of Central Avenue, no doubt marking at that point some part of the old Kohler and Frohling property.

69. *Alta California*, October 12, 1856. Since no wine from the 1856 vintage would have been available in October, the prize-winning wine had to be either from Fröhling's first or second vintage, a notable feat of precocity.

70. Henry Dalton, "Daily Occurences at Azusa," October 3, 1856, manuscript journal, Henry Dalton Papers, Huntington Library.

71. *Southern Vineyard*, December 22, 1859. A contract for this sort of operation has been copied out in the Henry Dalton Papers at the Huntington Library ("Daily Occurences at Azusa," August 22, 1864). On August 7, 1863, Dalton and Kohler and Fröhling signed a contract by which Kohler and Frohling would buy the entire crop of Dalton's vineyards and rent his cellars for the next year to store the wine produced. Dalton was to provide the labor for picking the grapes and making the wine, although the winemaking would be under the direction of a superintendent employed by Kohler and Frohling. They would pay 35 cents a gallon plus taxes for the wine produced. Dalton could add purchased grapes to the vintage, subject to Kohler and Frohling's approval of the quality of the grapes. The pomace and lees remaining from the vintage were Dalton's, presumably so that he could distill brandy from them.

72. Perkins, Stern and Co., "Catalog of California Wines." Kohler and Frohling set up their own still, "with all the latest European improvements," for the production of brandy at Los Angeles in 1862. See *Alta California*, October 13, 1862.

73. "California as a Vineland," 603–4. "Purple life-blood" is mere rhetoric: the juice of the Mission grape is colorless, like that of all grapes except for the few *teinturiers*. And the Indians must have been filling up the crusher, not the press.

74. From McKee ("Historic Winegrowers of Southern California"): "This plot [the Aguilar property] they immediately improved by cuttings imported directly from Europe—the first of record planted in Southern California after those brought in by Vignes." The importation attributed to Vignes is, as has been said, doubtful; the case for Kohler and Frohling may be a bit stronger, but there is no evidence. Documented importation of European varieties began, as has been noted, in Northern California in 1852.

75. California State Agricultural Society, *Transactions 1859*, 108.

76. Unidentified clipping in the Gallo file, Wine Institute, San Francisco.

77. "Wine in California: The Early Years," *Wayward Tendrils Quarterly* 21 (October 2011): 23. Richard Perkins was the backer of the firm; his son, Samuel, was the Perkins of Perkins and Stern. According to L. J. Rose, Jr., young Perkins was in charge of the store in Boston, while Charles Stern operated in New York. Perkins and Stern later handled the wine of L. J. Rose's Sunny Slope Vineyard as well as that of Kohler and Frohling. See Rose, *L. J. Rose of Sunny Slope*, 104.

78. Advertisement in the *Los Angeles Star*, May 4, 1861, quoted in Friis, *John Fröhling*, 33.

79. The railroad was not a boon at first. A memorial from Charles Kohler and other winemakers to the Central Pacific pointed out that, given the classification used by the railroad, it would cost $4.80 to ship by rail to Chicago a case of wine costing $2.50. At that rate the wine men would ship nothing by rail, since they had an established route by water as an alternative. No doubt the railroad gave way in this matter (*Alta California*, August 15, 1869). In the California State Agricultural Society's *Transactions 1874* (p. 333), a note on "the present rates of freight" from San Francisco states that the railroad rates are still "unsettled," but that "recent shipments by carloads have been made through to New York at one dollar and fifty cents (currency) per one hundred pounds." The basic rate by sail via Cape Horn was 10 cents a gallon.

80. Hardy, "Los Angeles," 200. Hardy, a successful winemaker in Australia, was a good judge of wine.

CHAPTER 4

1. B. D. Wilson to his second wife, Margaret Hereford Wilson, July 13, 1856, Benjamin Wilson Papers, Huntington Library. The more usual style of description is found in *Bonfort's Wine and Spirit Circular*, a New York publication. It rhapsodized that the San Gabriel Valley "is a second Garden of Eden, with many Eves. It can not be depicted by pen, nor illustrated by brush. The writer, the artist, the poet all feel the poverty of their professions as they stand before it. Nature in all her grandeur, in all her sublimity, in all her charm and beauty, adorned but not disguised by art" and so on. Quoted in Wait, *Wines and Vines of California*, 181.

2. Rose, Jr., *L. J. Rose of Sunny Slope*, 85.

3. Dakin, *A Scotch Paisano in Old Los Angeles*, 105.

4. Ibid., 108.

5. For years visitors to the Los Angeles Arboretum, on part of the old Santa Anita ranch, were shown a small adobe house identified as Hugo Reid's; that identification has now been discarded.

6. Brewer, *Up and Down California*, 14.

7. Hutton, *Glances at California*, 35.

8. There are eighteen entries under Wilson's name in W. W. Robinson's *Southern California Local History*, a survey of town development in Southern California. The record tracks him as the owner of property in what are now the areas of Beverly Hills, Culver City, Pasadena, San Pedro, Wilmington, San Marino, and Riverside. Local transactions for Los Angeles property recorded in the Benjamin Wilson Papers are with Isaac Ogier, Matthew Keller, Ozias Morgan, and Alexander Bell; no doubt there were many others.

9. His house and vineyard stood at the corner of Alameda and Macy Streets. Macy Street has now disappeared through the construction of Cesar Chavez Avenue. The site was, approximately, Alameda Street just to the east of today's Olvera Street.

10. Townsend, *The California Diary of General E. D. Townsend*, 105. One wonders why Keller is not on the list.

11. Edward Beale to B. D. Wilson, January 18, 1855, Benjamin Wilson Papers, Huntington Library.

12. Sullivan, "Wine in California: The Early Years; Los Angeles Wine, 1850–1870," *Wayward Tendrils Quarterly* 21 (October 2011): 21. Sullivan adds that Wilson's Swiss winemaker, Adolph Eberhart, kept "dabbling" with sparkling wine and won a premium at the 1867 state fair, but that sparkling wine was never a "serious part of the Lake Vineyard operation."

13. March 1855, quoted in Carosso, *The California Wine Industry*, 26n63 (no day given).

14. White to the *California Farmer*, September 22, 1855, in *California Farmer* 4 (October 5, 1855): 107. Wilson had moved his winemaking operations to his Lake Vineyard property, near San Gabriel, in 1855. But I think that White is mistaken in saying that the first sparkling wine was made there.

15. According to the report of the visiting committee of the California State Agricultural Society in 1858 (*Transactions 1858*, 293), Wilson then had at the Lake Vineyard (as he had renamed the Huerta de Cuati) 16,000 bearing vines and 22,000 young vines. The 16,000 presumably came with his purchase in 1854.

16. Deed to Huerta de Cuati, February 6, 1854, Benjamin Wilson Papers, Huntington Library.

17. Edward Beale to B. D. Wilson, January 18, 1855; and B. D. Wilson to Wiley Wilson, April

12, 1854, Benjamin Wilson Papers, Huntington Library.

18. The lake has since been filled in and transformed into Lacy Park; it is remembered by Lake Avenue in Pasadena, originally laid out by Wilson as Lake Vineyard Avenue.

19. B. D. Wilson to Margaret Wilson, August 15, 1856, Benjamin Wilson Papers, Huntington Library.

20. B. D. Wilson to Margaret Wilson, October 23, 1856, Benjamin Wilson Papers, Huntington Library.

21. Hobbs, Gilmore and Co. to B. D. Wilson, March 6, 1862, and June 24, 1862, Benjamin Wilson Papers, Huntington Library.

22. Hobbs, Gilmore and Co. to B. D. Wilson, July 5, 1862, Benjamin Wilson Papers, Huntington Library.

23. See Chapter 1, note 13. Captain Townsend noted on his visit to Los Angeles in October 1855 (*The California Diary of E. D. Townsend*, 106) that, besides the Mission, "other varieties are about being brought into use." This must mean that some nonbearing vines of other varieties were now in the Los Angeles vineyards, but we learn nothing more than that. Keller, as we have seen, was credited with twelve varieties in 1858; Townsend may mean those.

24. Henry Myles to B. D. Wilson, January 16, 1861, Benjamin Wilson Papers, Huntington Library.

25. Townsend, *The California Diary of E. D. Townsend*, 108. The "old German" was not Adolph Eberhart (who was Swiss), as he did not come to the Lake Vineyard until 1857.

26. Henry Myles to B. D. Wilson, January, 20, 1856; February 5, 1856; and February 22, 1856, Benjamin Wilson Papers, Huntington Library.

27. B. D. Wilson to J. DeBarth Shorb, April 10, 1868; April 20, 1869; April 26, 1869; and May 8, 1869, J. DeBarth Shorb Papers, Huntington Library.

28. Frank Bacon to Henry Bacon, [January 28, 1872]; and April 13, 1872, box 38, Henry Douglas Bacon Papers, Huntington Library.

29. McGinty, *Strong Wine*, 469.

30. The lack of capable help was long felt by winemakers throughout the state. A circular from California Winegrowers addressed to the federal government in 1870 asked that European winemakers be invited "by the thousands" to come to this country with "their experience, their industry, their families and their capital." See Carosso, *The California Wine Industry*, 94.

31. Henry Myles to B. D. Wilson, January 28, 1857, Benjamin Wilson Papers, Huntington Library.

32. Newmark, *Sixty Years in Southern California*, 319.

33. September 6, 1865, Benjamin Wilson papers, Huntington Library. Richard Steven Street (*Beasts of the Field*, 241) states that the vineyardists of Anaheim had begun to recruit Chinese immigrants from San Francisco in 1859, apparently the earliest such instance in Southern California. He also notes that Wilson was using Chinese labor as early as 1864.

34. J. DeBarth Shorb to George Dietz, November 10, 1872, J. DeBarth Shorb Papers, Huntington Library. Major Ben Truman described the wine as "a sweet wine much prized in the East and produced only upon a few tablones on the Mt. [i.e., Mound Vineyard]" (*Los Angeles Star*, April 4, 1874, quoted in Midge Sherwood, *Days of Vintage, Years of Vision*, 335). It sold at a price between those of Wilson's fortified and table wines. Presumably it had been well sulfured to prevent further fermentation of the residual sugar.

35. Reid, *History of Pasadena*, 336. Elizabeth Pomeroy (*Lost and Found*, 74) writes that Wilson's purpose was to find timber for fence posts and shingles, a much more sensible idea.

36. Adolph Eberhart to B. D. Wilson, February 23, 1864, Benjamin Wilson Papers, Huntington Library.

37. Sullivan, *Zinfandel*, 13.

38. Wilson Flint to B. D. Wilson, February 16, 1866, Benjamin Wilson Papers, Huntington Library.

39. Jancis Robinson, ed., *The Oxford Companion to Wine*, s.v. "Muscat of Alexandria."

40. J. DeBarth Shorb to Carlton Curtis, December 13, [1875,] J. DeBarth Shorb Papers, Letterbooks, vol. 1, Huntington Library. By the 1870s muscat wine was made at many different wineries in Los Angeles County.

41. J. DeBarth Shorb to B. D. Wilson, January 29, 1869, Benjamin Wilson Papers, Huntington Library. By "Frontiniac" Shorb must mean the Muscat de Frontignan, from the town of that name in the Languedoc, famous for its muscat wines. An alternative spelling is "Frontignac." Wine of that name ("La Frontignac") is listed among the sweet wines of California in the statistical summary published in *Report of the California State Board of Agriculture, 1911*, 182.

42. J. DeBarth Shorb to B. D. Wilson, January 28, 1872, Benjamin Wilson Papers, Huntington Library.

43. Sullivan, *A Companion to California Wine*, s.v. "Black Malvoisie."

44. Jancis Robinson, ed., *The Oxford Companion to Wine*, s.v. "Malvoisie."

45. J. DeBarth Shorb to B. D. Wilson, March 25, 1870, Benjamin Wilson Papers, Huntington Library.

46. Sullivan, *A Companion to California Wine*, s.v. "Thompson's Seedless."

47. One agent was the firm of Childs and Bartlett; John Wilson then took over and was succeeded by a Mr. Barber. See Adolph Eberhart to B. D. Wilson, May 12, 1866; J. Ross Browne to B. D. Wilson, September 12, 1866; and Carmick and Co. to B. D. Wilson, October 17, 1866, Benjamin Wilson Papers, Huntington Library.

48. It is said that Wilson broke the connection with Hobbs, Gilmore because Wilson, a sympathizer with the Confederate cause, felt that he was discriminated against by Hobbs, a "black Republican"—a term used at the time to label sympathizers with the antislavery movement. See John Walton Caughey, "Don Benito Wilson," 290.

49. Statement of account, box 31, Benjamin Wilson Papers, Huntington Library. The arithmetic does not work out; there must have been other credits not stated.

50. Hobbs, Gilmore to B. D. Wilson, September 24, 1863, Benjamin Wilson Papers, Huntington Library.

51. Unidentified clipping dated December 18, 1864, Bancroft Scraps, California Agriculture, vol. 18, part 4, Bancroft Library.

52. Margaret Wilson to J. L. Brent, April 10, 1866, Benjamin Wilson Papers, Huntington Library.

53. A characteristic lament occurs in a letter from Wilson to Shorb (December 20, 1868, J. DeBarth Shorb Papers, box 131, Huntington Library) about Wilson's wish to sell some property: "I would feel sorry to sell the property but I feel so totally unable to attend and have the property cared for and brought forward that it might be best for me to sell[,] as you know my troubles and age combined has dulled my spirits to that degree that I am not myself and never shall be again in this life[,] and to hold places of value and see them neglected only adds to my present sadness." Wilson's special burden was his only son, John, who became an alcoholic and died a suicide in 1870.

54. Rose, Jr., *L. J. Rose of Sunny Slope*, 49.

55. *Pacific Wine and Spirit Review,* June 5, 1891, 10.

56. J. DeBarth Shorb to B. D. Wilson, March 14, 1868, Benjamin Wilson Papers, Huntington Library. On the formation of B. D. Wilson and Co., see Shorb to Wilson, January 21, 1868 (Wilson Papers), and box 149, file 17 of the J. DeBarth Shorb Papers, Huntington Library. The inventory of property turned over by Wilson to B. D. Wilson and Co. in December 1867 gives a detailed picture of winery furnishings in Southern California at the time: the list runs from stills, tanks, press, crusher, and assorted cooperage to buckets, tin dippers, oak bungs, and two dozen grape baskets (box 149, file 18, Shorb Papers).

57. J. DeBarth Shorb to B. D. Wilson, January 21, 1868; March 2, 1868; March 5, 1869; and January 19, 1869, Benjamin Wilson Papers, Huntington Library.

58. J. DeBarth Shorb to B. D. Wilson, April 30, 1869, Benjamin Wilson Papers, Huntington Library.

59. J. DeBarth Shorb to B. D. Wilson, June 14, 1869, Benjamin Wilson Papers, Huntington Library. The firm of Morrow and Chamberlin was originally named Wilson, Morrow, and Chamberlin, but Wilson had his name removed this year (Sherwood, *Days of Vintage, Years of Vision*, 155). It was an article of faith among California wine men that most of the wine sold in New York as California wine was in fact manufactured in New York. "In the manufacture[,] carbonate of soda, protonitrate of mercury, solutions of borax, barytra water, and subacetate of lead are used, and both 'French' and 'California' wines are made and sold as such. Wines that are adulterated are first colored with Campeachy wood, beet root, indigo, Brazil wood, elderberries, cochineal, black mallons [*sic*], etc., and then adulterated by the use of sulphuric ether, sulphate of potassium, acetate of alum, bicarbonate of soda, alum, tannin, gelatine, aluminate of potash, etc." (Truman, "The Wines of California," January 30, 1887). The Californians said that the "wines" thus produced came from "brick vineyards."

60. J. DeBarth Shorb to B. D. Wilson, August 17, 1869, Benjamin Wilson Papers, Huntington Library.

61. J. DeBarth Shorb to A. P. Bacon, July 27, 1875, Letterbooks, vol. 2, J. DeBarth Shorb Papers, Huntington Library.

62. J. DeBarth Shorb to George Dietz, November 10, 1872, Letterbooks, vol. 1, J. DeBarth Shorb Papers, Huntington Library.

63. J. DeBarth Shorb to Charles Shaw, July 29, 1875, Letterbooks, vol. 2, J. DeBarth Shorb Papers, Huntington Library.

64. J. DeBarth Shorb to Samuel Lachman, July 29, 1875, Letterbooks, vol. 2, J. DeBarth Shorb Papers, Huntington Library.

65. J. DeBarth Shorb to J. D. Lyman, April 10, 1875, Letterbooks, vol. 2, J. DeBarth Shorb Papers, Huntington Library.

66. Rose, Jr., *L. J. Rose of Sunny Slope*, 83.

67. Untitled manuscript memoir by L. J. Rose, Jr., L. J. Rose Papers, box 1, p. 17, Huntington Library.

68. Rose, Jr., *L. J. Rose of Sunny Slope*, 133.

69. Ibid.

70. Workman, *The City that Grew*, 138–39.

71. Rose, Jr., *L. J. Rose of Sunny Slope*, 133. In an unsigned typescript titled "Life History of Hon. L. J. Rose" [by E. T. Harris] (box 3, L. J. Rose Papers, Huntington Library). It is said that "the universal voice of the small vineyard owners of Los Angeles County is that they have been indebted to Mr. Rose, more than to any or all other wine-makers, for keeping up the prices of wine grapes to living rates."

72. Nordhoff, *California for Health, Pleasure, and Residence*, 171.

73. According to Rose ("Appendix on Grape Culture," 225), the Blaue Elba, a dark-purple grape, made white wine "of the highest bouquet and quality." It was, he says, introduced by Jacob Keller of Anaheim, who gave cuttings to Rose. Rose supplied cuttings of the grape to William H. Workman for his Boyle Heights vineyard; Workman's son called it "the famous 'Blau Elba'" (Workman, *The City that Grew*, 183). Other judges were not convinced of the variety's merits. No grape of this name appears in *Wine Grapes* (2001), by Robinson, Harding, and Vouillamoz.

74. Rose, Jr., *L. J. Rose of Sunny Slope*, 80. Unsatisfactory Zinfandel may have been partly the result of winemaking practices. The judges at the Annual State Viticultural Convention in 1884 found that "Rose's San Gabriel Zinfandel No. 3," though a wine of "fine deep color, not fermented through, is rich in fruit but lacking delicacy; would, if well treated in the fermenting tank, result in a firm Zinfandel of good, full body" (*Report of the Third Annual State Viticultural Convention*, 12).

75. Salvator, *Los Angeles in the Sunny Seventies*, 154.

76. Malbeck (Malbec) and Pied de Perdrix are the same grape, also known as Cot in the region of Cahors; Petit Pineau is the name of a white grape (Menu Pineau). There was much confusion of names and identities of the many new varieties being introduced into the state.

77. Rose, "Los Angeles District: The State Commissioner's Report," 220. This was Rose's official report to the commission.

78. *Report of the Third Annual State Viticultural Convention*, 10. I cannot identify "Chauché noir."

79. Rose, Jr., *L. J. Rose of Sunny Slope*, 80. The accepted solution to the problem of sherry in California was not really a solution but a substitution. This was to heat the fortified base wine either by heated coils placed in the wine or by putting the wine in a heated room and "baking" it over some weeks. The process loosely resembles that used in the production of Madeira but is unknown in Jerez.

80. "Sunny Slope," typescript, box 3, L. J. Rose Papers, Huntington Library; also published in the *Illustrated Los Angeles Herald*, July 1882.

81. Prescott had just then been made the capital of the newly formed Arizona Territory and was also a mining center. It is about 350 miles from Rose's place.

82. Rose, "Cross-Country Reminiscences," p. 11, typescript, box 3, L. J. Rose Papers, Huntington Library. The article was published in the *Californian Illustrated Magazine*, December 1892.

83. Fifteen years later Rose ("Los Angeles District, *Pacific Wine and Spirit Review*, January 11, 1884, 221) noted that, although the Northern California wineries continued to ship by water through San Francisco, in the south "all our wines are now shipped by rail." The Santa Fe Railway had not yet arrived in Los Angeles when Rose made this statement, so Los Angeles wine shipped by rail had first to go to San Francisco, as did the wine shipped by water.

84. The association between Perkins, Stern and Co. and Kohler and Frohling came to an end in 1869. See B. D. Wilson to J. DeBarth Shorb, April 26, 1869, J. DeBarth Shorb Papers, Huntington Library.

85. Rose, Jr., *L. J. Rose of Sunny Slope*, 106.

86. After he had stepped back from running the winery, Rose sent his son, L. J. Rose, Jr., to New York to learn the trade at the Stern and Rose agency. Among other interesting encounters there, young Rose made the acquaintance of the celebrated Reverend Henry Ward Beecher, who "came regularly to the store every fortnight and ordered a gallon of port wine for sacramental purposes." Beecher enjoyed Rose's stories of California, and "would sit and chat with me for fifteen or twenty minutes, sipping a small glass of wine betimes" (Rose, Jr., *L. J. Rose of Sunny*

Slope, 130–31). Beecher's father, the Reverend Lyman Beecher, preached sermons against drink and co-founded the American Temperance Society. Americans, he declared, were "a generation of drunkards." Harriet Beecher Stowe, Henry's sister, is said to have been "always interested in temperance." She published "Temperance Tales" in 1859 (Ernest Cherrington, ed., *Standard Encyclopedia of the Alcohol Problem*, Westerville, OH, vol. 4 [1930]; *s.v.* "Stowe"). Henry apparently did some backsliding.

87. Workman, *The City that Grew*, 124.

88. "The Passing of L. J. Rose," *Pacific Wine and Spirit Review*, May 31, 1899, 22.

89. The Englishmen had, no doubt, been given exaggerated ideas about the prospects of the business. There were, according to one witness, some "big lies" told in promoting the sale (Evan Coleman to J. DeBarth Shorb, December 23, 1886, J. DeBarth Shorb Papers, Huntington Library). An account of how the estate was overvalued is given in "The Big Wine Syndicate," *Pacific Wine and Spirit Review*, September 21, 1889, 2.

90. The prospectus for L. J. Rose Company, Ltd., in an unidentified, undated [1886] cutting from a London paper, is in box 10 of the J. F. Crank Papers, at the Huntington Library. It affirms that "there is no other estate in the valley that can at present compare with Sunny Slope." The annual profit of the estate was said to have been $150,000, and that would have been expected to rise to $340,000 or more in five years.

91. *Pacific Wine and Spirit Review*, October 31, 1898, 7; and September 30, 1901, 32.

92. Rose, Jr., *L. J. Rose of Sunny Slope*, 164.

93. Newmark, *Sixty Years in Southern California*, 585.

94. Perkins, Stern and Co., "Catalog of California Wines."

95. Unidentified cutting dated November 5, 1864, Bancroft Scraps, California Agriculture, vol. 18, part 4, Bancroft Library.

96. Matthew Keller letter to the *Alta California*, January 1, 1867, reprinted in an unidentified cutting, Bancroft Scraps, California Agriculture, vol. 18, part 4, Bancroft Library.

97. Committee report to the Los Angeles Common Council, February 12, 1869, in John Albert Wilson, *History of Los Angeles County*, 109. Sainsevain Street is now called Commercial Street.

98. Newmark, *Sixty Years in Southern California*, 336–37. The Fair Oaks property had been sold by Benjamin Wilson to Eliza Johnston, widow of the Confederate general Albert Sydney Johnston, who was killed at Shiloh. She in turn sold it to her brother-in-law, Judge Eaton. The Fair Oaks vineyard was later absorbed into the Sierra Madre Vintage Company; see Chapter 7.

99. Truman, *Semi-Tropical California*, 120.

100. Rose, Jr., *L. J. Rose of Sunny Slope*, 48.

101. In 1872 Baldwin bought shares in Comstock mines for $2 each and sold them for $1,800 each.

102. Hawley, *The Present Condition, Growth, Progress, and Advantages of Los Angeles City and County*, 88.

103. Wait, *Wines and Vines of California*, 180. The figures are probably exaggerated.

104. Gudde, *California Place Names*. Apparently "Pasadena," abbreviated from the inordinately long original suggestion, means only "valley." One of the names proposed for the colony was "Muscat," after the most-planted variety of grape in Pasadena. See Zack, *Altadena*, 53.

105. The prospectus of the colony stipulated that in the first season of ownership 5 acres of grapes would be planted, and, in the second season, 5 more on each tract of land. See J. W. Wood, *Pasadena, California*, 55.

CHAPTER 5

1. Sullivan, "Wine in California: The Early Years," *Wayward Tendrils Quarterly* 21 (October 2011): 27.

2. John Albert Wilson, *History of Los Angeles County*, 156. The one with experience was probably Theodore Reiser, who is said to have served a three-year apprenticeship in winemaking in his native Baden (Friis, *Campo Aleman*, 61). Charles Kohler is reported as having said that many of the Germans "were practical viticulturists from the Rhine Valley," but Vincent Carosso, after citing that statement, went on to say that Kohler was "entirely wrong" (Carosso, *California Wine Industry*, 61). Since Kohler was one of the founders of Anaheim, the error is surprising.

3. According to Harris Newmark (*Sixty Years in Southern California*, 212), August Langenberger, son-in-law of Pacifico Ontiveros, used his influence with his father-in-law to complete the deal. Langenberger became one of the prominent winegrowers of Anaheim. The fact that Hansen had surveyed the ranch in 1855 no doubt helped to determine the purchase.

4. There were already vineyards in the region of the Santa Ana Valley; in 1846, Lieutenant Colonel William H. Emory (*Notes of a Military Reconnaissance*, 184) noted that the valley contained "many valuable vine yards and corn fields."

5. *Los Angeles Star*, January 30, 1858, quoted in John Albert Wilson, *History of Los Angeles County*, 155–56. The details of my account of the preparation of the site are largely taken from this source. The figure for the length of ditches seems incredible, but the total is carefully itemized in the newspaper article.

6. The officers of the Society wrote to the Patent Office in Washington asking for advice about the choice of grape varieties to plant (Paule, "The German Settlement at Anaheim," chapter 3). I do not know what advice might have been given—it could not have been based on any relevant experience—and in any case, there was no choice: the only thing available locally was the Mission grape.

7. The barrier was impenetrable in theory but not in fact. In 1862 the authorities ordered that the live fence be protected from the wildlife of the region by an outer line of cactus. During the great drought of 1862–65 mounted guards had to be posted outside the fence to fend off the assaults of cattle crazed by thirst; dozens of such animals were shot and killed. See Dickson, "The Founding and Early History of Anaheim, California," 31.

8. *Sacramento Union*, March 19, 1859, cited in Carosso, *California Wine Industry*, 64.

9. I follow the account given in Carosso, *California Wine Industry*, 61–65. Other versions differ on a number of important points.

10. Carosso, *California Wine Industry*, 65.

11. The federal census of 1870 lists thirty-seven proprietors of vineyards in Anaheim township, three of them women; the 1880 census lists sixty proprietors, five of them women. Most of these made wine.

12. Sullivan, "Wine in California: The Early Years," *Wayward Tendrils Quarterly* 21 (October 2011): 28.

13. Stern and Kramer, "The Wine Tycoon of Anaheim," 277.

14. *Alta California*, December 25, 1871.

15. John Albert Wilson, *History of Los Angeles County*, 181–82.

16. Peninou, *History of the Los Angeles Viticultural District*, 23–24.

17. Raup, *The German Colonization of Anaheim, California*, 134.

18. John Albert Wilson, *History of Los Angeles County*, 179.

19. Ibid.

20. Pachter, ed., *Abroad in America*, 180–81.

21. See the lists in Peninou, *History of the Los Angeles Viticultural District*. The list of thirty-seven Anaheim growers in the Perkins and Stern catalog of 1863 is entirely of German names.

22. Despite this disaster, the irrepressible and irresponsible Ben Truman, writing about Anaheim for the *New York Times* ("The Wines of California," February 20, 1887), found everything prosperous there. When he visited it just a week before, he found the place "greatly improved by hundreds of additions of vineyards….I find also that the wine business has always been on the increase, and that large quantities of the Mission and Zinfandel clarets, ports, sherries and Angelicas are sold annually, and that the Anaheim wine makers have 1,900,000 gallons on hand, with the possibility that some lots may have been overlooked." He does not mention any disease, although if he had actually visited Anaheim he would have been surrounded by dead vineyards. The "hundreds of additions of vineyards" is pure invention.

23. Pierce, *The California Vine Disease*, 71.

24. *Rural Californian* 10 (November 1887): 251. The expert was F. Lamson Scribner. He was accompanied by the distinguished French ampelographer Pierre Viala.

25. Pierce, *The California Vine Disease*, 209. Pierce has been called "the first professionally trained plant pathologist" to work in California. See Ralph E. Smith, quoted in Gardner and Hewitt, *Pierce's Disease of the Grapevine*, 3.

26. In the years 1935–46 Pierce's disease killed some 50,000 acres of vines in the Central Valley, more than in the Southern California devastation of the 1880s, although the later loss was a much smaller fraction of the whole (Gardner and Hewitt, *Pierce's Disease of the Grapevine*, 1). Most recently, Napa and Sonoma Counties suffered severe losses of vines to Pierce's disease in 2015 (*Wines and Vines*, January 2016, 20).

27. Reprinted from the *Anaheim Gazette* in *Pacific Wine and Spirit Review*, October 12, 1888, 29.

28. Raup, *The German Colonization of Anaheim, California*, 137.

29. According to Ernest Peninou (*History of the Los Angeles Viticultural District*, 25), the vineyards and wineries of Theo Reiser, William Koenig, Charles Lorenz, C. Rust, and Tim Boege survived the Pierce's disease devastation and continued in production down to Prohibition.

30. Pierce, *The California Vine Disease*, 65, 71.

31. The Almeria is a Spanish grape more valued for the table than for wine; Klaeber I am unable to identify. Most of the other grapes named have all had some role in California winemaking, although apart from Zinfandel none is important now. The native American varieties have long since disappeared from California vineyards.

32. Paule, "The German Settlement at Anaheim," chapter 4.

33. The practice of fortifying even table wines was apparently general. J. Ross Browne, a friend of California wine, in addressing a convention of Los Angeles winemakers in 1866, told them, "It would be better for you if you had never distilled a gallon of brandy, so far as your wine is concerned….The chief complaint is that there is too much spirit in the California wines" (unidentified cutting, October 8, 1866, Bancroft Scraps, California Agriculture, vol. 18, part 4, Bancroft Library). In the same year, the St. Louis Horticultural Society tasted five wines from Wilson's Lake Vineyard and rejected them as "doctored." They had apparently all been fortified, even the "hock" and the supposedly unfortified "Mound Vineyard" wine (Hyatt, *Hyatt's Hand-Book of Grape Culture*, 218–19).

34. Brace, *The New West*, 295.

35. Figures from "The California Wine Industry," Part V of *Report of the California State Board of Agriculture, 1911*, 191. In these totals, the figures for sweet wine are exact; those for dry wine are estimated.

36. Carosso, *California Wine Industry*, 95.

37. *Report of the California State Board of Agriculture, 1911*, 185. The numbers seem doubtful, but the trend was probably real enough.

38. U.S. Patent Office, *Report of the Commissioner of Patents for the Year 1861*, Agriculture section, 4.

39. Ibid., 483.

40. Ibid., 526.

41. The Los Angeles Viticultural District (mainly Los Angeles County) in 1858 had 2,753 acres of vines, nearly half of the state's total of 5,948 acres. Ten years later, the Los Angeles District had grown to 6,947 acres, but that now accounted for only 20 percent of the state total of 33, 316. The other districts (as identified by the Board of State Viticultural Commissioners in 1880) were El Dorado, Sonoma, Sacramento, Napa, San Francisco, and San Joaquin. Sonoma, the leading producer among the northern counties, is reported to have made 4,182,279 gallons of wine in 1869 to the 3,925,000 in Los Angeles. See Carosso, *California Wine Industry*, 189n52.

42. Truman, *Semi-Tropical California*, 94. Los Angeles was certainly the oldest district and had long been considered "best." The shift in reputation would have lagged behind the shift in production.

43. Salvator, *Los Angeles in the Sunny Seventies*, 68.

44. Carosso, *California Wine Industry*, 47. That act is still in force.

45. The tax, imposed as part of the Internal Revenue Act of 1862, was 5 cents on a gallon of wine. This may seem hardly worth a protest, until one realizes that a gallon of table wine in 1862 might fetch only 15 cents in the market.

46. California State Agricultural Society, *Transactions 1866 and 1867*, 36.

47. Carosso, *California Wine Industry*, 82.

48. The association's most notable work in this line was to sponsor the book *Grapes and Grape Vines of California*, published in San Francisco in 1877 and featuring ten color oleographs of different grape varieties from watercolors by Hannah Millard. The varieties illustrated are Mission, Johannisberg Riesling, Rose Chasselas, Muscat of Alexandria, Black Hamburg, Flame Tokay, Zinfandel, Sultana, Catawba, and Emperor—a strange selection by our current notions, and evidence of the still very limited knowledge of varietal character at the time. According to James Gabler (*Wine into Words*, 158), there are "only eight known perfect copies of the original publication," most of the edition having been taken apart for the sake of the illustrations. Should a complete copy of *Grapes and Grape Vines of California* appear on the market it would fetch a fabulous price.

49. Carosso, *California Wine Industry*, 92.

50. *Alta California*, September 1, 1858.

51. James Blake and William L. Simmons, "Report on Native Vines," in *Transactions 1859*, by California State Agricultural Society, 300–03.

52. Teiser and Harroun (*Winemaking in California*, 38) note this as "the first chemical analysis of California wine to appear in print," a "landmark in the progress of winemaking in California." The analyst, James Blake, an Englishman, was a physician practicing in Sacramento and San Francisco.

53. California State Agricultural Society, *Transactions 1859*, 301, 302.

54. Ibid., 302. "Verdot" is the Bordeaux grape Petit Verdot. Kleinberger is another synonym for the Elbling.

55. Sullivan, *Zinfandel*, 24–29.

56. *Report of the Sixth Industrial Exhibition of the Mechanics' Institute of the City of San Francisco…1868*, 69.

57. The Lenoir is a native American vine from the South, valued in California at this time because it is productive and its wine deeply colored. It is listed, with "La Frontignac," as among the sweet wines produced in California in the vintages of 1894–96. See *Report of the California State Board of Agriculture, 1911*, 192.

58. *Pacific Wine and Spirit Review*, July 17, 1885, 98.

59. "Appendix on Grape Culture" in Garey, *Orange Culture in California*, 226. *Wine Grapes*, by Jancis Robinson et al., identifies Burger as a synonym for Monbadon, a variety from the Charente in France. It is described as liking "hot dry climates" and as "suited to spur pruning"—exactly what it got in Southern California.

60. *Pacific Wine and Spirit Review*, January 30, 1885, 124.

61. Charles Sullivan (*Napa Wine*, 136) notes that Charles Lefranc, in the Santa Clara Valley, made California's first "Medoc," a blend of Cabernet and Malbec, in the 1860s. But the Bordeaux varieties did not catch on in north-coast vineyards until the 1880s.

62. An item in the *Pacific Wine and Spirit Review* (August 22, 1889, 185) reports on a 200-acre vineyard near Burbank being grown without irrigation as an "experiment." This was nearly thirty years after Rose had shown, only a few miles from Burbank, that it could be done.

63. Unidentified cuttings dated November 6, 1866; March 19, 1867; and June 12, 1869, in Bancroft Scraps, California Agriculture, vol. 18, part 4, Bancroft Library.

64. The modern view of the various techniques for sterilizing wine by heat is summed up in Jancis Robinson's *Oxford Companion to Wine*, *s.v.* "Pasteurization": "These techniques are relatively brutal…and are used only on ordinary wines which have no potential for improvement after bottle ageing."

65. Gabler, *Wine into Words*.

66. Hyatt and his work have been exhaustively studied by Gail Unzelman, in "Thomas Hart Hyatt: The Man and His Book," supplement to *Wayward Tendrils Quarterly* 23 (July 2013): 1–10.

CHAPTER 6

1. Rose, "Appendix on Vine Culture," 224.

2. Rose, "Los Angeles District," 220.

3. Figures from Sullivan, *A Companion to California Wine*, *s.v.* "California." Sullivan cautions that the figures are "best guesses." It should be noted that contradictory forces were at work in these years. Phylloxera was doing serious destruction in California, especially in the north, just at the time that new plantings were being made throughout the state. For the first half of the '80s, at any rate, planting outpaced destruction. The most spectacular instance was at Senator Leland Stanford's ranch called Vina, in Tehama County, where between 1882 and 1884 a million vines were set out.

4. California State Board of Agriculture, *Report of California State Board of Agriculture, 1911*, 191.

5. *San Francisco Chronicle*, December 19, 1879, quoted in John Albert Wilson, *History of Los Angeles County*, 66.

6. Rose, "Los Angeles District," 221.

7. Griswold, *Beauties of California*, n.p.

8. Descriptions of all four of these wineries may be found conveniently in Sullivan, *A Companion to California Wine*, and in Pinney, *A History of Wine in America*.

9. Letterbooks, vol. 2, February–November 1875, J. DeBarth Shorb Papers, Huntington Library.

10. The post office later awarded the name "Ramona" to a town in San Diego County; Shorb's Ramona disappeared into Alhambra.

11. See Shorb's letters to C. P. Huntington et al., October 7, 1875; to Smith's Sons, October 9, 1875; and to Charles Leoser, October 27, 1875, in Letterbooks, vol. 1, 1870–1875, J. DeBarth Shorb Papers, Huntington Library.

12. Details of the winery arrangements from an undated typescript [c. 1887?], box 149, J. DeBarth Shorb Papers, Huntington Library.

13. The name *Phylloxera vastatrix*, by which the insect has long been known, has now been officially replaced by an earlier name, *Daktulosphaira vitifoliae*, but the official name has not yet ousted the familiar name.

14. Jancis Robinson, ed., *The Oxford Companion to Wine*, s.v. "Phylloxera."

15. In Hawley, ed., *The Present Condition, Growth, Progress, and Advantages of Los Angeles, City and County*, 112.

16. In 1883 Shorb wrote ("Los Angeles Items," *Pacific Wine and Spirit Review*, November 23, 1883, 98) that the varieties chosen for next season's plantings in the company's vineyards were "Carignan, Mataro, Grenache, Riesling, Black Pinot, Black Burgundy and Lenoir." Black Burgundy and Black Pinot are both synonyms for Pinot noir. I do not know how the names might have been applied here. By this time in Southern California almost any well-known variety was available. In 1884 Shorb was selling cuttings of Roussillon (Grenache noir), Grenache, Mataro, Folle Blanche, and Carignan. See J. Stillman, of the Monte Vista Vineyard, San Bernardino County, to J. DeBarth Shorb, November 18, 1884, box 116, file 37, J. DeBarth Shorb Papers, Huntington Library.

17. Evan Coleman to J. DeBarth Shorb, August 5, 1882, J. DeBarth Shorb Papers, Huntington Library. The figure of 4,000 tons is probably one of Shorb's exaggerations. The practical aim was for 2,000 tons, and that quantity was reached only once, in 1883.

18. Evan Coleman to J. DeBarth Shorb, June 9, 1882, J. DeBarth Shorb Papers, Huntington Library.

19. The tonnage crushed in the early years was as follows: 1882, 1,927 tons; 1883, 2,074 tons; 1884, 1,733 tons; and 1885, 1,554 tons. See box 149, file 23, J. DeBarth Shorb Papers, Huntington Library.

20. Or 287 acres, as Shorb claimed in print (*Pacific Wine and Spirit Review*, June 18, 1884, 162). For the projected 400 acres, see Evan Coleman to J. DeBarth Shorb, February 9, 1884, J. DeBarth Shorb Papers, Huntington Library.

21. Evan Coleman to J. DeBarth Shorb, October 13, 1886, J. DeBarth Shorb Papers, Huntington Library. The biographical sketch of Shorb in J. M. Guinn's *Illustrated History of Los Angeles County* (p. 813) states that the San Gabriel Wine Company then owned 10,000 acres of land and cultivated 1,300 acres of grapes. Most of that grape acreage would have been in the established Lake and Mound Vineyards, not in the new vineyards of the San Gabriel Wine Company.

22. Evan Coleman to J. DeBarth Shorb, February 19, 1884, J. DeBarth Shorb Papers, Huntington Library.

23. Evan Coleman to J. DeBarth Shorb, April 30, 1883, J. DeBarth Shorb Papers, Huntington Library.

24. Evan Coleman to J. DeBarth Shorb, November 2, 1881; and October 12, 1884, J. DeBarth Shorb Papers, Huntington Library.

25. J. DeBarth Shorb to General [S.?] H. H. Clark, October 25, 1885, Letterbooks, vol. 9, 184, J. DeBarth Shorb Papers, Huntington Library.

26. *Pacific Wine and Spirit Review*, May 13, 1887, 19.

27. *Pacific Wine and Spirit Review*, April 15, 1887, 198.

28. Box 149, file 25, J. DeBarth Shorb Papers, Huntington Library.

29. E. L. Watkins to J. DeBarth Shorb, April 6, 1888, J. DeBarth Shorb Papers, Huntington Library.

30. J. DeBarth Shorb to Wilfred Neale, February 20, 1883, J. DeBarth Shorb Papers, Huntington Library.

31. F. W. Wood to J. DeBarth Shorb, June 9, 1884, J. DeBarth Shorb Papers, Huntington Library.

32. E. L. Watkins to J. DeBarth Shorb, July 11, 1885, J. DeBarth Shorb Papers, Huntington Library.

33. The winery's New York agency took a carload of claret in 1886 (F. W. Wood to J. DeBarth Shorb, February 4, 1886, J. DeBarth Shorb Papers, Huntington Library), but one hears little about claret after that date, and the quantities on hand in 1889 and 1892 were negligible: less than 2,000 gallons (box 149, J. DeBarth Shorb Papers, Huntington Library).

34. Charles F. Oldham to J. DeBarth Shorb, May 11, 1891, J. DeBarth Shorb Papers, Huntington Library. Oldham was interested in the San Gabriel wines because, as he had written a month earlier from London (April 8, 1891, ibid.), "California wines are becoming quite the rage here." Oldham, of the London firm of Grierson, Oldham, was the leading promoter of California wine in England. He bottled California wine under the Big Tree label, in flat-sided *Bocksbeutels* with the figure of a giant sequoia stump molded on one side.

35. Truman, "The Wines of California," March 13, 1887. There was a San Gabriel Vineyard Company, but not until after Prohibition. Truman must mean the San Gabriel Wine Company.

36. J. DeBarth Shorb to Evan Coleman, August 17, 1855, Letterbooks, vol. 9, 184, J. DeBarth Shorb Papers, Huntington Library.

37. Figures from file 23, box 149, J. DeBarth Shorb Papers, Huntington Library. In an item in the *Pacific Wine and Spirit Review* (November 23, 1883, 95), Shorb claims that the San Gabriel Wine Company made 400,000 gallons of wine in 1882 and would make 450,000 in 1883 "counting brandy by its equivalent in wine." He also states that "if everything is favorable" the company will plant 1,000 acres of vineyard in the coming season. Shorb was obviously not upon oath in saying such things.

38. F. W. Wood to J. DeBarth Shorb, May 22, 1886, J. DeBarth Shorb Papers, Huntington Library. From these figures it appears that San Gabriel wine was fetching almost 50 cents a gallon on average, a respectable figure for the times.

39. At Fresno in 1886 the Barton Winery made 400,000 gallons; the Fresno Vineyard, 440,000; the Eisen Vineyard, 300,000; and the Margaretta Vineyard, 230,000. See Benjamin C. Truman, "Fresno County's Productive Acres," from "The Wines of California" series, *New York Times*, February 27, 1887.

40. Paul Garrett, untitled typescript memoir, [1938,] p. 43, collection of John Barden, New Haven, CT.

41. F. W. Wood to J. DeBarth Shorb, December 16, 1885; E. L. Watkins to Shorb, April 17, 1888; Wood to Shorb, March 29, 1886; Wood to Shorb, March 1, 1886; and Wood to Shorb, March 31, 1886, J. DeBarth Shorb Papers, Huntington Library.

42. F. W. Wood to J. DeBarth Shorb, March 19, 1885; December 3, 1885; and December 8, 1885, J. DeBarth Shorb Papers, Huntington Library. In 1884 the San Gabriel Wine Company had advertised for a "Cellar Master, one who has had experience in preparing all kinds of California wines for the Eastern market" (*Pacific Wine and Spirit Review*, November 7, 1884, 24). Apparently they had no luck with this appeal and turned to local help. Watkins, from New Orleans, was the nephew of J. Lancaster Brent, before the Civil War one of the prominent lawyers of Los Angeles and during the war a Confederate general. Watkins worked first for Wilson,

Shorb, and Phineas Banning in their various interests in Wilmington, California, and he then became manager of the San Gabriel Wine Company. On the retirement of Evan Coleman, circa 1891, he was made vice president of the firm.

43. F. W. Wood to J. DeBarth Shorb, December 1, 1885, J. DeBarth Shorb Papers, Huntington Library.

44. F. W. Wood to J. DeBarth Shorb, December 11, 1885, J. DeBarth Shorb Papers, Huntington Library.

45. F. W. Wood to J. DeBarth Shorb, May 22, 1886, J. DeBarth Shorb Papers, Huntington Library.

46. Pinney, *A History of Wine in America*, 305.

47. F. W. Wood to J. DeBarth Shorb, June 9, 1884, J. DeBarth Shorb Papers, Huntington Library.

48. F. W. Wood to J. DeBarth Shorb, February 8, 1886, J. DeBarth Shorb Papers, Huntington Library. While Watkins was adding "cherry juice" to the San Gabriel ports, Major Benjamin Truman was instructing the readers of the *New York Times* ("The Wines of California," January 16, 1887) that "the port wine from Los Angeles County is undoubtedly the best, purest, and truest port used in this country."

49. Enclosure in F. W. Wood to J. DeBarth Shorb, March 1, 1886, J. DeBarth Shorb Papers, Huntington Library.

50. F. W. Wood to J. DeBarth Shorb, June 25, 1885, J. DeBarth Shorb Papers, Huntington Library.

51. F. W. Wood to J. DeBarth Shorb, December 3, 1885; December 11, 1885; and March 1, 1886, J. DeBarth Shorb Papers, Huntington Library.

52. Letterbook 9, 155–56, J. DeBarth Shorb Papers, Huntington Library.

53. F. W. Wood to J. DeBarth Shorb, May 22, 1886, J. DeBarth Shorb Papers, Huntington Library.

54. F. W. Wood to J. DeBarth Shorb, June 10, 1886, J. DeBarth Shorb Papers, Huntington Library.

55. F. W. Wood to J. DeBarth Shorb, April 16, 1887, J. DeBarth Shorb Papers, Huntington Library.

56. Evan Coleman to J. DeBarth Shorb, September 2, 1889, J. DeBarth Shorb Papers, Huntington Library.

57. *Pacific Wine and Spirit Review*, April 26, 1889, 53. Damage to the Alhambra region, where the company's vineyards were, was estimated at 92.85 percent. Damage in the San Gabriel region, where Wilson's and Shorb's vineyards were, was put at only 15 percent, so Shorb continued to have a source of grapes.

58. Ethelbert Dowlen to J. DeBarth Shorb, September 6, 1888, J. DeBarth Shorb Papers, Huntington Library.

59. Dowlen's report on the vineyards of the Los Angeles District, dated October 9, 1893, was published by the Board of State Viticultural Commissioners as *The Vineyards of Southern California*.

60. Evan Coleman to J. DeBarth Shorb, September 21, 1889, J. DeBarth Shorb Papers, Huntington Library.

61. *Pacific Wine and Spirit Review*, August 15, 1890, 12. One Los Angeles winemaker estimated that the crop in 1890 was "only about one-quarter that of 1886." See *Pacific Wine and Spirit Review*, January 26, 1891, 19.

62. Copy in J. DeBarth Shorb Papers, Huntington Library.

63. Isaias Hellman to Evan Coleman, February 13, 1893, J. DeBarth Shorb Papers, Huntington Library.

64. *Pacific Wine and Spirit Review*, April 23, 1897, 10; Dinkelspiel, *Towers of Gold*, 219.

65. Huntington had known the place since 1892, when he was entertained at San Marino by Shorb. He later said, "I thought then…that it was the prettiest place I had ever seen" (Thorpe, *Henry Edwards Huntington*, 97). The *Pacific Wine and Spirit Review* (April 30, 1903, 52) reported the sale in unfriendly terms: "A dispatch from Los Angeles announces the sale of the San Gabriel Wine Company's property to one of the hustling, bustling promoters of that lively section of the State. This property went for the measly sum of $11,000, and it is safe to say that 20 years ago, it could not have been bought for many times that sum.…It is to be sincerely regretted that this historical place upon which was planted one of the first vineyards that ever attained prominence in California, has gone into hands that will transform it into town lots, etc."

66. Untitled notes on Los Angeles and Riverside County wineries, [by C. Perelli-Minetti,] n.d., made for Ernest Peninou. Copy in the Gail Unzelman Collection, Santa Rosa.

67. *Pacific Wine and Spirit Review*, October 31, 1901, 89.

68. *Pacific Wine and Spirit Review*, December 31, 1902, 11. Wine tourism as we know it hardly existed in 1902, although Andrea Sbarboro at the Italian Swiss Colony winery in Asti, Sonoma County, entertained a steady stream of visitors in the 1890s and after, and Secondo Guasti, at the big Italian Vineyard Company winery in Cucamonga, encouraged visitors in 1912 (*Pacific Wine and Spirit Review*, February 28, 1912, 24). Probably others did too if they thought they had an attraction.

69. *Pacific Wine and Spirit Review*, July 31, 1903, 12.

70. Dolge, a German who founded the town of Dolgeville in upstate New York before coming to California, is said to have "opened a small winery on Spring Street" when he migrated to Los Angeles. See Cecilia Rasmussen, "L.A. Scene," *Los Angeles Times*, May 31, 1993, B3.

71. *Pacific Wine and Spirit Review*, December 21, 1888, 105.

72. Workman, *The City that Grew*, 239.

73. Pierce, *The California Vine Disease*, 65–71.

74. *Pacific Wine and Spirit Review*, October 8, 1889, 2.

75. Wait, *Wines and Vines of California*, 175.

76. Peninou, *History of the Los Angeles Viticultural District*, 25.

77. *Pacific Wine and Spirit Review*, April 5, 1893, 16.

78. E. L. Watkins to J. DeBarth Shorb, June 15, 1888, J. DeBarth Shorb Papers, Huntington Library.

79. This account of Nadeau gives me an opportunity to correct a mistake I made in an earlier work. In my *History of Wine in America: From the Beginnings to Prohibition* (1989), I say of Nadeau that he had been mayor of Los Angeles and died a suicide. I confused him with another native of Quebec among the early settlers in Los Angeles, Damien Marchesseault, who had been mayor of Los Angeles and who was a suicide. Nadeau was neither.

80. According to the WPA guide to the state (*California in the 1930s*, 90), over this short line connecting pueblo and port "ran a vainglorious black and gold locomotive called the *San Gabriel*, alongside of which the *vaqueros* used to race, shouting at it derisively and profanely in Spanish."

81. See Sherwood, *Days of Vintage, Years of Vision*, 404. The wines drunk at the banquet were, however, French: Veuve Clicquot, Roederer, Dry Monopole, etc. See the *Los Angeles Evening Express*, quoted in Frank B. Putnam, "Serape to Levi…Southern Pacific," 222.

82. The standard account of this episode is Glenn S. Dumke's *The Boom of the Eighties in Southern California*.

83. Newmark, *Sixty Years in Southern California*, 572.

84. Boyle Workman (*The City that Grew*, 231) notes that the Wolfskill lots were "the smallest in the city."

85. See Dumke, *The Boom of the Eighties in Southern California*, 47, 55, 57, 78–79, 83.

86. Agitation for the formation of a county separate from Los Angeles went back to 1869. It was motivated partly by the inconvenience of travel to Los Angeles, partly by the civic ambitions of the town of Santa Ana. See Dickson, "The Founding and Early History of Anaheim, California," 33; and Holt, "The Fruits of Viticulture in Orange County," 19.

87. Rudyard Kipling, then a young man, visited San Francisco in May and June of 1889; years later he wrote, "What I most distinctly remember of those days was being told that 'a place called Los Angeles' was dead (its boom had just busted) and would 'never do any more than raise jack-rabbits!'" (Rudyard Kipling to Mrs. Florence Jackson Stoddard, December 6, 1935, Library of Congress). Of course, that was the view from San Francisco; it was different in Los Angeles.

88. Ostrander, *The Prohibition Movement in California*, 63.

89. This view is developed at length in the well-known study *Southern California Country: An Island on the Land*, by Carey McWilliams.

CHAPTER 7

1. There was also a Mrs. Pinney, about whom I would like to know more.

2. There are other spellings of the name, but this appears to be the one settled on by the family.

3. Pelancoli's place was originally built by Giuseppe Covacci around 1855. It was built as a winery, with a basement cellar. It is now Casa la Golondrina Cafe. See Grenier et al., *Guide to Historic Places in Los Angeles*, 54.

4. *Los Angeles Herald* [c. 1877], excerpted in Spalding, *Los Angeles Newspaperman*, 55.

5. Giuseppe Gazza and Giuseppe Cavacci are said to have "operated several wine cellars on Olvera Street" in the 1850s. See Lothrop, *Chi Siamo*, 10.

6. Store ledger, p. 304, Matthew Keller Papers, Huntington Library.

7. Lothrop, "Italians of Los Angeles," 258.

8. *Pacific Wine and Spirit Review*, September 30, 1908, 11.

9. A list would include Accarnero [no first name], on Alpine Street; Ferdinando Bassolo, on Ord Street; the California Mission Winery of Antonio Moramarco, on Mission Road; the California Star Winery of Giuseppe Sormano and G. Borioli, on Macy at Lyon; Louis Carbone, on San Fernando Street; Domenico Destaso, New Depot Street; Vito Franco, Alpine Street; Giacinto Frontino, Bernard Street; Louis Guerrieri, Mission Road; Giovanni Guglielmo, Alpine Street; the Italian-American Vineyard Co. of Giovanni Demateis, at Alameda and Macy; the Lotito brothers, Cleveland Street; Antonio Pelancoli, Olvera Street; Lorenzo Pelancoli, Alameda Street; Giovanni Piuma, Avenue 19 at Humboldt; Primo Vintage Co., Utah Street on Boyle Heights; and Antonio Valla and Giacinto Tonini, at Olvera and Alameda. The San Antonio Winery, a late starter founded by Santo Cambianica in 1917, is the only survivor of the many Italian wineries in Los Angeles, although the Moramarcos are still in the wine business. San Antonio, through skillful promotion, has developed a big business but makes no wine in Los Angeles. It sells wines from many sources, including its own wines from grapes grown around Paso Robles, in Monterey County, and in Napa Valley.

10. *Pacific Wine and Spirit Review*, September 30, 1908, 11. The building now houses the restaurant Philippe's, a Los Angeles landmark famous for its French dip sandwich.

11. I have no information about John Bernard. He may have been related to the Swiss Jean Bernard who had a vineyard and winery in Los Angeles at Third and Alameda Streets in the 1870s. Jean Bernard died in 1889. His dictation among the H. H. Bancroft Papers (Bancroft Library) has little information about winemaking.

12. *Pacific Wine and Spirit Review*, September 21, 1895, 13. Three thousand tons of grapes would yield around 450,000 gallons.

13. *Pacific Wine and Spirit Review*, February 14, 1898, 22.

14. Ibid., 23. I am unable to identify the varieties called Marie Blanche and Monteraux.

15. Ibid., 22.

16. Of the 15,000 acres planted to vines in the Cucamonga region between 1900 and World War I, a third were Zinfandel. See Sullivan, *Zinfandel*, 183.

17. Peninou, *History of Los Angeles Viticultural District*, 29.

18. Pironi owned a wholesale wine business in Los Angeles as well as the West Glendale winery. He was one of the main customers for the wine of Justinian Caire's Santa Cruz Island Winery.

19. *Pacific Wine and Spirit Review*, July 31, 1904, 26.

20. *Pacific Wine and Spirit Review*, May 31, 1912, 13.

21. Guinn, *Illustrated History of Los Angeles County*, 783.

22. *Pacific Wine and Spirit Review*, June 30, 1898, 37.

23. Peninou, *History of Los Angeles Viticultural District*, 21.

24. *Pacific Wine and Spirit Review*, June 30, 1901, 32.

25. *Pacific Wine and Spirit Review*, October 31, 1901, 38; November 30, 1901, 38; and January 31, 1906, 56.

26. Macy Street no longer exists, having been obliterated by the construction of Cesar Chavez Avenue. Lyon Street is just a short distance to the east of the Metropolitan Transit Authority building.

27. *Pacific Wine and Spirit Review*, September 30, 1901, 42.

28. *Pacific Wine and Spirit Review*, August 31, 1903, 12.

29. Unidentified cutting dated November 14, 1868, Bancroft Scraps, Agriculture, vol. 18, part 4, Bancroft Library.

30. *Pacific Wine and Spirit Review*, September 30, 1902, 39; May 31, 1903, 16; and June 30, 1903, 15.

31. Peninou, *History of Los Angeles Viticultural District*, 26–28.

32. *Los Angeles Herald*, quoted in *Pacific Wine and Spirit Review*, August 22, 1889, 185.

33. Glen Dumke (*Boom of the Eighties*, 92) writes that, after Los Angeles, Pasadena was most affected by the boom of the 1880s: "Outside of Los Angeles itself, the frenzy struck hardest in Pasadena and the eastern valley."

34. The Marengo Ranch had an interesting history. Before the Civil War it had belonged to J. Lancaster Brent, a leading lawyer in Los Angeles, whose Southern sympathies led him to abandon Los Angeles in 1861 and return to the South, where he became a brigadier general in the Confederate army. After the war Brent did not return to California but remained in the South; his friend Benjamin Wilson sold the Marengo Ranch for him in 1868 to H. D. Bacon. Brent, an admirer of Napoleon, had named the ranch "Marengo," the site of Napoleon's

victory over the Austrians in 1800. The name is now that of a main street running north and south in Pasadena without quite reaching South Pasadena.

35. Later, when giving things Spanish names was fashionable, the post office was urged to "restore" the name to its alleged Spanish original, the nonsensical "La Manda," and for a time that was done. See Gudde, *California Place Names,* s.v. "Lamanda Park."

36. Sierra Madre Villa is now the name of a major north-south street in Pasadena. The Sierra Madre Villa and Lamanda Park regions lay between Allen Avenue on the west, Sierra Madre Villa on the east, Foothill Boulevard on the south, and an indefinite border in the hills to the north. Street names in the area today include Vinedo, Vineyard, Sunny Slope, Mataro, and Del Vina. Brigden Road, Allen Avenue, Hastings Ranch Drive, and Eaton Drive remember prominent winegrowers.

37. Guinn, *The History of California,* 25.

38. Salvator, *Los Angeles in the Sunny Seventies,* 159.

39. Zack, *Altadena,* 37.

40. On the sale of grapes to Rose, see Mary Agnes Crank, typescript memoir, J. F. Crank Papers, box 10, 13–14, Huntington Library. On the production of the vineyard in 1879, see John Albert Wilson, *History of Los Angeles County,* 132.

41. The articles of incorporation of the Sierra Madre Vintage Company, dated February 26, 1886, are in box 10 of the J. F. Crank Papers, at the Huntington Library.

42. Guinn, *Illustrated History of Los Angeles County,* 407.

43. *Pacific Wine and Spirit Review,* October 20, 1894, 29.

44. *Pacific Wine and Spirit Review,* June 30, 1901, 32; August 31, 1902, 39; and December 31, 1909, 40.

45. *Pacific Wine and Spirit Review,* May 31, 1907, 28.

46. *Pacific Wine and Spirit Review,* December 31, 1909, 17.

47. *Pacific Wine and Spirit Review,* May 31, 1907, 28.

48. Zack, *Southern California Story,* 149.

49. Matt Horman, "Then and Now: Sierra Madre History," online at "Sierra Madre Patch," http://patch.com/california/sierramadre, accessed June 6, 2012.

50. Brackett, *History of Pomona Valley,* 149. Brackett, a professor of mathematics, was one of the original faculty of Pomona College, founded in the boom year of 1887.

51. In the 1880s Pomona had a Maison Française "with a considerable clientèle of French colonists and visitors" (Brackett, *History of Pomona Valley,* 126).

52. Peninou, *History of the Los Angeles Viticultural District,* 48. See also Lehman, "Vines and Vintners of Pomona Valley," 57.

53. "Pomona and Her Environs," *Pomona Progress,* "Souvenir Edition" (February 1898): 40.

54. Peninou, *History of the Los Angeles Viticultural District,* 48.

55. Ibid., 49; obituary in *Pomona Progress Bulletin,* November 24, 1946.

56. Peninou, *History of the Los Angeles Viticultural District,* 51. The building has been declared a historical landmark by the city of Pomona. In the proceedings leading up to this designation it was stated that the building was erected "between 1906 and 1911" rather than in 1904 (City of Pomona Council Report, March 3, 2003, Special Collections, Pomona Public Library). I prefer the earlier date.

57. Brackett, *History of Pomona Valley,* 149.

58. Ibid., 441.

59. *Rural Californian*, November 1887, 256. He is remembered by Packard Drive in Pomona.

60. My account of Smith is drawn from his manuscript reminiscences, now part of the Lindley Bynum Collection in the Huntington Library.

61. Lehman, "Vines and Vintners of the Pomona Valley," 58.

62. *Pacific Wine and Spirit Review*, August 8, 1889, 167; and August 22, 1889, 182.

63. Quoted without citation in Peninou, *History of the Los Angeles Viticultural District*, 48.

64. *Pacific Wine and Spirit Review*, June 21, 1892, 16.

65. Smith reminiscences (Lindley Bynum Collection, Huntington Library), p. 10. A slightly different version of events is given by E. L. Watkins, who wrote that the Pomona Wine Company's entire stock of sweet wines was sold off at 25 cents a gallon (E. L. Watkins to J. DeBarth Shorb, March 26, 1892, box 125, J. DeBarth Shorb Papers, Huntington Library). The A. Mattei Winery in Fresno was not built until 1893, but Mattei may have been in the market for bulk wine before that.

66. Figures from *Report of the California State Board of Agriculture, 1911*, 191.

67. Peninou, *History of the Los Angeles Viticultural District*, 100.

68. *Report of the California State Board of Agriculture, 1911*, 193.

69. Guasti's fellow investors were Giovanni Demateis, Giacomo Barlotti, Ferdinando Bessolo, Carlo Demateis, Antonio Ferrario, Ambrogia Vignolo, Luigi Terrile, Leopoldo Schiappapietre, Antonio Signorio, and Antonio Dell'Acqua (untitled notes on Los Angeles and Riverside Counties Wineries [by Caesar Perelli-Minetti], Gail Unzelman Collection, Santa Rosa). It was, emphatically, the Italian Vineyard Company. Caesar Perelli-Minetti was the winemaker for the Cucamonga Pioneer Vineyard Association from 1934 to 1937.

70. *Pacific Wine and Spirit Review*, November 30, 1900, 31.

71. *Pacific Wine and Spirit Review*, December 31, 1900, 10.

72. *Pacific Wine and Spirit Review*, June 30, 1915, 25. Guasti had twenty-two varieties growing by 1911, including "four distinct varieties of muscats." See *Pacific Wine and Spirit Review*, October 31, 1911, 40.

73. *Pacific Wine and Spirit Review*, June 30, 1915, 25. The extravagant demand for barrels is explained by the fact that most California wine was shipped out as bulk wine in barrels.

74. *Pacific Wine and Spirit Review*, August 31, 1909, 38. It was reported in 1913 that there were then more than two hundred varieties being tested. See *Pacific Wine and Spirit Review*, September 30, 1913, 22.

75. Biane, "How Quality Can Be Controlled," 20.

76. The succession of firms is as follows: Perkins, Stern and Co., 1860–78; Stern and Rose, 1878–87; and Charles Stern and Sons, circa 1890 (based on the date November 13, 1890, printed on the letterhead of Charles Stern and Sons, J. DeBarth Shorb Papers, box 116, file 1, Huntington Library).

77. Bundschu, "In Memoriam," 70–71.

78. The seed of the Ontario International Airport was the purchase by the city of the Benton Ballou vineyard in 1940, with the purpose of developing the land as an airport. See Hofer, "Cucamonga Wines and Vines," 141.

79. Ostrander, *The Prohibition Movement in California*, 15.

80. Workman, *The City that Grew*, 165.

81. *Pacific Wine and Spirit Review*, October 31, 1908, 29.

82. Typical among such histories is *I Can Remember Early Pasadena*, by Jennie Hollingsworth

Giddings (1949). The book has a splendid jacket photograph showing embryo Pasadena set in the midst of vineyards. The book itself has not a single mention of grapes or wine. The author manages to write a chapter on Benjamin Wilson, whom she knew, without mentioning the fact that his residence was a vineyard and his business was making wine. Similarly, in *Pasadena, California: Historical and Personal* (1917), author John W. Wood manages to write 565 dense pages without mentioning grapes or wine, although he writes about Wilson, Shorb, Stoneman, Kewen, Baldwin, Rose, and others, all of them engaged in growing grapes and making wine on a large scale. How did these writers explain such falsification to themselves?

83. Clarke, "Prohibition in Southern California," 377.

84. It was held that such an ordinance assumed a legislative power that a town or city did not have.

85. Clarke, "Prohibition in Southern California," 378.

86. Ostrander, *The Prohibition Movement in California*, 71.

87. Reid, *History of Pasadena*, 240ff. According to Michele Zack (*Altadena*, 89), there were five California wines offered.

88. Clarke, "Prohibition in Southern California," 381.

89. *Pacific Wine and Spirit Review*, December 5, 1891, 24.

90. *Pacific Wine and Spirit Review*, January 31, 1914, 60.

91. Ostrander, *The Prohibition Movement in California*, 141.

92. *Pacific Wine and Spirit Review*, April 30, 1913, 19.

93. When Prohibition put an end to this work, Stoll founded a journal called *The California Grape Grower*, which, after Repeal, became *Wines and Vines*, still a leading trade journal.

94. It is often said that the success of the Prohibition movement was owing to America's entrance into the First World War, when temperance became a patriotic duty. That idea was no doubt a powerful influence, but the necessary work had already been done, largely through the activity of the Anti-Saloon League.

CHAPTER 8

1. National Prohibition Act, Section 29, Title II.

2. Garrett, "The Right to Make Fruit Juices," 2–3.

3. *Wickersham Report*, 1:28. The official title of this document, written by the National Commission on Law Observance and Enforcement, is *Enforcement of the Prohibition Laws: Official Records*. The more common title, *Wickersham Report*, comes from the commission's chairman, George Wickersham, a former U.S. attorney general.

4. Teiser and Harroun, "The Volstead Act, Rebirth, and Boom," 58.

5. Peninou, *History of the Los Angeles Viticultural District*, 100. The 12,500 acres reported for Los Angeles County in 1912 had shrunk dramatically by 1920. I can only guess why. Many growers, on the passage of the constitutional amendment in 1919 and before the terms of the Volstead Act were known, pulled up their vines and planted other crops. In Los Angeles County there was also a powerful wave of immigration. Los Angeles, the city, grew from 310,198 in 1910 to 576,673 in 1920; for the county in the same years, the growth was from 504,131 to 936,455. No doubt much vineyard land was needed to accommodate such growth.

6. Driscoll, *Pomona Valley Community Book*, 72.

7. U.S. Department of the Treasury, Bureau of Industrial Alcohol, *Statistics Concerning Intoxicating Liquors, December 1933*, 64.

8. Ibid., table 69.

9. Ibid., 64.

10. U. S. Bureau of Prohibition, *Statistics Concerning Alcoholic Liquors*, for the years 1927, 1929, and 1930.

11. The basic permit was Form 1405, "Permit Issued Under the National Prohibition Act and Regulations Issued Thereunder." California wineries must also have held a state permit.

12. The Revenue Act of 1916 required wineries to be bonded. The BW number is now regarded as determining whether a winery is actually a wine-producing facility.

13. There is something called "waterberry" in grapes, but that is a disease, not a kind of grape.

14. The quantity of wine that could be produced under a given permit had to be specified because the coverage of the required bond was adjusted to the quantity of wine produced: the bigger the permitted production, the more costly the bond.

15. Peninou, *History of the Los Angeles Viticultural District*, 41–42.

16. *California Grape Grower* 13 (October 1932): 3.

17. The Grignolino grape is from the Piedmont region of northern Italy, the district from which Guasti came, and it was always a favorite of Guasti's. He won a gold medal for his Grignolino wine at the Panama-Pacific International Exposition in 1915. See Sullivan, *Companion to California Wine, s.v.* "Grignolino."

18. Franklin D. Roosevelt to Marvin H. McIntyre, April 18, 1933, Franklin D. Roosevelt Papers, Roosevelt Library, Hyde Park, New York.

19. The winemaker was Angelo Lispi, whose Imperial Winery is discussed in the next chapter.

20. Roosevelt, *Public Papers and Addresses of Franklin D. Roosevelt*, vol. 2: *The Year of Crisis 1933*, 512.

21. Sullivan, *A Companion to California Wine, s.v.* "Thompson Seedless."

22. Schoonmaker and Marvel, *American Wines*, 46. Other estimates were dramatically lower.

23. Jefferson Peyser, legal counsel for the Wine Institute from its creation in 1934, recalled of his work with the federal authorities that "some of those federal people could never understand. They never quite got over the fact that Prohibition had been repealed, and they did treat the industry for a number of years just like bootleggers" (Peyser, *The Law and the California Wine Industry*, 13–14). On his retirement from the University of California, Davis, in 1974, after a nearly forty-year tenure, the distinguished enologist Maynard Amerine said the biggest change that had occurred during his career was that "the wine industry has become respectable." See Hiaring, "One of the World's Great Wine Scholars Retires June 30," 26.

CHAPTER 9

1. The brief accounts that follow are from information in the records of the Bureau of Alcohol, Tobacco, and Firearms (now the Alcohol and Tobacco Tax and Trade Bureau), mainly for the years from 1920 to 1940, now in Special Collections at the Shields Library, University of California, Davis.

2. Figures from *Wine Review* 4 (March 1936): 11; and *Wines and Vines* 20 (March 1939): 5. Over a longer stretch of time the mortality was even worse. Between 1934 and 1940 there were, by my count, 101 named wineries in Los Angeles County; by 1950 only 8 survived. Those survivors were mostly small, and all were Italian: Matteo Brusso, Garvey (F. Cambianica), Old Mill (Mazetti), San Antonio (S. Cambianica), San Gabriel (Demateis), Vernaci, Viotti, and West Coast Winery (Lotito). San Antonio is the lone survivor today.

3. The suggestion is one of several put forth in Simone Cinotto's *Soft Soil, Black Grapes: The Birth of Italian Winemaking in California*.

4. *Wine Review* 2 (April 1934): 4.

5. Frank De Bartolo claimed that the orange wine he made for the Hendrickson Winery in 1934 was the first of its kind to be commercially successful. See De Bartolo file, BATF records, Shields Library, University of California, Davis.

6. While still in Glendale, Verry also offered a wine called "philery," whatever that is. It was perhaps white wine from the pink-skinned Moschophilero ("Fly-Lover") grape widely grown in Greece and sometimes known as "philery" or "filery." But was the grape ever grown in California?

7. *Wine Review* 4 (November 1936): 22.

8. Not all of the wine produced was made at the Los Angeles winery. The Santa Fe Vintage Co. contracted with the Cucamonga Pioneer Vineyard Association in 1953 to deliver 4,000 tons of grapes to be crushed at the latter's winery on Haven Avenue in Cucamonga; the contract was renewed in the two following years. See Hofer, "Cucamonga Wines and Vines," 204–05.

9. Untitled notes on Los Angeles and Riverside Counties Wineries made by [Caesar Perelli-Minetti] (copy, Gail Unzelman Collection).

10. *Wine Review*, November 1937, 27.

11. *Wine Review*, July 1937, 20.

12. Figures from *Wines and Vines* 16 (July 1935): 22; *Wines and Vines* 17 (September 1936): 4; and *Wines and Vines* 19 (September 1938): 22.

13. Both Concannon and Almadén had "Chateau Yquem" wines. The authorities denied the use of such a name on the grounds that it had not been used as a "generic" name before Prohibition. In contrast, "Burgundy," "claret," "Sauterne," and like names had been so used and were therefore allowed—and still are.

14. Some of the buildings that once housed the Lombardi Winery, Santa Fe Vintage Co., and California Mission Vintage Co. still survive, although they have long since been turned to other uses. So far as I can determine, no trace of the Piuma/Pacific establishment remains.

15. Untitled notes on Los Angeles and Riverside Counties Wineries made by [Caesar Perelli-Minetti] (copy, Gail Unzelman Collection).

16. Ibid.

17. Pacific Wines won prizes for its "Chateau Yquem" and its port at the Los Angeles County Fair, and there may have been other Los Angeles prizewinners there, but none appears in the reports of the Sacramento judgings.

18. The original 1941 WPA guide was reprinted by the University of California Press in 2011 as *Los Angeles in the 1930s*.

19. The photograph is of the tasting room at Inglenook Winery in the Napa Valley, and the gentleman standing is Carl Bundschu, then the manager of Inglenook. That the compilers of the WPA guide did not hesitate to use an inauthentic photograph confirms my point about the general ignorance of and indifference to Los Angeles winemaking—but who's to know? It may be that the authors of the guide supposed that the photo was in fact of the local scene, although that is doubtful. Probably they asked the Wine Institute for a suitable photograph and were furnished with the one of Inglenook out of the institute's stock supply, no questions asked.

20. Figures from Pitt and Pitt, *Los Angeles A to Z*.

21. *Wines and Vines* 27 (April 1946): 71.

22. Maria Briano, January 28, 1943, in Briano File, box 102, BATF records, Shields Library, University of California, Davis.

23. U.S.D.A., National Agricultural Statistics Service, 2015.

24. *Los Angeles Times*, November 18, 2015.

25. But Jones's facility was not, as stated on the company's website, "the first commercial winery to be bonded in the city of Los Angeles since Prohibition." There were many in the 1930s, as we have seen. The claim is more evidence, as if it were needed, of how completely the history of Los Angeles winemaking has been forgotten.

APPENDIX I

1. Munson, *Foundations of American Grape Culture*, 89.

2. Ibid., 87.

3. Hedrick, *The Grapes of New York*, 136. The title of the work is misleading; it is in fact an encyclopedic treatment of all native American grapes.

4. Munson, *Foundations of American Grape Culture*, 87.

5. Ibid., 89.

6. Hedrick, *The Grapes of New York*, 135.

7. Winkler, Cook, Kliewer, and Lider, *General Viticulture*, 3.

8. Teiser and Harroun, *Winemaking in California*, 1.

9. Hilgard, "The Agriculture and Soils of California," 503.

10. Forbes, *California*, 172.

11. Bancroft, *History of California*, 4:135.

12. Ibid., 4:228–29n.

13. Quoted in S. B. Buckley, "The Grapes of North America," in U.S. Patent Office, *Report of the Commissioner of Patents for the Year 1861: Agriculture*, 483.

14. Bancroft, *History of California*, 1:619n.

15. Keller, U.S. Patent Office, *Report of the Commissioner of Patents 1858*, 346.

16. From the *California Farmer* 15 (March 15, 1861): 1.

17. J. DeBarth Shorb to B. D. Wilson, October 28, 1873, Benjamin Wilson Papers, Huntington Library.

18. Sullivan, *Napa Wine*, 129.

19. *San Francisco Merchant* 11 (November 30, 1883): 117.

20. Board of State Viticultural Commissioners, *First Annual Report*, 47.

21. That *V. californica* is not resistant to phylloxera has been disputed. George Gale (*Dying on the Vine*, 280n13) says the vines grafted to roots of *V. californica* that succumbed to phylloxera (as did those of Professor Hilgard at Mission San José) were on *californica* roots from vines that had already been hybridized with vinifera vines. Their resistance had thus been compromised. "Pure *californica*," Gale adds, "is as resistant as standard rootstocks." Gale cites as his authority a paper by Granett, De Benedictis, and Marston titled "Host Suitability of *Vitis californica* Bentham to Grape Phylloxera *Daktulosphaira vitifolia* Fitch," *American Journal of Enology and Viticulture* 43 (1992): 249–52. These authors point to the fact that *V. californica* survives in large numbers in regions where phylloxera has long been known. They observed no phylloxera on the roots of any specimens they examined. Perhaps Munson and Hedrick both examined hybridized vines without knowing it. But the question of resistance appears to be not yet finally settled. At least, I doubt that anyone today would risk grafting to *V. californica*.

22. Board of State Viticultural Commissioners, *First Annual Report*, 51.

23. Sullivan, "Wine in California: The Early Years," *Wayward Tendrils Quarterly* 22 (January 2012): 27.

SOURCES AND WORKS CITED

MANUSCRIPTS AND SPECIAL COLLECTIONS

Bancroft Library, University of California, Berkeley
    Benjamin Hayes Scrapbooks
    Bancroft Scraps: California Agriculture
John Barden, New Haven, CT
    Paul Garrett memoir
Huntington Library, San Marino
    Henry Douglas Bacon Papers
    Lindley Bynum Collection
    J. F. Crank Papers
    Henry Dalton Papers
    Matthew Keller Papers
    L. J. Rose Papers
    J. DeBarth Shorb Papers
    Benjamin Wilson Papers
    Lewis Wolfskill Papers
Pomona Public Library, Special Collections
    Local information on winemakers
University of California, Davis
    Bureau of Alcohol, Tobacco, and Firearms Records, c. 1919–1940
Gail Unzelman Collection, Santa Rosa
    Untitled notes on Los Angeles and Riverside Counties wineries [by
    Caesar Perelli-Minetti]
Wine Institute, San Francisco

Irving McKee. "Historic Winegrowers of Southern California, 1850–1890." Unpublished typescript. San Francisco: Wine Institute, n.d. [1950?].

NEWSPAPERS AND SPECIALIZED PERIODICALS

Alta California
Bonfort's Wine and Spirit Circular
California Farmer and Journal of Useful Sciences
California Grape Grower
Los Angeles Semi-Weekly News
Los Angeles Star
Pacific Wine and Spirit Review; earlier title: *San Francisco Merchant*
Rural Californian
The Southern Vineyard
Wayward Tendrils Quarterly
Wine Review
Wines and Vines

OTHER PRINTED WORKS

Apostol, Jane. "Don Mateo Keller: His Vines and His Wines." *Southern California Quarterly* 84 (Summer 2002): 93–114.

Ayers, James J. *Gold and Sunshine: Reminiscences of Early California.* Boston: Richard C. Badger, [1922].

Bancroft, Hubert Howe. *California Pastoral, 1769–1848.* San Francisco: The History Company, 1888.

———. *History of California.* 7 vols. San Francisco: The History Co., 1884–90.

Beck, Warren A., and Ynez D. Haase. *Historical Atlas of California.* Norman: University of Oklahoma Press, 1974.

Bess, Michael. "Early Agriculture in Pomona Valley." *Pomona Valley Historian* 6 (April 1980): 47–63.

Biane, Marius. "How Quality Can Be Controlled." *Wines and Vines* 19 (April 1938): 20.

Blake, William. *Report of a Geological Reconnaisance in California.* New York: H. Ballière, 1858.

Bolton, Herbert Eugene. *Fray Juan Crespi: Missionary Explorer on the Pacific Coast, 1769–1774.* Berkeley: University of California Press, 1927.

————. "The Mission in the Spanish-American Colonies." *American Histori-cal Review* 23 (1917–18): 42–61.

Bowman, J. N. "The Vineyards in Provincial California." *Wine Review* 11 (April–July 1943).

Brace, Charles Loring. *The New West: or, California in 1867–1868.* New York: G. P. Putnam and Son, 1869.

Brackett, F. P. *History of Pomona Valley, California.* Los Angeles: Historic Record Company, 1920.

Brady, Roy. "Alta California's First Vintage." In *The University of California Sotheby Book of California Wine,* edited by Doris Muscatine, Maynard A. Amerine, and Bob Thompson. Berkeley: University of California Press; London: Sotheby Publications, 1984.

Brewer, William. *Up and Down California in 1860–1864.* Edited by Francis P. Farquhar. New Haven: Yale University Press, 1930.

Bryant, Edwin. *What I Saw in California.* 1848. Reprint, Palo Alto, CA: Lewis Osborne, 1967.

Buffum, Edward Gould. *Six Months in the Gold Mines.* Philadelphia, 1850. Reprint, Ann Arbor: University Microfilms, 1966.

Bundschu, Charles. "In Memoriam." *Pacific Wine and Spirit Review* 46 (January 31, 2004): 70–71.

"California as a Vineland." *Atlantic Monthly* 13 (May 1864): 600–04.

California Board of State Viticultural Commissioners. *First Annual Report.* San Francisco: Edward Bosqui and Co., 1881.

————. *Grape Growers and Wine Makers of California.* Sacramento: State Office, 1888.

————. *Report of the Third Annual State Viticultural Convention.* San Francisco: The San Francisco Merchant [,1884].

————. *The Vineyards of Southern California.* Sacramento: J. Johnston, Super-intendent of State Printing, 1893.

California State Agricultural Society. *Transactions 1858.* Sacramento: State Printer, 1859.

————. *Transactions 1859.* Sacramento: State Printer, 1860.

————. *Transactions 1866 and 1867.* Sacramento: State Printer, 1868.

————. *Transactions 1872.* Sacramento: State Printer, 1873.

————. *Transactions 1874.* Sacramento: State Printer, 1875.

California State Board of Agriculture. *Report of the California State Board of Agri-culture, 1911.* Sacramento: Superintendent of State Printing, 1912.

California State Register and Year Book of Facts. San Francisco: Henry B. Langley and Samuel A. Mathews, 1857–59.

California State Vinicultural Association. *Grapes and Grape Vines of California.* San Francisco: Edward Bosqui, 1875.

Carosso, Vincent P. *The California Wine Industry, 1830–1895.* Berkeley: University of California Press, 1951.

Caughey, John W. "Don Benito Wilson: An Average Southern Californian." *Huntington Library Quarterly* 2 (April 1939): 285–300.

———. "The Jacob Y. Stover Narrative." *Pacific Historical Review* 6 (1937): 164–81.

Cinotto, Simone. *Soft Soil, Black Grapes: The Birth of Italian Winemaking in California.* New York: New York University Press, 2012.

Clarke, E. P. "Prohibition in Southern California." *Overland Monthly,* n.s. 15 (April 1890): 376–84.

Cleland, Robert Glass. *The Cattle on a Thousand Hills: Southern California, 1850–1880.* 2nd ed. San Marino, CA: Huntington Library, 1951.

Cole, Martin, and Henry Welcome, eds. *Don Pio Pico's Historical Narrative.* Translated by Arthur P. Botello. Glendale, CA: Arthur H. Clark Co., 1973.

Dakin, Susanna Bryant. *A Scotch Paisano in Old Los Angeles: Hugo Reid's Life in California, 1832–1852, Derived from His Correspondence.* Berkeley: University of California Press, 1939.

Dale, Harrison Clifford, ed. *The Ashley-Smith Explorations.* 1918. Revised, Glendale, CA: Arthur H. Clark Co., 1941.

Dana, Richard Henry. *Two Years Before the Mast.* Edited by J. H. Kemble. 2 vols. Los Angeles: Ward Ritchie Press, 1964.

———. *Two Years before the Mast and Twenty-Four Years After.* London: Sampson Low, Son, and Marston, 1869.

Davies, David. "An Emigrant of the Fifties." *Historical Society of Southern California Quarterly* 19 (September–December 1937): 99–120.

Davis, William Heath. *Seventy-Five Years in California.* Edited by Harold A. Small. San Francisco: J. Howell Books, 1929.

Dickson, Lucille F. "The Founding and Early History of Anaheim, California." *Annual Publications of the Historical Society of Southern California* 11, no. 2 (1919): 26–37.

Dinkelspiel, Frances. *Towers of Gold: How One Jewish Immigrant named Isaias Hellman Created California.* New York: St. Martin's Press, 2008.

Driscoll, Roy L. *Pomona Valley Community Book.* Pomona: Arthur H. Cawston, 1950.

Duhaut-Cilly, Auguste. *A Voyage to California, the Sandwich Islands, and Around the World in the Years 1826–1829.* Translated and edited by August Frugé and Neil Harlow. Berkeley: University of California Press, 1999.

Dumke, Glenn S. *The Boom of the Eighties in Southern California.* San Marino: Huntington Library, 1944.

El Pueblo: Los Angeles before the Railroads. Los Angeles: Security Trust and Savings Bank, 1927.

Emory, William H. *Notes of a Military Reconnaissance from Fort Leavenworth, in Missouri, to San Diego, in California.* Washington, D.C.: Wendell and Van Benthuysen, 1848. Reprint, Albuquerque: University of New Mexico Press, 1951.

Engelhardt, Zephyrin. *San Gabriel Mission and the Beginnings of Los Angeles.* San Gabriel, CA: Mission San Gabriel, 1927.

Forbes, Alexander. *California: A History of Upper and Lower California.* London: Smith, Elder and Co., 1839.

Forbes, Mrs. A. S. C. "When Los Angeles Was the 'City of Vineyards.'" *Annual Publications of the Historical Society of Southern California* 15 (1–2): 339.

Friis, Leo J. *Campo Aleman: The First Ten Years of Anaheim.* Santa Ana: Friis-Pioneer Press, 1983.

———. *John Fröhling: Vintner and City Founder.* Anaheim: Mother Colony Household, Inc., 1976.

Gabler, James. *Wine into Words: A History and Bibliography of Wine Books in the English Language.* 2nd ed. Baltimore: Bacchus Press, 2004.

Gale, George. *Dying on the Vine: How Phylloxera Transformed Wine.* Berkeley: University of California Press, 2011.

Gardner, M. W., and William B. Hewitt. *Pierce's Disease of the Grapevine: The Anaheim Disease and the California Vine Disease.* Berkeley and Davis: University of California, Department of Plant Pathology, 1974.

Garey, Thomas A. *Orange Culture in California, with an Appendix on Grape Culture by L. J. Rose.* San Francisco: Published for A. T. Garey, Pacific Rural Press, 1882.

Garrett, Paul. "The Right to Make Fruit Juices." *California Grape Grower* 4 (July 1923): 2–3.

Gates, Paul W. *California Ranchos and Farms, 1846–1862.* Madison: State Historical Society of Wisconsin, 1967.

Geiger, Maynard. "The Building of Mission San Gabriel, 1771–1828." *Southern California Historical Quarterly* 50 (Spring 1968): 33–42.

Giddings, Jennie Hollingsworth. *I Can Remember Early Pasadena.* Pasadena: privately printed, 1949.

Granett, J., J. De Benedictis, and J. Marston. "Host Suitability of *Vitis californica* Bentham to Grape Phylloxera *Daktulosphaira vitifolia* Fitch." *American Journal of Enology and Viticulture* 43 (1992): 249–52.

Grenier, Judson, Doyce B. Nunis, Jr., Jean Bruce Poole, et al. *Guide to Historic Places in Los Angeles.* Dubuque, IA: Kendall/Hunt Publishing Co., 1978.

Griffin, John. "A Doctor Comes to California." Edited by George Wolcott Ames, Jr. *California Historical Society Quarterly* 21 (December 1942): 333–57.

[Griswold, N. W.] *Beauties of California.* San Francisco: H. S. Crocker and Co., 1884.

Gudde, Erwin G. *California Place Names: The Origin and Etymology of Current Geographical Names.* 3rd ed. Berkeley: University of California Press, 1969.

Guinn, J. M. *History of California and an Extended History of Its Southern Coast Counties.* Los Angeles: Historic Record Co., 1907.

———. *Illustrated History of Los Angeles County.* Chicago: Lewis Publishing Co., 1889.

———. "The Plan of Old Los Angeles." *Annual Publications of the Historical Society of Southern California* 3 (1895): 40–50.

Gumprecht, Blake. *The Los Angeles River: Its Life, Death, and Possible Rebirth.* Baltimore: Johns Hopkins University Press, 1999.

Hardy, Thomas. "Los Angeles." *San Francisco Merchant* 16 (October 8, 1886): 200.

Harlow, Neal. *California Conquered.* Berkeley: University of California Press, 1982.

Hart, James D. *Companion to California.* Rev. ed., Berkeley: University of California Press, 1987.

Hawley, A. T., ed. *The Present Condition, Growth, Progress, and Advantages of Los Angeles City and County.* Los Angeles: Mirror Printing, Ruling and Binding House, 1876.

Hedrick, Ulysses Prentiss. *The Grapes of New York.* Albany, NY: J. B. Lyon, 1908.

Hendricks, Rich. "Viticulture in El Paso del Norte during the Colonial Period." *Agricultural History* 78 (2004): 181–200.

Hiaring, Philip. "One of the World's Great Wine Scholars Retires June 30th." *Wine and Vines* 55 (April 1974): 22–36.

Hilgard, Eugene. "The Agriculture and Soils of California." *USDA Annual Report, 1878*. Washington, D.C.: Government Printing Office, 1879, pp. 476–507.

Hittell, John S. *The Resources of California*. San Francisco: A. Roman and Co., 1863.

Hofer, James D. "California Wines and Vines: A History of the Cucamonga Pioneer Vineyard Association." M.A. thesis, Claremont Graduate School, 1983.

Holt, Raymond M. "The Fruits of Viticulture in Orange County." *Southern California Historical Society Quarterly* 28 (March 1946): 7–33.

Humboldt, Alexander von. *Political Essay on the Kingdom of New Spain*. New York: I. Riley, 1811.

Hutton, William R. *Glances at California, 1847–1852*. San Marino: Huntington Library, 1942.

Hyatt, Thomas Hart. *Hyatt's Hand-Book of Grape Culture*. San Francisco: H. H. Bancroft, 1867.

Jackson, Sheldon G. *A British Ranchero in Old California: The Life and Times of Henry Dalton and the Rancho Azusa*. Glendale and Azusa, CA: Arthur H. Clark Co. and Azusa Pacific College, 1977.

Jacobson, Jean L. "Upsides of Wild Fermentation." *Wines and Vines* 93 (April 2012): 34–39.

Janssens, Augustin. *The Life and Adventures in California of Don Augustin Janssens, 1834–1856*. Edited by William H. Ellison and Francis Price. San Marino: Huntington Library, 1953.

Jones, Idwal. *Vines in the Sun*. New York: William Morrow, 1949.

Jore, Léonce. "Jean Louis Vignes of Bordeaux, Pioneer of California Viticulture." *Southern California Historical Society Quarterly* 45 (1963): 289–303.

Larkin, Thomas O. *The Larkin Papers: Personal, Business, and Official Correspondence of Thomas Oliver Larkin, Merchant and United States Consul in California*. Edited by George P. Hammond. 10 vols. Berkeley: University of California Press, 1951–1964.

Layne, J. Gregg. "Annals of Los Angeles." *California Historical Society Quarterly* 13 (1934): 195–234, 301–54.

Leggett, Herbert B. *Early History of Wine Production in California*. San Francisco: Wine Institute, 1941.

Lehman, Anthony. "Vines and Vintners of the Pomona Valley." *Southern California Quarterly* 54 (1972): 55–65.

Lothrop, Gloria Ricci. *Chi Siamo: The Italians of Los Angeles.* Pasadena: Tabula Rasa Press, 1981.

———. "Italians of Los Angeles: An Historical Overview." *Southern California Historical Quarterly* 85 (2003): 249–300.

McWilliams, Carey. *Southern California Country: An Island on the Land.* New York: Duell, Sloan and Pearce, 1946.

M'Kee, Andrew. "The Grape and Wine Culture of California." *U.S. Patent Office Annual Report 1858.* Washington, D.C.: Government Printing Office, 1859, pp. 338–44.

Mechanics' Institute. *Report of the Sixth Industrial Exhibition of the Mechanics' Institute of the City of San Francisco…1868.* San Francisco: Mechanics' Institute, 1868.

Munson, Thomas Volney. *Foundations of American Grape Culture.* Denison, TX: T. V. Munson and Son, 1909.

Nelson, Howard J. "The Two Pueblos of Los Angeles: Agricultural Village and Embryo Town." *Southern California Quarterly* 59 (Spring 1977): 1–11.

Neuerberg, Norman. "The Beginnings of the Wine Industry in California." *La Gazeta del Archivo* [Archive of the Santa Barbara Mission] (Fall 1993): 10–12.

Newmark, Harris. *Sixty Years in Southern California, 1853–1913.* 3rd ed. Boston: Houghton Mifflin Co., 1930.

Nordhoff, Charles. *California for Health, Pleasure, and Residence.* New York: Harper's, 1872.

Ostrander, Gilman. *The Prohibition Movement in California, 1848–1933.* Berkeley: University of California Press, 1957.

Pachter, Mark, ed. *Abroad in America: Visitors to the New Nation, 1776–1914.* Reading, MA: Addison-Wesley Publishing Co., 1976.

Palóu, Francisco. *Life of Fray Junípero Serra.* Translated by Maynard A. Geiger. Washington, D.C.: Academy of American Franciscan History, 1955.

Paule, Dorothea Jean. "The German Settlement at Anaheim." M.A. thesis, University of Southern California, 1952.

Peninou, Ernest P. *History of the Los Angeles Viticultural District.* Santa Rosa, CA: Nomis Press, 2004.

Peninou, Ernest P., and Sidney S. Greenleaf. *Directory of California Wine Growers and Wine Makers in 1860.* Berkeley: Tamalpais Press, 1967.

Perkins, Stern and Co. "Catalogue of California Wines." New York, 1863.

Peyser, Jefferson E. *The Law and California Wine.* Interview by Ruth Teiser. Berkeley: Regional Oral History Office, Bancroft Library, University of California, 1974.

Phelps, William Dane. *Alta California, 1840–1842.* Edited by Briton Cooper Busch. Glendale, CA: Arthur H. Clark Co., 1983.

Phillips, George Harwood. *Vineyards and Vaqueros: Indian Labor and the Economics of Southern California, 1771–1877.* Norman, OK: Arthur H. Clark Co., 2004.

Pierce, Newton B. *The California Vine Disease: A Preliminary Report of Investigations.* U.S.D.A. Division of Vegetable Pathology. Bulletin No. 2. Washington, D.C.: Government Printing Office, 1892.

Pinney, Thomas. *A History of Wine in America: From the Beginnings to Prohibition.* Berkeley: University of California Press, 1989.

Pitt, Leonard, and Dale Pitt. *Los Angeles A to Z: An Encyclopedia of the City and County.* Berkeley: University of California Press, 1997.

Pomeroy, Elizabeth. *Lost and Found: Historic and Natural Landmarks of the San Gabriel Valley.* Pasadena: Many Moons Press, 2000.

"Pomona and Her Environs." *Pomona Progress,* "Souvenir Edition." February 1898: 40.

Putnam, Frank B. "Serape to Levi...Southern Pacific." *Historical Society of Southern California Quarterly* 38 (September 1956): 211–24.

Raup, Hallock F. *The German Colonization of Anaheim, California.* Berkeley: University of California Press, 1932.

Reid, Hiram. *History of Pasadena.* Pasadena: Pasadena History Co., 1895.

Revere, Joseph Warren. *A Tour of Duty in California; Including a Description of the Gold Region.* New York and Boston: C. S. Francis and Co., 1849.

Robinson, Alfred. *Life in California.* 1846. Facsimile reprint, New York: Da Capo Press, 1969.

Robinson, Jancis, ed. *The Oxford Companion to Wine.* 3rd ed. Oxford: Oxford University Press, 2006.

Robinson, Jancis, Julia Harding, and José Vouillamoz. *Wine Grapes: A Complete Guide to 1,368 Vine Varieties, Including Their Origins and Flavors.* New York: Ecco, 2012.

Robinson, W. W. *Los Angeles from the Days of the Pueblo.* San Francisco: California Historical Society, 1981.

———. *Ranchos Become Cities.* Pasadena: San Pasqual Press, 1939.

————. *Southern California Local History.* Edited by Doyce B. Nunis, Jr. Los Angeles: Zamorano Club, 1994.

Roosevelt, Franklin D. *The Year of Crisis 1933, vol. 2. Public Papers and Addresses of Franklin D. Roosevelt.* Edited by Samuel I. Rosenman. New York: Random House, 1938.

Rose, L. J. "Appendix on Grape Culture," in *Orange Culture in California,* by Thomas A. Garey. San Francisco, 1882.

————. "Los Angeles District: The State Commissioner's Report." *Pacific Wine and Spirit Review* 11 (January 11, 1884): 220–1.

Rose, L. J., Jr. *L. J. Rose of Sunny Slope, 1827–1899.* San Marino: Huntington Library, 1959.

Rowland, Donald E. *John Rowland and William Workman: Southern California Pioneers of 1841.* Spokane, WA: Arthur H. Clark Co.; Los Angeles: Historical Society of Southern California, 1999.

Salvator, Ludwig Louis. *Los Angeles in the Sunny Seventies.* 1878. Translated by Marguerite Eyer Wilber. Los Angeles: Bruce McAllister and Jake Zeitlin, 1929.

Schoonmaker, Frank, and Tom Marvel. *American Wines.* New York: Duell, Sloan and Pearce, 1941.

Scott, Paul T. "Why Joseph Chapman Adopted California and Why California Adopted Him." *Historical Society of Southern California Quarterly* 38, no. 3 (1956): 239–46.

Serra, Junípero. *Alta California's First Census and Directory.* Translated by Antonine Tibesar. Edited by Doyce B. Nunis, Jr. Los Angeles: Zamorano Club, 2004.

Servín, Manuel P. "The Secularization of the California Missions: A Reappraisal." *Southern California Quarterly* 47 (June 1965): 133–49.

Shaler, William. *Journal of a Voyage between China and the North Western Coast of America Made in 1804 by William Shaler.* Edited by Lindley Bynum. Claremont, CA: Saunders Studio Press, 1935.

Sherwood, Midge. *Days of Vintage, Years of Vision.* 2 vols. San Marino, CA: Orizaba Publications, 1982, 1987.

Shorb, J. DeBarth. "Los Angeles Items." *Pacific Wine and Spirit Review* 11 (November 23, 1883): 98.

Spalding, William Andrew. *Los Angeles Newspaperman.* Edited by Robert V. Hine. San Marino: Huntington Library Press, 1961.

Stern, Norton B., and William M. Kramer. "The Wine Tycoon of Anaheim." *Western States Jewish Historical Quarterly* 9 (April 1977): 262–78.

Street, Richard Steven. *Beasts of the Field: A Narrative History of California
Farmworkers, 1769–1913.* Stanford: Stanford University Press, 2004.

Sullivan, Charles. *A Companion to California Wine: An Encyclopedia of Wine and
Winemaking from the Mission Period to the Present.* Berkeley: University of
California Press, 1998.

———. *Like Modern Edens: Winegrowing in Santa Clara Valley and Santa Cruz
Mountains 1798–1981.* Cupertino: California History Center, 1982.

———. *Napa Wine: A History from Mission Days to Present.* 2nd ed. San Francisco: Wine Appreciation Guild, 2008.

———. "Wine in California: The Early Years." *Wayward Tendrils Quarterly*
20ff (April 2010–October 2015).

———. *Zinfandel: A History of a Grape and Its Wine.* Berkeley: University of
California Press, 2003.

Teiser, Ruth, and Catherine Harroun. "The Volstead Act, Rebirth, and
Boom." In Doris Muscatine et al., eds. *The University of California/
Sotheby Book of California Wine.* Berkeley: University of California
Press, 1984.

———. *Winemaking in California.* New York: McGraw-Hill Book Co., 1983.

Thorpe, James. *Henry Edwards Huntington.* Berkeley: University of California
Press, 1994.

Townsend, E. D. *The California Diary of General E. D. Townsend.* Edited by
Malcolm Edwards. Los Angeles: Ward Ritchie Press [, 1970].

Truman, Benjamin C. *Semi-Tropical California: Its Climate, Healthfulness, Productiveness, and Scenery.* San Francisco: A. L. Bancroft, 1874.

———. Series titled "The Wines of California." *New York Times,* January 16,
1887; January 30, 1887; February 27, 1887; and March 13, 1887.

United States Bureau of Prohibition. *Statistics Concerning Alcoholic Liquors.*
Washington, D.C.: Government Printing Office, 1927, 1929, 1930.

United States Department of Agriculture. *Annual Report of the Commissioner of
Agriculture 1878.* Washington, D.C.: Government Printing Office, 1879.

United States Department of the Treasury, Bureau of Industrial Alcohol.
Statistics Concerning Intoxicating Liquors, December 1933. Washington,
D.C.: Government Printing Office.

United States National Commission on Law Observance and Enforcement.

Enforcement of the Prohibition Laws. 5 vols. Washington, D.C.: Government Printing Office, 1931.

United States Patent Office. *Report of the Commissioner of Patents 1858.* Government Printing Office, 1859.

———. *Report of the Commissioner of Patents for the Year 1861.* Washington, D.C.: Government Printing Office, 1862.

Wait, Frona Eunice. *Wines and Vines of California.* San Francisco, 1889. Reprint, Berkeley: Howell-North Books, 1973.

Webb, Edith Buckland. *Indian Life at the Old Missions.* Los Angeles: Warren F. Lewis, 1952.

White, Michael. *California All the Way Back to 1828.* Edited by Glen Dawson. Los Angeles: Glen Dawson, 1956.

Wilson, Iris. *William Wolfskill, 1798–1866: Frontier Trapper to California Ranchero.* Glendale, CA: Arthur J. Clark Co., 1965.

Wilson, John Albert. *History of Los Angeles County.* Oakland: Thompson and West, 1880.

Winkler, A. J., J. A. Cook, W. M. Kliewer, and L. A. Lider. *General Viticulture.* 2nd ed. Berkeley: University of California Press, 1974.

Wolcott, Marjorie Tisdale, ed. *Pioneer Notes from the Diaries of Judge Benjamin Hayes.* Los Angeles: privately printed, 1929.

Wood, John Windell. *Pasadena, California: Historical and Personal.* Pasadena: self-published, 1917.

Wood, William Maxwell. *Wandering Sketches of People and Things in South America, Polynesia, California, and Other Places Visited.* Philadelphia: Carey and Hart, 1849.

Workman, Boyle. *The City that Grew.* Los Angeles: Southland Publishing Co., 1936.

WPA. *California in the 1930s: The WPA Guide to the Golden State.* 1939. Reprint, Berkeley: University of California Press, 2013.

WPA, Federal Writers Project. *Los Angeles in the 1930s: The WPA Guide to the City of Angels.* 1941. Reprint, Berkeley: University of California Press, 2011.

Zack, Michele. *Altadena: Between Wilderness and City.* Altadena: Altadena Historical Society, 2004.

———. *Southern California Story: Seeking the Better Life in Sierra Madre.* Sierra Madre: Sierra Madre Historical Preservation Society, 2009.

INDEX

The extensive notes following the main text have not been indexed. Readers are advised that a note attached to a particular reference may be an addition to the subject in question.

Index

ABOUT THE AUTHOR

Thomas Pinney is emeritus professor of English at Pomona College. He has published scholarly work on George Eliot, Lord Macaulay, and Rudyard Kipling, and several books on American wines including the two-volume *A History of Wine in America* (University of California Press). The second volume of this definitive wine history won the 2006 International Association of Culinary Professionals Award for best book on wine, beer, or spirits.

ABOUT THE CALIFORNIA HISTORICAL SOCIETY BOOK AWARD

In 2013, after a twenty-year collaboration and with a shared commitment to finding new and inclusive ways to explore California's history, the California Historical Society and Heyday established the California Historical Society Book Award as a way of inviting new voices and viewpoints into the conversation. Each year we bring together a jury of noted historians, scholars, and publishing experts to award a book-length manuscript that makes an important contribution both to scholarship and to the greater community by deepening public understanding of some aspect of California history. For more information, visit www.heydaybooks.com/chsbookaward or www.californiahistoricalsociety.org/publications/book_award.html.

CALIFORNIA
HISTORICAL
SOCIETY since 1871

ABOUT THE CALIFORNIA HISTORICAL SOCIETY

Founded in 1871, the California Historical Society (CHS) is a nonprofit organization with a mission to inspire and empower people to make California's richly diverse past a meaningful part of their contemporary lives.

PUBLIC ENGAGEMENT

Through high-quality public history exhibitions, public programs, research, preservation, advocacy, and digital storytelling, CHS keeps history alive through extensive public engagement. In opening the very heart of the organization—our vast and diverse collection—to ever wider audiences, we invite meaning, encourage exchange, and enrich understanding.

CHS COLLECTIONS

CHS holds one of the state's top historical collections, revealing California's social, cultural, economic, and political history and development—including some of the most cherished and valuable documents and images of California's past. From our headquarters in San Francisco to the University of Southern California and the Autry National Center in Los Angeles, we hold millions of items in trust for the people of California.

LIBRARY AND RESEARCH

Open to the public and free of charge, our North Baker Research Library is a place where researchers literally hold history in their hands. Whether you're a scholar or are simply interested in learning about the history of your neighborhood, city, or community, you have hands-on access to the rich history of our state.

PUBLICATIONS

From our first book publication in 1874, to our ninety-year history as publisher of the *California History* journal, to the establishment of the annual California Historical Society Book Award in 2013, CHS publications examine the ongoing dialogue between the past and the present. Our print and digital publications reach beyond purely historical narrative to connect Californians to their state, region, nation, and the world in innovative and thought-provoking ways.

SUPPORT

Over the years, the generosity and commitment of foundations, corporations, cultural and educational institutions, and private donors and members have supported CHS's work throughout the state.

LEARN MORE

www.californiahistoricalsociety.com

HEYDAY
into California

ABOUT HEYDAY

Heyday is an independent, nonprofit publisher and unique cultural institution. We promote widespread awareness and celebration of California's many cultures, landscapes, and boundary-breaking ideas. Through our well-crafted books, public events, and innovative outreach programs we are building a vibrant community of readers, writers, and thinkers.

THANK YOU

It takes the collective effort of many to create a thriving literary culture. We are thankful to all the thoughtful people we have the privilege to engage with. Cheers to our writers, artists, editors, storytellers, designers, printers, bookstores, critics, cultural organizations, readers, and book lovers everywhere!

We are especially grateful for the generous funding we've received for our publications and programs during the past year from foundations and hundreds of individual donors. Major supporters include:

Anonymous; Arkay Foundation; Judith and Phillip Auth; Judy Avery; Richard and Rickie Ann Baum; Randy Bayard; BayTree Fund; Jean and Fred Berensmeier; Nancy Bertelsen; Edwin Blue; Beatrice Bowles; Philip and Jamie Bowles; Peter Boyer and Terry Gamble Boyer; Brandt-Hawley Law Group; John Briscoe; California Humanities; The Campbell Foundation; John and Nancy Cassidy; The Christensen Fund; Lawrence Crooks; Chris Desser and Kirk Marckwald; Frances Dinkelspiel and Gary Wayne; Steven Dinkelspiel; The Roy and Patricia Disney Family Foundation; Tim Disney; Patricia Dixon; Gayle Embrey;

Richard and Gretchen Evans; Megan Fletcher, in honor of J. K. Dineen; Patrick Golden and Susan Overhauser; Wanda Lee Graves and Stephen Duscha; Whitney Green; Walter & Elise Haas Fund; Penelope Hlavac; Nettie Hoge; Michael Horn, in memory of Gary Horn; Humboldt Area Foundation; JiJi Foundation; Claudia Jurmain; Kalliopeia Foundation; Marty Krasney; Abigail Kreiss; Guy Lampard and Suzanne Badenhoop; Thomas Lockard and Alix Marduel; David Loeb; Judith Lowry-Croul and Brad Croul; Praveen Madan and Christin Evans; Joel Marcus; Malcolm and Rina Margolin; William, Karen, and John McClung; Michael McCone; Nion McEvoy and Leslie Berriman, in honor of Malcolm Margolin; Judy Mistelske-Anklam and William Anklam; Karen and Tom Mulvaney; National Wildlife Federation; The Nature Conservancy; Eddie Orton; The Ralph M. Parsons Foundation; Alan Rosenus; The San Francisco Foundation; San Manuel Band of Mission Indians; Greg Sarris; Save the Redwoods League; Stanley Smith Horticultural Trust; Roselyne Swig; Tappan Foundation; Thendara Foundation; Michael and Shirley Traynor, in honor of Malcolm Margolin; The Roger J. and Madeleine Traynor Foundation; Al and Ann Wasserman; Sherry Wasserman and Clayton F. Johnson; Lucinda Watson; Peter Wiley and Valerie Barth; Mina Witteman; and Yocha Dehe Wintun Nation.

GETTING INVOLVED

To learn more about our publications, events and other ways you can participate, please visit www.heydaybooks.com.